Transition, Institutions, and the Rural Sector

RURAL ECONOMIES IN TRANSITION

Series Editors

Zvi Lerman
The Hebrew University of Jerusalem
Csaba Csaki
The World Bank and the Budapest Economics University
Johan Swinnen
Katholieke Univesiteit Leuven

Much of the world's rural population lives in transition countries that are attempting to transform their economies from the centrally planned socialist system to a market-oriented system. The Rural Economies in Transition series evaluates the deep impact these transformations are having in Central and Eastern Europe, the former Soviet Union, and Asia. Based on original empirical work by international teams at the cutting edge of research, each volume presents the results of one complete empirical study devoted to a single country or region. The editors have designed the series to provide agricultural, development, and political economists, as well as scholars in other disciplines, with authoritative and up-to-date factual information about rural transition. The editors welcome manuscript submissions from scholars engaged in original empirical research in the field.

Titles in the Series

Private Agriculture in Armenia, by Zvi Lerman and Astghik Mirzakhanian
Transition, Institutions, and the Rural Sector, edited by Max Spoor
Romanian Agriculture and Transition toward the EU, edited by
　　Sophia Davidova and Kenneth J. Thomson

Transition, Institutions, and the Rural Sector

Edited by Max Spoor

LEXINGTON BOOKS
Lanham • Boulder • New York • Oxford

LEXINGTON BOOKS

Published in the United States of America
by Lexington Books
A Member of the Rowman & Littlefield Publishing Group
4720 Boston Way, Lanham, Maryland 20706

PO Box 317
Oxford
OX2 9RU, UK

British Library Cataloguing in Publication Information Available

Library of Congress Cataloging-in-Publication Data

Transition, institutions, and the rural sector / edited by Max Spoor.
    p. cm. – (Rural economies in transition)
   Includes bibliographical references and index.
   ISBN 0-7391-0546-9 (cloth: alk. paper)
   1. Land reform—Europe, Eastern. 2. Land reform—Former Soviet republics.
  3. Land reform—Asia, Central. 4. Europe, Eastern—Economic conditions. 5. Former
Soviet republics—Economic conditions. 6. Asia, Central—Economic conditions.
I. Spoor, Max. II. Series.

HD1333.E85 T73 2003
338.1'0947—dc21   2002037985

Printed in the United States of America

Dedicated to Friso, Saskia
and Francisca

Contents

List of Abbreviations

ACE	Action for Cooperation in Economics (EU-Program)
ADB	Asian Development Bank
ADF	Albanian Development Fund
AFADA	Albanian Fertilizer and Agri-Input Dealers Association
AFE	Analytical Centre of Agri-Food Economics
ALP	Agricultural Labor Productivity
AWU	Annual Work Unit
CEE	Central and Eastern Europe
CIS	Commonwealth of Independent States
CMEA	Council for Mutual Economic Assistance
CPIA	Country Policy and Institutional Assessment
DFID	Department of International Development
EBRD	European Bank for Reconstruction and Development
EC	European Commission
ECA	Europe and Central Asia
EIU	Economist Intelligence Unit
EU	European Union
FAO	Food and Agricultural Organization
FDI	Foreign Direct Investment
FSU	Former Soviet Union
GAO	Gross Agricultural Output
GDP	Gross Domestic Product
GNP	Gross National Product
IFAD	International Fund for Agricultural Development
IMF	International Monetary Fund
INSTAT	Institute for Statistics
IPRS	Immovable Property Registration System
ISS	Institute of Social Studies
KAFC	Kyrgyz Agricultural Finance Cooperation
MOAF	Ministry of Agriculture and Food
NDC	New Developing Countries (in Europe)
NGO	Nongovernmental organization
NIS	Newly Independent States
NSI	National Statistical Institute
NSO	National Statistical Office
OECD	Organization for Economic Cooperation and Development
PPAP	Participatory Poverty Alleviation Project
PPP	Purchasing Power Parity
RNFE	Rural nonfarm economy
SAPARD	Special Pre-Accession Assistance for Agriculture and Rural Development
SME	Small and mediumsized enterprise
SSO	State Statistical Office
TACIS	Technical Assistance to the Commonwealth of Independent States
UNDP	United Nations Development Program
UNRISD	United Nations Research Institute for Social Development
USAID	United States Agency for International Development
USSR	Union of Socialist Soviet Republics
WUA	Water User Association

Introduction

Max Spoor

Ten years after the collapse of the USSR, in December 1991, a critical review is warranted of the transition experience in Eastern Europe (the CEE and FSU) in terms of its impact on institutions and markets, in particular with regard to the–often ignored–agricultural and rural sector. Macro policies have focused on market and price liberalization, deregulation, and privatization, although the latter has taken a myriad of forms when it concerns land. There are major differences in this respect between some of the CEE countries and the FSU, in terms both of reforms and performance.

However, the real "Achilles heel" in transition strategies towards the rural sector has been the issue of missing markets and institutions. While original expectations were focused on the positive effects of price and market liberalization, very little attention was given to the buildup of markets and their corresponding institutions. Various unexpected phenomena, such as increased barter trade, regional self-sufficiency tendencies, increased dependency on household plot production, and stagnation in the emergence of a viable commercial and peasant farm agriculture, can be observed. The dramatic situation of the agricultural (and rural) sector in quite a number of transition countries is such that lessons have to be drawn from transition policies and their impact.

In global terms, the 1990s saw some of the most profound and widespread societal changes of the twentieth century. For the economies in transition, since the fall of the Berlin Wall or even before that event, these changes have caused problems of a particular, often complex, nature. They are mostly studied in a vacuum of theoretical propositions, since even the nature of the term "transition," the economic, social, and political transformation process towards a market economy and a pluralistic democratic society, is problematic. However, as part and parcel of a learning-by-doing process, a growing number of comparative and detailed case studies of transition, contribute to our understanding of the complexities of this process.

With countries such as China, Vietnam, Laos, Cambodia, and Mongolia, the Central and East European economies and the successor states of the FSU, there are nearly thirty transition economies in total, of which many can also be considered developing countries. Although the rural sector is important in most of them, and particularly in the Asian transition countries, it has nevertheless been the Cinderella of reform, the stepchild that did not receive adequate attention in the economic reforms. In the 1990s, reform was, primarily directed towards macroeconomic stabilization, the extractive industry, the finance sector, and the restructuring of international trade. Lessons from the Chinese and Vietnamese experiences, which have a longer transition path, were paid insufficient attention, or were misinterpreted, as demonstrated through the expectation that by the mid-1990s a substantial part of agricultural output in Russia would be produced by a thriving peasant sector.

In the early 1990s, there was a tendency, supported by the mainstream Washington Consensus, to focus exclusively on privatization, liberalization, and deregulation, while the very important institutional dimension of the transition was underestimated or ignored. Perhaps there was a naïve belief in the appearance of markets when these measures were implemented. And in fact, markets did appear, but often not in the forms the economics literature would have predicted, as many of them were inefficient, monopolistic, fragmented, operating with high transaction costs, and under strong political interference in combination with criminal influence over parts of marketing chains. Public and private institutions, understood as organizations that are essential for a working market economy, were weak and only slowly developing. Institutions, understood as the "rules of the game," building a new legislative framework with enforcement mechanisms, were even further away. Even though many countries produced large numbers of decrees and laws, most remained paper tigers, in the absence of enforcement mechanisms.

Now, after more than a decade of reform, it is generally accepted that policy reforms need to be more focused on the building of public and private institutions, which will improve the working of markets. At the moment, markets clearly do not work in favor of small producers in rural areas. Land markets are very important, but rather than increasing the welfare of these farmers, they often bring greater insecurity. Rural financial services are even crucial, as they can provide the options for investments and the introduction of improved technology in farm production, while institutions that promote savings can contribute importantly to accumulation (as the Chinese experience has shown in terms of rural household savings).

Since former cooperative structures have withered away, rural extension and marketing services are necessary to reconstruct forward and backward linkages with farm production. A whole spectrum of new institutions, of public, private and mixed character, is needed in order to link the emerging private, and often small-scale farm economy, with other sectors of the economy, improving productivity and reducing marketing costs. Processes of land consolidation (in cases where fragmentation has been extreme) and the formation of new forms of association, comparable with the well-known single purpose cooperatives in

Western Europe around a century ago, are needed to promote viable farm structures and improved marketing channels. In some of the EU-accession countries these aspects of agrarian transformation have already improved. However, there are many transition economies, regions and sub-sectors of the agricultural economy, in which producers have retrenched into self-sufficiency production, using backward technologies in order to subsist, with few prospects for the future.

Nonfarm employment creation in rural areas is not only important in order to stop, or at least delay, the increasing rural-urban migration. It is also crucial to build a healthy rural economy, with a processing industry for agricultural products, and with consumer good and farm implement industries that fuel the farm economy. A dynamic agricultural economy is extremely important for rural areas, both for the more urbanized societies in Eastern Europe, and for the Asian developing countries. An issue that has been causing increasing concern in rural development during transition, is rural "de-development"–the depopulation of the countryside through rural-urban migration, leaving behind hardly viable small farms, increasing rural poverty and deprivation. Poverty alleviation is indeed given priority, but while this might be needed in the short-run, poverty can only be attacked in a sustainable manner through improved productivity, employment creation, and the construction of marketing structures. In various parts of the FSU, in particular in Moldova, the Central Asian states and on the Caucasus, and in the New Developing Countries (NDC) of Europe, such as Albania, Macedonia, parts of Bosnia-Herzegovina and Kosova, rural poverty is a growing problem. It is important to resolve this, not only in order to construct a sustainable growth model in the long-run, but also in order to avoid the dangers of social unrest, exclusion and conflicts.

This edited volume presents state of the art work in the field of rural transformation in the "transition economies," bringing together papers written by renowned scholars in the field of agrarian transition, and some young researchers. The book includes a number of analytical comparative studies focusing on the lessons to be drawn from transition, combined with case studies from various countries, such as Albania, Armenia, Bulgaria, the Central Asian States and Mongolia, Kyrgyzstan, Russia, and Uzbekistan. The authors use different points of departure in their studies, emphasizing structural phenomena, the political economy of reform, initial conditions, and the institutional environment. Where the authors clearly agree, after more than a decade of policy reform and research in this field, is that a return to the blueprint approach of the early 1990s should be avoided. The initial, somewhat naïve, belief in a rapid transformation overlooked or ignored the enormous institutional gap between the former centrally planned economies and the market economies that were to be constructed. This book contributes to filling this gap in research on rural transformation in the transition economies. The volume is divided into two parts, the first presenting comparative studies of agrarian reform during the past decade of transition, with the second containing detailed country case studies.

Ellman, in the first chapter, sets the tone for a critical analysis of the "transition experience" of the first decade, by comparing expectations and reality. The original expectations for the agricultural sector included the end of shortages, an increase in output, the collapse of large-scale agriculture and the emergence of commercial agriculture. Indeed, the restructuring of relative (and absolute) prices made an end to the "shortage economy," but in an exclusionary manner. Output contracted, the heirs of the large-scale farms remained dominant, in particular in the CIS countries, and commercial agriculture was very slow to develop. What is more surprising, is the technical regress in the sector, the emergence of widespread subsistence oriented *minifundia* and the use of barter in exchange relations. These phenomena were quite unexpected, making agriculture to "fall outside the transition paradigms." In hindsight it can be concluded that the reforms, particularly those that were dominant in the former Soviet Union, did not depart from a solid view of the reality of agricultural production under "state socialism." There was rational opposition against reforms, in particular privatization of land, and even more importantly, there was a naïve expectation with the reformers that markets would emerge overnight. In conclusion, Ellman states that the reforms have been of a hasty nature, and calls for "more research and less prescription."

In the next chapter, which provides a detailed overview of land reform experiences, Lerman states that the inefficiency of the huge farms and the collective organization of production were the common characteristics of socialist agriculture. Reforms had to produce transferable private property rights and a more efficient and competitive sector, focusing on land reform and farm restructuring. However, the decade of transition has produced an "East/West" (CIS/CEE) divide, which is expressed in substantial differences in the legal attitude towards land ownership, transferability of land and land allocation strategies. This can be shown through the use of a land-policy index. Lerman upholds that the strategies towards the distribution (and/or restitution) of physical land plots, work out much better than the use of (non-physical) shares, such as was done in large CIS countries such as Russia and Ukraine. Even stronger, he argues that there is a positive correlation between the degree of individualization of agriculture and its output performance. In most countries a dual (or bimodal) agrarian structure has remained. Also with regards to the "East/West" divide this is clearly present, as in particular in the CIS very large farms (the heirs of the *sovkhozy* and *kolkhozy*) dominate. The reasons are amongst others the safe environment, market failure, and continued political interference, in particular by the regional and local political elite. His conclusion is that stronger reforms have led to a better performance, and that transferability of land and secure land tenure remain pivotal elements of reform.

In the following chapter, also concerned with the lessons that can be drawn from ten years of rural transition, Swinnen argues that there are three patterns. These can be observed in Central Europe (Czech Republic, Slovakia and Hungary), in the FSU (Russia, Ukraine and Belarus), and in Asia (China, Vietnam, with Albania added to this group). Gross agricultural output declined in the first two and rose in the last group of countries, while agricultural labor productivity rose in the first and the last, but declined in the second. He distinguishes the impact of initial conditions (pre-reform development and pre-reform distortions) and that of reform policies. Using principle component and regression analyses, he provides a detailed picture of the different effects of the various policies that were implemented and draws some interesting comparative lessons from the "transition dynamics" of the past decade. As Swinnen states, one has to be careful in choosing the indicators measuring performance, and there is no single optimal transition path. There are some essential ingredients for successful performance during transition, which includes macroeconomic stability, the reform of property rights, the creation of market (or exchange) institutions, and the enforcement of contracts. Although not all of these ingredients have to be in place at the same time, institution building needs to be well adapted to local circumstances. Finally, he agrees with the previous author that performance was better in those cases where "landowners," rather than "share-owners" emerged after land reform.

The final chapter in Part I, is a comparative study written by the editor of the volume, the focus being on land privatization and farm restructuring in the Central Asian region (with Kazakhstan, Kyrgyzstan, Uzbekistan and in this particular case including Mongolia). Spoor argues that land reforms have shown great diversity and have produced various outcomes. There were, however, common grounds to the stagnation during the final stages of the Soviet regime, such as low (land and labor) productivity and free-rider behavior in the collective organization of agricultural enterprises. Also the administrative state-order system and the social, rather than productive focus of the large farms, contributed negatively to performance. Spoor analyzes the macroeconomic situation, which was in most of the region rather dramatic during the first half of the decade of transition. This is followed by a critical overview of two important aspects of agrarian reform, privatization of land and farm restructuring. Although there have been some far-reaching reforms in Kyrgyzstan and Mongolia, overall the privatization of land was a gradual process, or even absent in some cases. Large-scale farms remain sometimes dominant, though most often operating very inefficiently. Whenever small-scale "family" farms emerged, or private herds (such as in Mongolia), the institutional gap makes their survival problematic. The lack of viable public, private, or mixed institutions that promote land (or rental) markets, provide credit and other services, and manage water resources, is the real bottleneck for the newly emerging peasant farms.

In Part II of this volume, a series of case-studies of agricultural transition are presented, highlighting–on the basis of very recent fieldwork–various aspects of meso- and micro-institutional development and revealing existing bottlenecks. Serova and Khramova report on a survey undertaken in three Russian *oblasts*, Pskov, Tambov and Rostov, amongst large-scale and private farms. The chapter analyzes the (non)-functioning of emerging factor markets, of land, inputs, machinery, capital and of farm output. Land markets are still in an embryonic stage of development, with rental markets for land being more dynamic. Lack of sound legislation is seen as the main limitation. There is a strong reduction in the use of inputs and machinery. In particular private farms blame high prices and opportunistic behavior of traders. The banking system is poorly developed, with high interest rates and complicated banking procedures. Finally, barter trade in farm output diminished, although large-scale farms have a practice of mutual debt offsets, and buyers of farm produce seem to be more diversified, in particular after the crisis of 1998.

In a second contribution on Russia, Visser focuses on farm restructuring, property relations and household strategies. Although at the surface the land privatization was rather cosmetic (see also Lerman's chapter), since the mid-1990s one can observe gradual, but fundamental changes within the farms. His analysis is based on a farm survey conducted in the less-endowed Pskov region (also present in the research of Serova and Khramova), looking to what determines success or failure of particularly the large-scale farms, which have remained dominant, and the role of the growing sector of household enterprises. Asset stripping is quite generalized and even a form of "parasitic symbiosis" has developed between the two categories. Some enterprises seem to be able to contain the process of decay. Continued and trusted leadership, high wages and a strong labor regime are important factors in this success. Visser discusses various scenarios that represent the current development within large-scale farms. These include a return to centralization, a shift to peasant farms (with all the difficulties of the inhospitable market environment), a form of contractual symbiosis between management and employees, and the continuation of parasitic behavior, as part of a downward spiral of decay.

A team of authors, Kopeva, Doichinova, Davidova, Gorton, Chaplin, and Bezemer, presents in the next chapter a case-study of agricultural diversification in Bulgaria. Land reform has produced fragmentation of the previously existing large farms into very small ones, of which two-thirds do not produce for the market. As little systematic study is available of alternative sources of income, a survey was undertaken covering two regions, Plovdiv and Varna, with peri-urban and rural sub-regions represented in the sample. In the occupation of household members, agriculture still represents the mainstay, followed by non-agricultural self-employment. Permanent off-farm work is still uncommon and migration (contrary to expectations) is not an important phenomenon. Developing a nonagricultural business is the preferred option for diversification of income by households. Interestingly enough, and contrary to other countries in the CEE region, those who were full-time in agriculture had the highest income. This hides the fact that many households, whose land assets are insufficient, are forced to search for alternative sources of income, not having been successful enough. The authors are, however, optimistic about future options for diversification of income, given existing levels of education and infrastructure.

Continuing in Southeast Europe, Childress presents an analysis of the national land consolidation program and the development of agricultural services in Albania. This is another example of a land reform that has led to land fragmentation, in this case through physical redistribution. There are efforts underway to encourage consolidation of fragmented landholdings, and to improve the agricultural services environment. In the absence of well-established land markets, the focus is actually on taking away obstacles for land transactions, promoting exchanges, rentals, purchase and sales of land. Subsidizing transaction costs is a good way of doing this, and at the same time promoting forms of associations between small-holders. He argues on the basis of field work that there is an interest in land consolidation, that the costs of fragmentation are high, but that costs of undertaking land transactions and risks are seen as often prohibitive by the small farmers, who for 80-90 percent produce for self-sufficiency. The agricultural services environment is equally important, and taken its poor state, needs substantial improvements in order to provoke more commercially oriented farming. Childress discusses in detail the efforts in both fields undertaken in Albania, and the risks that exist for continued fragmentation and stagnation of the reform process.

The following chapter takes our investigative journey into the rural areas of Central Asia and the Caucasus. Taking a political economy approach, Kandiyoti looks at pathways of farm restructuring in Uzbekistan. She sets out by placing agrarian reform in the specific context of mediation between state and society. For the case of Uzbekistan, cotton is a heavily contested sub-sector, crucial for both employment, budget revenue and foreign exchange earnings. It was exemplary for the tensions between the Center (Moscow), the local elites and their constituencies. After independence these tensions transformed, but did not vanish, with external pressures to start agrarian reform adding to the complex playing field. Cotton was and still is a main source of revenue, controlled through a (quasi)-quota system and a combination of low output and high input prices. While one would have expected an improvement in the terms of trade for the agricultural sector, they deteriorated in the past decade. Gradual reforms in Uzbekistan have led to the transformation of existing collective structures into *shirkats* (joint stock companies); peasant (*dekhan*) farmers, who are still within their boundaries; and a small section of independent farmers. Kandiyoti analyzes two paths of farm restructuring, one in which a similar "parasitic symbiosis" (see chapter by Visser in this volume) seems to exist between the large farm structure and the household plots, and the other in which outright liquidation leads to the emergence of independent farms, who are still facing substantial problems.

The next chapter deals with the rural nonfarm economy (RNFE) in Armenia. The two authors, Bezemer and Davis, analyze this important part of the rural economy, which–given the growing agricultural surplus labor–should be a focal point in economic strategies to stimulate rural development and overcome rural poverty. In various transition countries the RNFE already provides a substantial share of household income. In Armenia, where a redistributive land reform took place in the early 1990s and generally holdings are very small, agricultural unemployment is widespread. Nonfarm income is important (be it from pensions, salaries or remittances). However, as Bezemer and Davis note, there is no dynamic nonfarm economy in Armenia. In a recent survey in three regions, the nature of the RNFE is investigated, in particular with regard to its potential to alleviate poverty through nonfarm employment. They conclude that the capacity of these micro, small and medium enterprises is still rather limited in terms of employment generation and that they are closely linked to food processing and food product trading. They receive little or no support from public institutions, and see as a major bottleneck their limited access to credit.

That same bottleneck, namely the availability of credit for agricultural (or rural) producers, is the topic of the final chapter of Part II, in which Pelkmans analyzes the effectiveness of "transition aid" to Kyrgyzstan in this specific field. This country has been a leading reformer in the context of the FSU, and had to cope with a very severe contraction of the economy in the early 1990s. Agrarian reform in Kyrgyzstan shows much of the earlier analyzed abnormalities, in which local elites got hold of much of the privatized assets and asset stripping was a rule rather than an exception. The institutional (services) environment was not favorable to the newly established private farmers, lacking extension services, input markets and credit institutions. Pelkmans looks at an innovative aid project in this missing field, in which micro-credit was provided to groups of poor farmers, as an example of micro-institution building. The project, although successful in some ways, encountered substantial problems, caused by the predominance of individual interests, speculative in nature or driven by legitimate food security objectives, that were countering an economic (re)use of the credit. It also had to struggle with corruption and nepotism, albeit at a micro-level. This analysis leads Pelkmans to caution in case aid is provided, and equally questions the often ill-prepared reforms that have been quite harmful in creating an institutional vacuum in rural areas.

In conclusion, as this volume's title expresses the importance of institutions, the contributions presented in the book underline this, in part by analyzing macro- and sectoral policies in a comparative setting, but particularly looking to micro-institutional change, development and still existing gaps and bottlenecks. The latter are manifold, and mainly affect the emerging small farm sector. The "East/West" divide, taking into account that some CEE countries have moved from "transition" to "pre-accession" to the EU, is growing, which should be a matter of serious concern. Agriculture still remains the mainstay of large sections of the population, in particular in the former Soviet Union. Lessons from transition show that the rural and agricultural sector needs very specific and well-designed attention, mainly focused on institutional transformation and buildup. In its absence not only the above divide will grow, but also the urban/rural divide in transition economies will become more profound, contributing to "de-development" of the countryside, marginalization and eventually, to social instability.

The contributions in this volume, with the exception of one paper, were originally presented at a conference, carrying the same title as this book. This conference, organized by the Centre for the Study of Transition and Development (CESTRAD), Institute of Social Studies, was held in The Hague, The Netherlands, 10-11 December 2001.[1] After the conference a short, but intensive process of selection, revisions and editing took place, which led to the relatively expeditious production of the underlying volume. The editor is grateful for the very fruitful and enthusiastic cooperation that he encountered in working with the contributors, the editorial staff of Lexington Books, one of the editors of the Series "Rural Economies in Transition" Zvi Lerman, and the assistance rendered by Andy Brown in the language editing.

CESTRAD, The Hague, July 2002

1. The Conference was co-financed by CESTRAD, the Institute of Social Studies (ISS), The Hague, and the Research School for Resource Studies for Development (CERES), Utrecht, which is acknowledged here. The assistance rendered by Maureen Koster and Francisca Quilaqueo in organizing the conference is also highly appreciated.

Expectations and Reality: Reflections on a Decade of Agricultural Transformation

Michael Ellman

The outcome of the first decade of agricultural transformation has been substantially different from what was expected by the international financial institutions and most Western economists. This can be seen by comparing *expectations* and *reality*, and also by looking at the *unexpected results* of the transformation.

The expectations were for the end of shortages (as disequilibrium prices were eliminated), more output (as the inefficient communist system was abolished), the collapse of large-scale agriculture (as its political support was overthrown), and the emergence of commercial agriculture (the natural kind of agricultural organization in a market economy). The first of these expectations was in fact generally met. However, it was partly met in the way wishes are granted in horror stories. An important contribution to overcoming shortages was made by the sharp reduction in demand resulting from the fall in real incomes and mass impoverishment. The second expectation was not met at all. Output generally declined (Lerman, 1998: 308). As far as the third expectation was concerned, the outcome was generally mixed. Although household and family farming grew in importance, large-scale agriculture proved surprisingly resilient and remains important in many countries (Bezemer, 2001). As far as the fourth expectation is concerned, this turned out to be a slow process which generally remains far from complete.

Not only were expectations not entirely fulfilled, but there were a number of striking unexpected results. These concern technical regress, subsistence agriculture, barter, and the tenacity of old forms and networks.

The old system made extensive use of machinery and chemicals (e.g. artificial fertilizers, pesticides). As a result of the worsening terms of trade of agriculture this proved impossible for the new "marketized" agriculture. Hence in many countries there was a revival of pre-industrial technology (e.g. the horse in Russia) and a growth in labor-intensity. Although part of the decline in the consumption of chemicals and machinery was economically rational and led to an increase in their productivity, part of it was simply technical regress resulting from the poor financial position of agriculture. Subsistence agriculture, a pre-capitalist phenomenon, turned out to be remarkably important and persistent. In many countries it became a major form of food production.

A very striking phenomenon was the growth and importance in agriculture–mainly in the CIS countries–of barter. The exchange of food products for other food products, agricultural inputs or manufactured consumer goods, was widespread in the CIS countries in the 1990s.

Another important unexpected phenomenon was the tenacity of old forms and networks. Many of the old *kolkhozy* and *sovkhozy*, although they changed under the pressure of circumstances, refused to disappear completely as expected by their enemies. This was not just a matter of inertia and path dependence. By 1995, in East German agriculture, there appeared to be no efficiency advantage to family farms compared with large-scale farming (Mathijs and Swinnen, 2001). Not only organizational forms but also personal networks inherited from the old regime remained important. Old networks in rural areas frequently persisted as their members helped each other.

Lessons from Transition

What lessons can be learned from these developments? It seems to me that there are four main lessons. First, the developments which have taken place in agriculture fall outside the transition paradigm. Transition was imagined as a linear change from a traditional communist system to a modern market economy as more and more market–and hence socially and technologically advanced–elements were introduced. However, phenomena such as barter, subsistence production and technical regress fall entirely outside this paradigm. Evidently something else has been happening other than "transition."

Second, many of the initial reformers failed to take sufficient account of the evolution of state socialism. The expectation that socialized agriculture would collapse as soon as the "artificial" political support for it was removed, partly derived from images of the use of terror to impose it and–in the USSR– the ghastly famine which was experienced in its initial period. Not enough attention was paid to the *evolution* of agricultural policy under state socialism. This led to a situation, for example, where in the Brezhnev period Soviet agriculture was receiving substantial subsidies and social benefits from the state. Hence the rural population had something to lose from radical change.

Third, there exists a rational rural opposition to land privatization (Leonard, 2000). Rural inhabitants may well think that land privatization, which turns them into landless laborers and the former farm chairmen and directors, and urban conglomerates and individual urban capitalists into estate owners, is a retrograde development. This is not necessarily an irrational sentiment but may be entirely rational for the victims of rural change.

Fourth, successful market-oriented production is a social construct and has to be built up over time. In the early transformation period Jeffrey Sachs wrote that one has only to clear away the old unnatural state socialist system, and a healthy market economy would spring up on its own (Sachs, 1993: xii). This is in fact a reformulation of the well-known observation of Adam Smith that the division of labor is based on the natural propensity of human beings to trade (Smith, 1910: 12). This, however, is and was an illusion. Productive activity in a healthy market economy is the result of a long development, in which people learn to work together to achieve technical progress and high productivity.

Conclusions

What conclusions can we draw from this experience? It seems to me that there are two important ones. First, the Popperians were right. As was pointed out in 1993:

> Today's Popperians apply yesterday's Popperian critique of hasty attempts to implement a utopia to the new situation. They stress that far-reaching social transformations inevitably take time. They urge the need to take into account the concrete situation in specific countries and emphasize that policies frequently produce unintended effects. Plans to introduce capitalism in 500 days strike them as completely absurd. The Popperians anticipate a long and difficult process of socio-political-economic transformation which may take decades and with no guarantee of success (Ellman et al., 1993).

Second, some humility on the part of Western "experts" is appropriate. Instead of imagining that we know all the answers, and telling people all over the world how they should run their affairs, we should recognize the limits of our knowledge and the importance of unintended consequences. We should study what has happened and analyze its causes. "More research and less prescription" should be our slogan.

A Decade of Transition
in Europe and Central Asia:
Design and Impact of Land Reform

Zvi Lerman

The former socialist countries in Europe and Central Asia (the ECA countries) entered the transition in 1989-91, with a common institutional and organizational heritage in agriculture. Most land, regardless of its legal ownership, was cultivated collectively in large-scale collective and state farms that managed thousands of hectares and employed hundreds of member-workers. The commercial production from the collective and state sector was supplemented by subsistence-oriented individual agriculture, derived from rural household plots of less than one hectare. This created a distinctly dual agricultural structure; product markets and input supply channels were largely controlled by state organizations within an administrative command framework; production targets were set centrally; and budget constraints to penalize under-performers virtually did not exist.

This, in effect, was the Soviet model of socialist agriculture that had dominated the region since the late 1920s in CIS and since the early 1950s in CEE. Only Poland and the former Yugoslavia partially deviated from this common pattern: here large-scale collective farms never achieved the same prominence as in other socialist countries, and their agriculture remained largely based on small individual farmers throughout the decades following World War II. Yet pervasive central controls plagued farmers in Poland and Yugoslavia in exactly the same way as in all other socialist economies.

The well-documented persistent inefficiency of socialized agriculture was an inevitable result of the command economy, which insulated the farms from market signals, imposed central targets as a substitute for consumer preferences, and allowed farms to function indefinitely under soft budget constraints without proper profit accountability. Yet this inefficiency also can be attributed to two "micro-level" factors, which sharply distinguished socialist agriculture from agriculture in market economies: exceptionally large farms and collective organization of production. The typical farm size in socialist countries was an order of magnitude larger than the average in land-rich market economies, such as the United States or Canada. The excessive size was reflected not only in large land endowments, but also in the large number of workers employed (in absolute terms and per hectare of land). Such large farms are a rarity in market economies; they are relatively inefficient due to high transaction costs (including the cost of monitoring labor and various agency costs associated with hired management) and can survive in a competitive environment only under special circumstances. As for the other micro-level factor, collective farms–in the form of production cooperatives or communes–virtually do not exist today in market economies, again because of their inherent inefficiency stemming from a variety of behavioral and governance features.

Related to these micro-level factors was also the issue of ownership and transferability of land. The stylized model of agriculture in market economies is characterized by a predominance of individual or family farms–not collectives–that operate on privately owned land and enjoy fully transferable use rights. In some socialist countries (the fifteen republics of the Soviet Union and Albania), all land was nationalized and held in exclusive ownership by the state. In CEE countries, only a small portion (up to about 20 percent) of the land was expropriated by the state after World War II; most land remained formally in private ownership, but landowners had no control over the disposition of their land. In either group of countries, regardless of ownership, land was locked into fixed collective use patterns. Land transfers among users could be initiated only by central authorities. Even in Poland and Yugoslavia, where land largely remained in individual cultivation (and in private ownership), transactions were rendered virtually impossible by administrative barriers and land could not flow from less efficient to more efficient users.

Because of this common heritage, efficiency considerations suggested a fairly uniform conceptual framework for agricultural reform in all transition countries. On the macro level, the reform framework called for the elimination of central controls, price liberalization, and the introduction of hard budget constraints. On the micro level, it included a shift from collective to individual agriculture and a general downsizing of corporate farms, in line with the established experience of market economies. The abolition of collective agriculture was to be accompanied by privatization of land rights, which in Western thinking implies transferable property rights and well-functioning land markets. Ultimately, these actions were to change the entire system of producer incentives, leading to a more efficient and competitive agriculture.

Without in any way detracting from the importance of actions on the macroeconomic level, it was progress on the sectoral micro-level of the reform agenda that had the potential for a significant impact on the agrarian rural population. Individual responsibility and direct accountability were expected to cure the free riding, shirking, and moral hazard that make collective organizations generally inefficient. Smaller farm sizes were expected to be more manageable and less wasteful, reducing the level of monitoring and other transaction costs between managers and workers that are typically high in large organizations. Property rights associated with private ownership of land (or secure tenure) were expected to induce farmers to put a greater effort into production. Finally, transferability of use rights was expected to facilitate the flow of land from less efficient to more efficient producers, or more concretely from passive landowners (such as pensioners in an ageing population) to energetic active operators.

The Divergence of Land Policies

In this conceptual framework, transition to the market should involve radical reconfiguration of the land resources in former socialist countries, including changes in both property rights and land-use patterns. These issues are usually characterized under the rubric of land reform and farm restructuring. The agrarian policies of transition countries related to land reform and farm restructuring should be evaluated against the basic attributes of market agriculture, namely private land ownership, transferability of use rights, and individual or noncollective organization of production.

An examination of these attributes reveals that, despite far-reaching commonalities imposed by the communist regimes on societies and economies, the agricultural sectors in CEE and CIS are in fact following divergent paths of market reforms, which is gradually creating a sharp "East/West divide" between the two sub-blocs in the formerly Soviet-dominated region. Since the common institutional and organizational heritage dictated a conceptually common framework for transition in all these countries, the divergence appears to be associated with differences in the specifics of implementation, which in all likelihood stem from inherent cultural, social, and political differences that persisted throughout the Soviet era, albeit hidden below the veneer of the socialist fraternity of nations.

The three main components of land policies in the region include the legal attitude toward private land ownership, transferability of land, and land-allocation strategies. Most transition countries allow private ownership of potentially all farmland, and agricultural land remains largely state-owned only in Belarus and parts of Central Asia. Private ownership, however, is not synonymous with the right to transfer land among users. The ten CEE countries, plus the four "small" CIS countries (Armenia, Georgia, Moldova, and Azerbaijan), recognize private ownership of land and have no legal barriers to land transactions. In this respect, these fourteen countries have the most liberal land policies. Russia and Ukraine, which control the bulk of farmland resources in the region, legally recognize private land ownership, but the buying and selling of land is restricted in practice, and land transactions are mainly limited to leasing. Kyrgyzstan recognized private land ownership following the June 1998 referendum, but immediately imposed a five-year moratorium on all transactions in land (thus moving backward in terms of measures of transferability compared with the pre-referendum period, when land was state-owned but use rights were secure for ninety-nine years and transferable). The remaining countries of Central Asia and Belarus generally do not recognize private land ownership, but they differ in their attitude toward land transactions. Land-use rights are transferable in Kazakhstan and Tajikistan. Turkmenistan, Uzbekistan, and Belarus prohibit any transactions in land.

Private ownership of land is the norm in market economies, and it is certainly an appropriate goal for countries in transition. Yet successful market agriculture can develop on state-owned land (it suffices to recall the case of Israel, where most land is leased by the state to farmers for terms of forty-nine or ninety-nine years). Security and transferability of tenure appear to be more important determinants of productivity and efficiency gains than legal property rights. The experience in developed market economies indicates that many farmers are "operators" and not "landowners:" they cultivate land that they do not own. Thus, farmers in Belgium, France, and Germany rent more than 60 percent of the land they cultivate, while the overall "tenancy rate" in the fifteen countries of the European Union is 40 percent. In Canada, 30 percent of farmed land is not owned by the farmers, and in the United States, only 35 percent of farmed land is fully owner operated: another 55 percent is a mixture of own land with land leased from others and 10 percent is cultivated by farmers who do not own any land. In ranking the land privatization policies in transition countries, one should give separate scores for two dimensions of the process: one score for actual legal recognition of private ownership of land (as in a market economy) and another, totally independent, score for transferability of land and security of tenure. Transferability is important no less, and perhaps even more, than private ownership for the development of land markets that enable the farmers to adjust the size of their holdings and allocate resources to the most efficient producers.

Restrictions on land transferability are a real barrier to the flow of resources from less efficient to more efficient users and thus an obstacle to overall efficiency improvement in agriculture. However, pragmatic considerations suggest that temporary moratoria on buying and selling land in transition countries may be necessary from political or social considerations. Policymakers in CIS and CEE are often concerned that the immediate exposure of the new landowners to the full range of land market transactions after decades of collectivism may have negative social consequences, which may involve excessive concentration of land in the hands of speculators and foreign owners.

Thus, Kyrgyzstan motivated the moratorium imposed simultaneously with the introduction of private land ownership in 1998 by the need to let the new landowners get used to the entire set of their property rights and fully recognize the implications of their decisions. Psychologically, people need a delay period to adjust to the new reality before making irrevocable decisions. To borrow an example from an area outside of agriculture, many recipients of mass privatization vouchers in Russia in the early 1990s blindly rushed to sell them to speculators and professional investors. They did not recognize the long-term value of the new asset and precipitously converted it into something familiar–cash. These early "voucher sellers" understood the implication of their irrevocable decision only much later, when gradual normalization had led to steep increases in the value of stock of the privatized companies, which they could have owned if they had not sold the vouchers.

In Kazakhstan, unscrupulous managers of farm enterprises took advantage of the total lack of asset management experience among the rural population to entice the new shareholders to sell their land shares. In this way, large segments of the rural population were stripped of their main asset and land was concentrated in the hands of a small number of farm bosses. This negative effect could probably have been avoided had the government of Kazakhstan temporarily restricted the buying and selling of land and limited transferability to short or perhaps medium-term lease transactions. Such approach to transferability of land would allow rural people to postpone irrevocable decisions to a later stage, when the economic situation has normalized and they have become more aware of the implications of land transactions. To ensure that the temporary moratorium quickly achieves the intended educational effect, it should be accompanied by appropriate information campaigns explaining property rights and land-market transactions to the new landowners.

Another dimension of land policy in transition countries is the land-allocation strategy. All CEE countries plus the "small" CIS countries allocate land to beneficiaries in the form of physical plots. In Russia, Ukraine, Kazakhstan, and other CIS countries, beneficiaries usually receive paper shares that certify their entitlement to a certain amount of land within the local farm enterprise, without specifying a concrete physical plot. In addition to paper shares, rural families in CIS cultivate small household plots of less than one hectare–a long-standing tradition in the former Soviet Union that dates back to the 1930s.

Allocation of physical land plots is clearly a better option in terms of potential transferability and impact on land markets. Ownership of a plot of land allows one to decide whether to farm it, sell it in return for a one-time lump sum, or perhaps lease it to somebody who can operate it more profitably, thus retaining the property rights "just in case" while earning a stream of future returns. If one holds a paper share, it represents fractional ownership in a large tract of jointly shared land, which in reality is managed and controlled by somebody else (typically the former collective farm in the village). Realizing land disposition options as a shareholder is much more difficult. The easy way is simply to leave the land share in the large farm that is already cultivating the land (as it always did in the past). Any other alternative will require negotiating with the current operator to identify, survey, and mark a physical plot of land that can be withdrawn for individual use from the jointly shared tract. Eventually, if the negotiations go well, the shareholder will end up in the same place as a person in a country that allocated land plots to beneficiaries from the start. Only this will have taken much longer and may involve considerable uncertainty as to the final outcome. In a ranking of land policies, allocation of physical plots scores much better than distribution of paper shares.

The last difference in land policy between CEE and CIS concerns the privatization strategy. The CEE countries (except Albania) have chosen to privatize land by restitution to former owners. The CIS countries (and Albania) have adopted the "land to the tiller" strategy: land is privatized to workers without any payment and in an equitable manner. Hungary and Romania are two CEE countries that used a mixed strategy: land was restituted to former owners and also distributed without payment to agricultural workers in the interest of social equity.

This restitution-distribution dichotomy is commonly explained by the different length of time since nationalization or collectivization–eighty years in CIS and fifty years in CEE. This explanation clearly carries a lot of weight, but a number of prominent counter-examples cast doubts as to its general validity. Thus, in CIS, Moldova, Ukraine, and Belarus rejected the concept of restitution, although the western parts of these countries were integrated into the Soviet Union after World War II, at the same time as the Baltic States, and the memory of private land ownership was much fresher than in Russia.

In CEE, Albania deviated from the general practice of its neighbors and opted for distribution rather than restitution. Perhaps the choice of restitution over distribution was determined more by the desire to make a clean break with the Soviet past than by the memory of land ownership. In other words, this was probably a strictly political decision, and not necessarily driven by rational economic considerations.

Examination of the impacts of restitution and distribution does not indicate anything that recommends one strategy over the other. Both are guided by clear justice principles, although the beneficiaries turn out to be different (former owners under restitution, "the tiller" under distribution). The distribution procedure, with its strict egalitarian foundations, may be simpler to design, as it does not require any decisions concerning former ownership rights. Yet both procedures are equally complex to implement if extended to the ultimate stage of physical allocation of land plots to individuals. True, restitution typically ends with allocation of physical plots of land, which is the preferred allocation strategy according to our "scorecard."

Table 1. Differences in the Implementation of Land Policy in Transition Countries

	Potential private ownership	Privatization strategy	Allocation strategy	Transferability	Land-policy index[*]
Rom	All	Rest+distribution	Plots	Buy/sell, lease	10.0
Hun	All	Rest+distribution	Plots	Buy/sell, lease	10.0
Bul	All	Restitution	Plots	Buy/sell, lease	9.2
Est	All	Restitution	Plots	Buy/sell, lease	9.2
Lat	All	Restitution	Plots	Buy/sell, lease	9.2
Lit	All	Restitution	Plots	Buy/sell, lease	9.2
Cz	All	Restitution	Plots	Buy/sell, lease	9.2
Svk	All	Restitution	Plots	Buy/sell, lease	9.2
Alb	All	Distribution	Plots	Buy/sell, lease	9.2
Arm	All	Distribution	Plots	Buy/sell, lease	9.2
Gru	All	Distribution	Plots	Buy/sell, lease	9.2
Mol	All	Distribution	Plots/shares	Buy/sell, lease	8.5
Az	All	Distribution	Plots/shares	Buy/sell, lease	8.5
Rus	All	Distribution	Shares	Lease	6.7
Ukr	All	Distribution	Shares	Lease	6.7
Kyr	All	Dist/conversion	Shares	Moratorium	5.4
Kaz	HH plots	None	Shares	Use rights	5.4
Taj	None	None	Shares	Use rights	2.5
Tur	All	None; virgin land to farmers	Leasehold	None	4.0
Uzb	None	None	Leasehold	None	0.6
Bel	HH plots	None	None	None	1.3
Pol	All	Sell state land	Plots	Buy/sell, lease	9.6

[*] On a scale of 0 to 10: land policy index 10 corresponds to ideal market attributes, 0 to no market attributes. For computational details of the land-policy index see Lerman, Csaki, and Feder (2001), chapter 2.

But distribution is not necessarily restricted to paper shares. Albania, Armenia, and Georgia followed a strict "land to the tiller" strategy, and yet it took the form of distribution of physical plots to individuals. Azerbaijan is preparing to launch a similar procedure. Moldova is currently in the middle of a large-scale "share conversion" process that allocates physical plots to shareholders. Whether a country adopts restitution to former owners or distribution to agricultural workers, the major determinants remain the allocation strategy (plots or paper shares), the legal status of private ownership, and the transferability or tradability of use rights and property rights. Restitution and distribution get the same mark on our scorecard.

Table 1 summarizes the differences in land policies across the ECA countries–recognition of private ownership of land, transferability of property and use rights, allocation of land in physical plots or paper shares, privatization by restitution or distribution. To quantify these differences, we have ranked the land policies on a scale of 0 to 10, where ten corresponds to the ideal attributes: private land ownership, full transferability, allocation in the form of physical plots (see the last column in table 1). In this ranking of land policies, the CEE countries as a group get a score of 9 out of 10 and the CIS countries a score of 6. This is indeed a significant divergence.

Individualization of Agriculture

Market economies are characterized by predominance of individual or family farms, with a smaller share of commercially oriented corporate farms. How have the divergent land policies affected the transition from collective to individual agriculture in CEE and CIS? Individual agriculture is possible without land privatization, and land privatization does not necessarily create individual farmers. Yet primarily because of differences in land allocation strategies–paper shares versus physical plots–the extent of individual cultivation in CIS is substantially lower than in CEE (figure 1). On average, 16 percent of agricultural land is cultivated individually in household plots and family farms across CIS, compared with 63 percent across the CEE countries (up from 4 percent and 14 percent respectively in the pre-transition decade). Although in CIS the share of individual agriculture in land is relatively modest, its contribution to the agricultural product has been steadily increasing over time and now approaches (and in some countries exceeds) 50 percent of total agricultural output.

Land-policy decisions, and especially the specific land-allocation strategy (physical plots versus certificates of entitlement), determine the resulting mix between corporate farms and individual agriculture. Countries that have opted for allocation of land in the form of physical plots (whether through restitution to former owners or distribution to workers) have a larger individual sector than countries that distribute land entitlements in the form of paper shares.

Figure 1. Share of Agric. Land in Individual Use in CEE and CIS, 1997

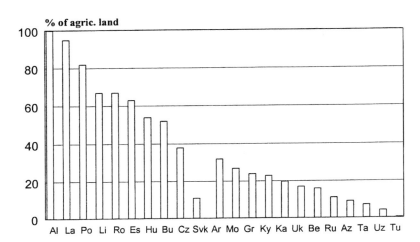

% of agric. land

There is a strong correlation between the land-policy choices of countries and the degree of individualization in agriculture. A higher land-policy score goes with a higher individualization rate: the CEE countries get 9 out of 10 for land policy and the degree of individualization is 63 percent; the CIS countries get 6 out of 10 for land policy and the degree of individualization is 16 percent. This is not surprising, as we have discussed the impacts of land policies on the shift of resources from collective to individual farming.

Perhaps more importantly, there is also a fairly strong association between the degree of individualization and agricultural performance. All six countries showing positive growth in agricultural output between 1992 and 1997 have a relatively high share of land in individual cultivation (more than 50 percent for CEE countries and more than 20 percent for CIS countries). Among the 16 countries that did not achieve agricultural growth, 10 have a relatively low degree of individualization. A regression analysis of the agricultural output growth (1992-97) versus land in individual use (in 1997) provides a fit with slope coefficient b = 0.32, significant at 10 percent (p = 0.08, R^2 = 0.14). It thus seems that more market-compliant land policies lead to higher individualization of agriculture, which is in turn associated with agricultural growth.

The positive impacts of individualization are also evident at the rural household level. In CIS, the process of land reform consists of two main components: the assignment of paper shares to the rural population and actual allocation of land for augmentation of household plots. While a land share corresponds to an endowment of 10-20 hectare, the average household plot is less than 1 hectare after enlargement.

Yet a bird in the hand is better than two in the bush: the land share remains on paper, while the household plot is allocated in physical form for real individual cultivation. The average plot size virtually doubled in the early 1990s, the number of plots increased significantly, and the share of total agricultural land in household plots rose from 4 percent in the 1980s to 16 percent in the late 1990s. The household plot is mainly a source of food for the family, but 10-20 percent of the output is sold for cash in nearby markets.

The cash revenue from these sales augments the income of rural families, and the household plot contributes altogether 40-50 percent of the family budget (including the value of homegrown products consumed by the family). Some families increase the household plot even further by leasing additional land from friends and neighbors. Others pool the land resources of parents, grandparents, and married children to create relatively large holdings. Surveys of rural households show that the larger the plot, the greater the surplus available for cash sales and the greater the contribution to family income.

Table 2. Characterization of Well-Being and Optimism amongst Independent Farmers and Employees of Corporate Farms in CIS (percent of respondents)

	Independent farmers	Farm employees
Change of family's material situation in recent years		
Improved	42	8
Unchanged	34	51
Deteriorated	24	41
Adequacy of family income at present		
Sufficient for subsistence (or worse)	45	70
Adequate for basic necessities	45	29
Comfortable–no material difficulties	10	1
Perception of family's economic future		
Better	43	14
Unchanged	47	55
Worse	9	31

Source: World Bank surveys for Russia, Ukraine, and Moldova 1994-98.

Private farmers cultivating land independently outside the collectivist framework are another segment of the rural population that appears to enjoy the benefits of individualization in CIS. Private farmers in most cases are former farm-enterprise employees who have decided to leave the collective and take the fate of their families in their hands. The employees remaining in farm enterprises come basically from the same population as private farmers, but they have a different set of attitudes and priorities. They prefer the relative safety of the traditional collective framework to the risks and uncertainties of independent farming. This may be attributed to personal attitudes toward risk, which are determined, among other factors, by age, education, and skills. Both groups give a fairly low evaluation of the general standard of living in their countries. Yet their responses in numerous surveys show that on the whole private farmers are better off and more optimistic than employees of collective enterprises (table 2). Since private farmers represent the ultimate individualization of agriculture, their positive assessment of family well-being–at least relative to the individuals who have decided to stay in the collective rather than face the risks of personal initiative–is evidence of the benefits of individual farming.

Persistence of Collective and Corporate Farm Structures

Despite reallocation of land to the individual sector in the process of land reform, large collective and corporate farms still play a much more prominent role in CEE and CIS than in market economies, where agriculture is primarily based on family farms. Various collective, cooperative, and corporate forms of farm organization continue to manage nearly 40 percent of agricultural land in CEE and 80 percent in CIS. As a result, the distribution of farm sizes in most transition countries retains the sharp duality that traditionally characterized socialist agriculture: a high proportion of very small farms (mainly household plots) control a relatively small proportion of land, and a small proportion of very large farms control a large proportion of land, if not most of the land (Table 3). This dual or bimodal distribution of land is at a sharp variance with the distribution observed in market economies (United States, Canada, the countries of the European Union), where most of the land is concentrated in mid-sized farms and the two extreme tails of very small and very large farms are much less prominent.

Although large collective or corporate farms remain prominent throughout the region, important differences are beginning to emerge between their organizational forms in CIS and CEE. Most large farms in CIS continue to operate like the former collectives, without significant change in size or management, although they are now registered under a variety of "market sounding" names (joint-stock societies, limited liability companies, partner-ships) and are not called *kolkhozy*.

The corporate farms in CEE–now called "companies," not "cooperatives"–are substantially smaller than the original collectives (averaging less than 1,000 hectare, down from 3,000-5,000 hectare before the transition). They are beginning to show greater sensitivity to market signals, including the ability to adjust the labor force to operating needs in the interest of higher profitability. Overall, the CEE corporate farms appear to be developing the basic attributes of market-oriented operation that are still not observed in most large farms in CIS. These emerging differences in farm organization are linked to differences in the philosophy of agricultural transition. Policy-makers in CIS essentially perceive market agriculture as based on the successors of former collective and state farms, which are to be subjected to a "horizontal" transformation toward improved productivity but otherwise remain largely unchanged in scale and scope.

Table 3. Concentration of Land: Percentage of Agricultural Land in the Top 10 Percent of Largest Farms

Country	Percentage of farm land	Farm structure characterized
Armenia	10	
Georgia	10	over-
Latvia	20	fragmented
Lithuania	30	
USA	**35**	
Canada	**38**	
EU15	**40**	
Slovenia	40	
Poland	40	"normal"
Romania	50	
Estonia	60	
Czech Republic	82	
Bulgaria	90	
Hungary	92	
Slovakia	97	sharply dual
Russia	95	
Ukraine	90	
Kazakhstan	99	

Source: Official country statistics.

Politicians in CEE, on the other hand, appear to have recognized the need for radical changes in the farm-enterprise sector, including the introduction of hard budget constraints and the enforcement of strict bankruptcy procedures for failing farms. This radically changes the organizational behavior of farm enterprises and sharpens their response to market forces. While CIS policies show a definite bias toward successor farm enterprises at all levels of government, CEE policies often favor individual farms and show a negative bias toward large corporate farms, thus forcing them to shift even further toward new market-oriented forms of behavior.

As noted in the previous section, individualization of agriculture has positive impacts at both the sectoral and the household level. Yet there has been no rush into individual farming by members of former collectives, and on the whole large corporate farms have not disintegrated. Different motivations are possible for the mutually exclusive decisions to farm one's land individually or "collectively." Individual risk preferences provide one explanation. A collective or cooperative farm may generate lower income but in a relatively safe, nonvolatile environment. This in itself is sufficient for some individuals to forgo the potentially higher incomes of individual farming that are necessarily associated with much higher uncertainty. In CIS, the privatized land resources represented by the individual shares are typically left by the shareowners in joint cultivation in the former collective farm or some corporate successor. Overall, a very small proportion of rural residents opt for exit from collectives and the individual farming sector is mainly growing through the increase of household plots assigned to collective farm employees. Another explanation, particularly relevant in CEE, is that many of the new landowners created through restitution left farming long ago and now have jobs and property in urban areas. They have no immediate personal use for their restituted land, and yet they would like to keep this newly found asset in their ownership rather than sell it. Entrusting the land to a larger corporation or cooperative in return for lease payments makes good economic sense. These new landowners, of course, also have the option of leasing their land to other private individuals, but this may be perceived as riskier than leasing to a large organization, which is regarded as a more reliable source of lease payments.

There are, however, at least two other broad sets of reasons that may create barriers to transition from collective to individual agriculture. One may be characterized as market failure or, more modestly, market imperfection. The other is related to regional and local power play and politics.

There is generally no evidence of economies of scale in primary agricultural production, while individual or family farms are easier to organize and operate than corporations. This accounts for the predominance of individual farming in market economies, where an individual farm is not necessarily a very small farm: the optimal farm size is determined in each particular case by the managerial capacity of the farmer, and it may be quite large for highly capable individuals. Corporate farms normally develop in special niches, where the corporate form of organization and the relatively large scale of operation have clear advantages. Thus, poultry and pig production are easily amenable to industrialization and corporatization, especially if integrated with processing.

Yet, in an imperfectly competitive environment, large farms may have easier access to input supplies, product-marketing channels, and credit facilities. This gives them a practical advantage relative to smaller individual farms and encourages the creation of large corporate farms in higher proportions than in a perfect market environment. Such market imperfections are observed in all market economies, and individual farmers typically overcome them through the creation of service cooperatives. A service cooperative is a large corporation that interfaces between the member-farmers and the imperfect market to exploit the special advantages enjoyed by large-scale operations. It can wield the combined power of the productive resources of 300 to 500 members when negotiating with input suppliers, product marketers, or banks, while the members keep their individual identity in production. The two-tier structure of individual family farms supported by a network of service cooperatives is a common phenomenon in market economies. It evolves naturally in any community of individual farmers who seek to overcome barriers to competition and access to market services.

The situation is more complex in CEE and CIS. The markets in transition countries are still far from perfect, and the established large corporate farms that have had decades of experience operating in the former socialist environment indeed may have substantial advantages in access to these imperfect markets compared with newly created and relatively inexperienced individual farmers. As a result, there is little motivation for individuals to exit from existing collectives and corporations and force their breakup through the creation of family farms. Potential farmers report in field interviews that, in the prevailing environment, they will be strongly disadvantaged relative to the established large corporate farms that succeeded the former collectives. Farmers interviewed in areas where individual farms are created in sufficient numbers display strong psychological resistance to the formation of service cooperatives: they see too much similarity between the collective organization that they have left behind and the cooperative organization advocated as a market solution for their difficulties. As a result, they prefer to fight it out on their own, individually, from a position of inferiority relative to the large farms, and unwittingly forgo the strengths and benefits that true voluntary cooperation imparts to the individual members.

Closely related to the whole issue of market imperfections is the question of power politics at the local and regional level. In many countries, especially in CIS, the regional political system still retains many of the crude interventionist features that characterized the socialist command economy. Even if the central government no longer interferes directly in farm operations through plans and targets, the regional authorities often preserve the traditional pattern of prescription and proscription. Although regional governments no longer command central budgets that they can distribute among their favorite farms, they often have access to other resources and authority mechanisms that can be used to force compliance with behavior in their interest.

There is a symbiotic relationship between the management of large collective and corporate farms, on the one hand, and the regional authorities, on the other. The large farms still represent the organized backbone of agriculture in each region, and even though they often produce less than 50 percent of agricultural output, they are much easier for the local authorities to control and tax than the thousands and tens of thousands of individual households. The organizational logic that fueled the collectivization strategy in the Soviet Union in the 1930s and then in Central Eastern Europe in the 1950s remains equally valid today: it is easier for the authorities to deal with a small number of large farms when trying to meet budget targets, food availability objectives, and other procurement goals. In return for the rents and payoffs that the local authorities extract from the large collective farms, their managers are rewarded with preferential access to inputs and credits, as well as personal prestige and other perquisites. This interplay between managers of large collective farms and regional authorities acts to preserve the existing farm structure, suppressing the expected shift from collective to individual farming and to viable corporate farms that act like business entities accountable to their shareholders.

This phenomenon has largely disappeared in countries and societies that became highly democratized during the transition. Yet in less democratized countries with strong remnants of the former authoritarian mentality it persists and, together with market imperfections, plays a role in shaping the farm structure. Generalization is impossible, due to lack of data, but the specific case of Russia demonstrates that agriculturally productive regions, where large collective farms are still a potentially rich source of payoffs for the regional authorities, have little tendency to reform. Farms in agriculturally poor regions, on the other hand, are less attractive as a cash source or provider of strategic agricultural products (e.g. grain) for the regional authorities and there is a higher likelihood that they will be left alone to adjust and adapt to the new environment, possibly breaking up into a large number of smaller units or even individual farms in the process.

This prediction is borne out by the election results in Russia, where the fertile agricultural provinces form the "Red Belt" that consistently returns the conservatives to power (table 4). It is also supported by recent empirical findings of a World Bank study in Russia, which shows that the agricultural sector in the fertile Saratov *oblast* is much less reformed than the agricultural sector in the less fertile Leningrad *oblast.*

Barriers to individual farming and the persistence of large-scale collective or corporate farming in CEE and CIS may thus be explained by various factors: the personal risk preferences of individual landowners, lack of alternative occupation opportunities, market imperfections, cronyism and special relations between regional authorities and farm managers, and the desire of local authorities to use the farm sector as a tool for social and political objectives. All these factors play a certain role, but their specific importance or weight varies from country to country, depending on local conditions. In combination, they maintain the proportion of collective and corporate farms in transition countries at a higher level than in established market economies.

Table 4. Average Economic Indicators for Regions with Predominantly Communist and Predominantly Democratic Voting Patterns in Russia's 1999 Duma Elections

Share (%)	Most communist regions (29.4% of the national vote)	Most democratic regions (16.7% of the national vote)
Agriculture in regional GDP	15	6
Labor in agriculture	17	6
Budget to agriculture	7	3
Urban population	62	80

Note: The two political-preference categories include the twenty-five regions with the highest percent of votes for the bloc of eight communist parties and for the bloc of five democratic parties, respectively. The numbers are averages for the regions in the two categories. All differences are statistically significant at 5 percent.
Source: P. Schreinemachers, 2001 (unpublished).

Performance and the Policy Environment

Agricultural performance in CEE and CIS is correlated with the degree of individualization of agriculture, which in turn depends on each country's choice of land policies. Yet the discussion in the preceding section has highlighted a range of additional factors that impact on the shift from collective to individual farming, and thus probably on agricultural performance. The most general among these factors are the market environment and the socioeconomic norms that govern the human relations within the agricultural sector.

Land policies are just one component of the market environment for agriculture. Additional factors include liberalization of price and trade policies, farm restructuring and development of land-reform institutions, privatization and de-monopolization of agro-processing and input supply, development of rural financial systems, and establishment of a market-oriented institutional frame-work. A country scorecard can be constructed for each of these factors, like the scorecard for land policy discussed above. Averaging the scores for each of these components produces an index that reflects the level of market reforms in agriculture (referred to as the ECA index). This index is more general than the land-policy score used previously, as it incorporates additional dimensions of agricultural reform beyond land policy. The results, however, are essentially the same: countries with a higher score on the agricultural market reform index show better agricultural performance.

A similar positive association is observed when relating agricultural per-formance to the Country Policy and Institutional Assessment (CPIA) index, which is based on four groups of policy variables that are not directly related to agriculture: macroeconomic management and sustainability reforms; policies for sustainable and equitable growth; policies for reducing inequalities; and public sector management. A more comprehensive aggregate index incorporating in addition the Freedom House Freedom Index, which includes assessment of democratization and corruption, and the Euromoney Creditworthiness Index, which assesses the development of financial institutions and the risk level associated with each country's transition policies, demonstrates that higher scores on the index are associated with smaller decline in agricultural output.

The CEE countries receive consistently higher scores than the CIS countries on all policy-related indices. An average index incorporating five standard policy indices (with equal weights) produces a score of 6.6 for ten CEE countries and 3.8 for twelve CIS countries. More advanced policies go hand in hand with better economic results. In terms of performance, agricultural output in 1997 is practically at the 1992 level for CEE and 17 percent below the 1992 level for CIS. In terms of overall economic performance, CEE countries show a healthy 8 percent growth in GDP between 1992 and 1997, while the CIS countries register a drop of 25 percent in GDP during the same period. Finally, in terms of developments in agricultural employment, labor productivity in CEE rose 25 percent following a 16 percent reduction of total agricultural labor, while in CIS labor productivity dropped 21 percent following a 9 percent increase in total agricultural labor. The relationship between reform policies and performance across different subgroups of countries in CEE and CIS is illus-trated in table 5.

Table 5. Performance Ranking and the Policy Index by Groups of Countries in CEE and CIS

	Change in GDP	Change in Agric Output	Change in Agric Labor	Change in Agric Labor Productivity	Performance Ranking (1=best, 5=worst)	Policy Index[#] 1997-98
West CEE (4)[*]	Up	Down	Sharp down	Up	1	7.3
East CEE (4)[**]	Down	Steady	Steady	Steady	2	6.0
Transcaucasia (3)	Down	Up	Sharp up	Down	3	4.3
European CIS, Kazakhstan (5)	Down	Down	Down	Down	4	4.1
Central Asia (4)	Down	Down	Up	Down	5	3.0

[*] Czech Republic, Slovakia, Hungary, Estonia.
[**] Bulgaria, Romania, Latvia, Lithuania
[#] On a scale of 1 to 10: higher values imply closer to market environment. Calculated as simple average of five policy-oriented indices: the ECA Index (Csaki and Nash, 1998), the Freedom Index (Karatnycky et al., 1997), the Liberalization Index (de Melo et al., 1996), the Creditworthiness Index (*Euromoney*, September 1998), and CPIA Index (internal World Bank documents; the methodology of calculation is available from the authors on request).

The tangible differences in agricultural and economic performance between the two groups of countries are clearly related to differences in the general policy environment, as well as differences in land policy. It is very likely that the political, social, and macroeconomic factors characterizing the different policy environments in the CIS and CEE, as reflected in the policy-oriented indices, have in fact influenced their different land-reform decisions.

Land reform alone may have been insufficient to trigger and sustain the divergent trend, but combined with political commitment and resolve it has produced the patterns of divergent performance that we observe today. Countries that decisively implement market-oriented policies–in agriculture, in the whole economy, and in society in general–are outstripping the reluctant reformers in terms of both agricultural indicators and overall economic growth. The main message is that market reforms in general, with land reform as part of the overall policy package, have been reflected in better agricultural and economic performance.

Implications for Agricultural Strategies

Our analysis suggests that policy-makers aiming for a transition from the former socialist structure to an efficient and viable farm sector should place the emphasis on individual agriculture and corporate entities operating under hard budget constraints and strict business orientation. We cannot ignore the evidence of market economies: agriculture is predominantly organized around individual farms, with a small share of corporate farms, and certainly not collective or labor-managed farms. Albania, Armenia, Georgia, Moldova, and more recently Azerbaijan and Kyrgyzstan are examples of countries that are moving toward complete individualization. In these countries, governments and the international community should support the process by developing the institutional tools of individual land management, including titling, registration, extension, and farmer education.

In countries where fast transition towards individualization is not feasible for social and political reasons (e.g., Russia, Ukraine, Belarus, Central Asia), the strategy should focus on creating the conditions which provide inducement to the breakup of the large corporate farms into farms of the most efficient size, given local circumstances–farms that typically will be much smaller and certainly more manageable and will operate under hard budget constraints. Various subsidization avenues allowing "restructured" farms to avoid being exposed to market discipline need to be curtailed, as these only serve to slow the transition process and sustain farms that are not economically viable. This also implies that central governments need to induce local authorities to cease viewing corporate farms as a tool of social policy (e.g. a source of lifetime employment for the rural population or a source for producing cheap food).

A level playing field is required that allows farms of all structures and sizes to operate if they can maintain viability under market conditions. The procedure for breakup of nonviable corporate structures needs to be in place, thus facilitating the emergence of smaller or individual farms where larger farms have failed. Identification of land ownership or land rights entitlements with distinct tracts of land is an important ingredient of such a procedure.

Dismantling large farm enterprises, as implemented in Albania, Armenia, Georgia, and to a certain extent Romania, is the most direct path, but not the only path to the creation of an agriculture dominated by family farms. Distribution of land and asset shares can serve the same purpose, as is becoming evident in Moldova. To be effective, however, the first stage of allocating paper shares must be followed by a second stage in which land and assets are distributed to individuals in kind. This is the only way to achieve genuine restructuring of the former socialist farms. A possible strategic direction that combines the advantages of individual enterprise with economies of scale of corporate organization is to support a two-tier agricultural system. In this system, land and production are managed by individuals, whereas services are provided by corporations or cooperatives. This is similar to the system practiced in the Israeli *moshav*. It is also similar to recent developments in Russia, where according to anecdotal evidence some former farm enterprises act as a service shell for household plots, which are responsible for all production. The extent to which these service shells evolve into genuine service cooperatives for individual producers will ultimately depend on the elimination of subsidized input deliveries by local authorities and introduction of hard budget constraints requiring strict repayment of all debt.

Table 6. Lessons of Transition in the Farm Sector

General patterns of success

- Privatization without true reorganization does not lead to performance break-throughs
- Better agricultural performance goes with
    o larger individual sector
    o greater liberalization
    o better performance of the overall economy
    o greater political commitment to reform
- Change varies across the region depending on
    o government's commitment to reform (both executive and legislative branches)
    o regional and local acceptance of new ownership modes and farm structures
    o presence of hard budget constraints for corporate farms
    o emergence of supporting market services
- CEE countries as a group have undertaken more of the steps associated with better performance and are outperforming the CIS

Lessons for governments and the international community

- Achieving agricultural potential is not possible without true restructuring of farms
- Subsidization cannot be effective in the absence of performance criteria, transparency, a well-defined time frame, and well-conceived targeting
- Formal privatization and formal adoption of reform do not necessarily imply real change in farm operation and performance
- Local power-group alliances involving regional governments and the former collective farm leaders can stall change as the old pattern of farm organization and operation may suit their interests

As we have noted previously, an individual farm is not necessarily a small farm. To exploit the full potential of individual farming, the strategy must ensure relatively free transferability of land from the state to private users (either in ownership or in long-term leases) and, more importantly, among private users. This naturally involves development of land-market institutions, including titling, registration, full cadastral services, and possibly also mortgage banking. Yet these technical aspects on their own are not enough. Governments in the region need to be convinced of the importance of land transactions for efficiency and productivity improvement.

While there is much concern among various observers and policy-makers regarding the damage of excessive land fragmentation and the need for land consolidation, transferability of land should be recognized as the recipe for curing these problems. Land policy should aim for elimination of restrictions on land transactions (including prohibition on corporate and foreign land owner-ship, which persists in some CEE countries) and lowering of fiscal and adminis-trative barriers (taxes, fees, bureaucratic requirements).

The thrust to promote transferability of land by international bodies must be managed so as to avoid possible conflicts with countries that do not wish to recognize private land ownership. Experience throughout the world shows that in most cases transferability and security of tenure are more important than formal ownership for efficiency and productivity increases. The proven capacity of rental markets to improve land allocation suggests that excessive focus on convincing ideologically stubborn governments to relent in this regard may be counter-productive. Rather, progress on legitimizing rental markets and providing the legal and enforcement apparatus for long-term leases may prove to be a more feasible objective in the medium term. The general lessons and conclusions that we draw from a decade of transition in CIS and CEE are schematically summarized in table 6.

A related issue is the disposition of large areas that for various reasons (typically relating to political, historical, and ideological factors) are maintained under state ownership. The ultimate objective is to privatize the ownership of such land, but as has been argued above, long-term leases to private operators provide for a fairly efficient utilization of such land. The focus of the policy discussion should be on ensuring that the access to such land is available to all potential operators, rather than only or preferentially to those who intend to manage very large farms. Competition in accessing leases from the state is also necessary to avoid a hidden subsidy (through artificially low rent) to farm entities that ultimately would not be viable.

Lessons from Ten Years
of Rural Transition

Johan F. M. Swinnen

It is now more than a decade ago that the Berlin Wall fell and signalled the beginning of a vast set of changes throughout the countries of the former Soviet Bloc. Economic and institutional reforms in the Communist world started more than twenty years ago further east: first in China in the late 1970s and later in Vietnam. The changes affected society in a multitude of ways. They affected the way the political and economic system operated but also the social organization of society, the psychology of the people living in the countries, and the culture of day-to-day life. Below, the focus will be on how these changes affected the rural economy and the agricultural and food sector.

When looking at the transformation of the rural economies and the agri-food sector of transition economies, similar characteristics and diverging patterns can be observed. It is from confronting the similarities and the diverging experiences that one can learn and try to identify the factors affecting the economic behaviour of the systems. Performance differs strongly among transition countries. One can distinguish three "extreme" patterns in agricultural transition, for the first nine years of transition (figures 1 and 2).

- *Pattern I* ("Central Europe"): a strong decline in gross agricultural output (GAO) coincides with a strong increase in output per worker, because of a strong outflow of labor from agriculture. This is the pattern followed by the Czech Republic, Slovakia and Hungary: GAO declines by around 30 percent during the first years of transition, but stabilizes after four years. At the same time, agricultural labor productivity (ALP) increases rapidly: around 10 percent annually during the first nine years of transition.
- *Pattern II* ("Russia"): a strong decline in GAO coincides with a strong decline in ALP. Russia, Ukraine and Belarus are typical examples of this pattern, as are several other Newly Independent States (NIS). On average, output fell by almost 50 percent in these countries and labor productivity by around 30 percent.
- *Pattern III* ("China"): a strong increase in GAO coincides with an, albeit slower, increase in ALP. Examples are China, Vietnam, and, in Europe, Albania. On average, output increased by more than 50 percent in China and Vietnam, while labor productivity increased by 25 percent.

Figure 1. Gross Agricultural Output (GAO) during First Nine Years of Transition[*]

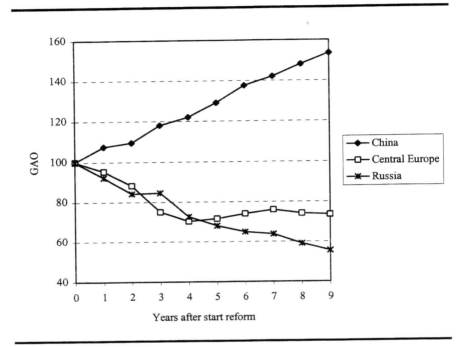

Years after start reform

Source: Own calculations based on data from OECD and FAO
[*] "China" is the average for China and Vietnam; "Central Europe" is the average for the Czech Republic, Slovakia and Hungary; and "Russia" is the average for Russia, Ukraine and Belarus.

The causes of these differences in performance include both variations in reform policies and in initial conditions.[1] While most recognize the impact of both, there has been a fierce debate on the relative importance of the various factors, which has been most intense on the implications of the reforms in China for reforms elsewhere. The Chinese reforms have resulted in extraordinary growth and are argued to have been successful because they were "gradual," in contrast to CEE and FSU reforms (Roland and Verdier, 1999).

However, others have argued that the difference in structural characteristics of the Chinese economy at the outset of transition makes it a unique situation, with very little policy lessons to be learned for the CEE and FSU transition countries (Sachs and Woo, 1994).

Figure 2. Agricultural Labor Productivity (ALP) during First Nine Years of Transition*

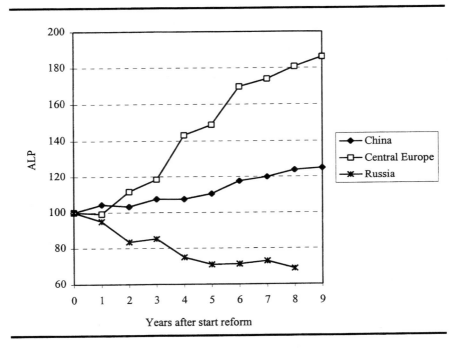

Years after start reform

Source: Own calculations based on data from OECD, FAO, ADB and national statistics.
* "China" is the average for China and Vietnam; "Central Europe" is the average for the Czech Republic, Slovakia and Hungary; and "Russia" is the average for Russia, Ukraine and Belarus.

Impact of Initial Conditions

Initial conditions vary substantially among countries. At the outset of transition, China and Vietnam had the lowest GNP/capita level. Related to the level of development, the share of agriculture in employment was considerably higher in China (around 70 percent) than in Russia (less than 20 percent), and was the lowest in Central Europe (13 percent). China and Vietnam had a very labor-intensive agriculture. The man/land ratio was higher than one, compared to less than 0.15 in Central Europe and Russia (see table 1).[2]

In Central Europe and East Asia, the collectivization of agriculture and introduction of central planning occurred after the Second World War, while in Russia this was in the 1920s and 1930s. Experience with private and individual farming was hence more likely to be present than in Russia. In Russia and other

FSU countries land was nationalized during the socialist era, while in Central Europe most collective farm land was legally owned by individuals. In China, the collective farms had legal and effective property rights while in Vietnam land was state-owned but the effective property rights were controlled by the collective farms. Finally, pre-transition agriculture in all countries was characterized by the dominance of large-scale farms[3] (table 1).

In China and Vietnam agriculture was heavily taxed, while in most of the CEE region and the FSU, agriculture was generally supported with heavy subsidies. Also, pre-reform, China and Vietnam mainly traded with non-CMEA countries, while the Soviet Union formed the backbone of the CMEA system, trading mainly with other socialist countries. The Central European countries were somewhat less integrated, but still a large part of their trade volume went through the CMEA system.

To estimate the impact of initial conditions, we used a combination of a principal component (PC) analysis and regression analysis in Macours and Swinnen (2000b).

Figure 3. Classification by Principal Components of Initial Conditions: Index of Pre-Reform Development (PC1) and Index of Pre-Reform Distortions (PC2)

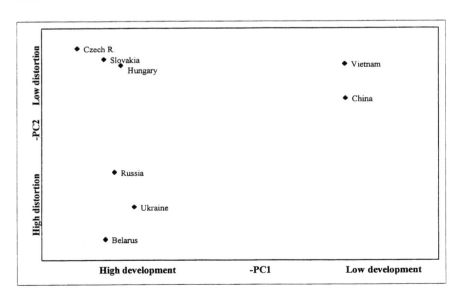

Source: Macours and Swinnen (2000b)

Table 1. Initial Conditions and Policies in the Transition Patterns*

	Patterns		
	Central Europe	Russia	China
Initial Conditions (IC)			
GNP/capita PPP	7670	6803	950
Share of agr. In employment	13	17	70
Agric. labor intensity	0.13	0.09	1.49
Legal land ownership	individuals °	state	state
Pre-reform agr. price policy	subsidized	subsidized	taxed
Years under central planning	42	73	32
Reform Policies (RP)			
Land reform procedure	restitution °	share distr.	phys. distr.
Property rights reform	fast	slow	Fast
Policy Outcomes (PO) #			
Relative price change	-41	-60	+24
Use rights	strong	weak	Strong
% agr. land in individual farms	16	11	99
Overall liberalization index	0.86	0.60	0.15

- The values are the averages of the representative countries from each pattern (the Czech Republic, Slovakia and Hungary for "Central Europe"; Russia, Ukraine, and Belarus for "Russia", China and Vietnam for "China").
° Part of the land in Hungary was owned by collective farms and (therefore) only one-third of Hungarian land was restituted; the rest was privatized through compensation bonds and physical distribution.
Five years after start of the reforms.

Source: Macours and Swinnen (2001)

We show that six indicators of initial conditions (see table 1) can be captured by two principal components:

- PC1 has high negative weight for income level, and high positive weights for labor intensity and the importance of agriculture in the economy, and can therefore be interpreted as an *index of the level of development* at the beginning of transition.

- PC2 has high positive weights for years under central planning and integration in the CMEA, and a high negative weight for land in private ownership pre-reform, and can be interpreted as an *index of the level of distortions* at the beginning of transition.

Figure 3 plots all the countries according to these indices of development (PC1) and distortion (PC2). The three patterns of transition, based on performance, can be clearly distinguished within this classification of initial conditions: Central Europe with a higher level of development (PC1) and lower pre-reform distortions (PC2). Russia, Ukraine and Belarus differ mostly from this first group by higher pre-reform distortions.

China and Vietnam had a much lower level of development than the two other groups, and medium levels of distortions. Our regressions show that during the first years of transition, agricultural *output* developments were to an important extent determined by initial conditions, both directly and indirectly, through their effect on policy outcomes.

However, the results of the estimations also suggest that (exogenous) reform policy choices played an important role in determining labor *productivity* developments during the first years of transition. After correcting for the endogenous part of the different policy outcomes, the establishment of strong use rights and the overall liberalization of the economy has a significant positive effect on ALP.

Impact of Reform Policies

The relative price changes following price and trade liberalization have importantly affected the post-reform output developments. With subsidy cuts and the collapse of the CMEA trading system, this resulted in a dramatic fall of relative prices for farms, and in output.

Figure 4 shows a positive relationship between the relative price changes and the output changes after the first five years of the reform. Importantly, the only TCs where GAO has increased during transition are the countries where relative prices have increased–and vice versa. Macours and Swinnen (2000a) estimate that terms of trade effect explains 40-50 percent of the fall in average crop output in eight CEE countries during transition.

The shift from collective farming to individual (family) farming had a positive impact on agricultural output. Monitoring problems are among the reasons why there is less incentive to work on a cooperative farm than on an individual farm. On an individual farm the farmer's income is directly related to the performance of the farm, and is therefore a greater incentive to increase the labor effort. This causes an increase in the productivity of labor as well as in the intensity with which the other inputs are used, as was also found in other studies on China (Lin, 1992) and Vietnam (Pingali and Xuan, 1992).

Figure 4. Output and Price Changes after Five Years of Reform in Fifteen Transition Countries

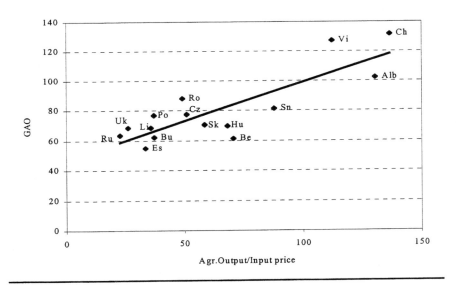

Source: Macours and Swinnen (2001)

Interestingly, the shift to individual farms had a negative impact on average labor productivity in agriculture. This was because the positive impact of the greater labor effort on productivity and of lower monitoring costs was more than offset by other effects, such as the fragmentation of assets induced by the break-up of collective farms. The substitution of other inputs by labor contributed to the negative relationship with average labor productivity. This can be caused both by the increase in the marginal productivity of labor, *ceteris paribus*, with the shift to individual farms and by a change in the relative price of labor vis-à-vis the cost of other inputs. The latter is reinforced by capital constraints and credit market imperfections, which are widespread during agricultural transition. Finally, in situations of food insecurity, worker owners will prefer individual farming rather than leaving agriculture.

Privatization and land reform affected performance differently, depending on their impact on property rights and on the environment. In respect to property rights one can distinguish between use rights and transfer rights. Transfer rights have been established in the CEE region, and, since 1994, also in Russia. Although land transfers have occurred on some occasions in China, there is no legal framework guaranteeing the transfer right of land. However, even in the TCs where land transfer rights are legal, land sales are *de facto* largely absent during the period we are analyzing. Nevertheless, leasing or transfer of use rights had an important impact on land allocation.

The restitution process in Central Europe and the land distribution process in China created stronger individual use rights than the share distribution process in Russia and Ukraine. Despite the allocation of land shares to members, the land remains in joint cultivation pending a further restructuring decision by the "shareowners" (Lerman, 1997). Significant transaction costs limit the effective use rights of the individual owners.

These differences are important since the transfer of effective use rights to individuals generally induced a decline in output and an increase in productivity. The creation of effective use rights caused profit-maximizing behavior with hard budget constraints. This resulted in a reduction of surplus input use and therefore a decline in output. At the same time it improved the allocation and efficiency of input use, causing an increase in productivity.

The impact of privatization on productivity depends on liberalization in the rest of the economy. In particular, slow liberalization resulted in significant rigidities in the capital and labor market, reducing both the inflow of capital for working capital and investments, and the outflow of surplus labor. Macours and Swinnen (2000a) conclude that because of these market imperfections the direct efficiency impact of privatization in countries such as Romania and Bulgaria was negative. It was positive in the Central European countries, such as Hungary and the Czech Republic, where liberalization removed factor market imperfections to a greater extent. In countries such as Romania and Albania, productivity gains from privatization arrived primarily indirectly through the shift to individual farming.

Furthermore, in Central Europe strong productivity gains occurred despite a relatively limited shift to individual farming. Compared to Russia and Ukraine where large-scale farms continued to dominate, farms in Central Europe generally have undergone more effective restructuring, including both management reform and operation adjustments. In contrast, Lerman and Csaki

(1997) report that, despite some downsizing in restructured farms, internal reorganization has not produced far-reaching results in Russia and Ukraine and the collective framework has preserved most of its traditional function. As a result of this lack of restructuring, Sedik, Trueblood, and Arnade (1999) measure a decline in farm efficiency during transition in Russia.

Finally, organization and contract disruptions caused a decline in output and productivity during transition. External disruptions resulted from the collapse of the CMEA trading system. Internal disruptions resulted from the breakup of the strong integrated system of supply chains, with the central planner as enforcement mechanism. The breakup of this contracting system with privatization, restructuring, and liberalization, in the absence of alternative contract enforcement mechanisms and information distribution systems caused important drops in output and investment (McMillan, 1997). Several explanations of this result focus on the disruptions of relation-specific investments, due to information problems, search frictions, and absence of contract enforcement mechanisms.

Roland and Verdier (1999) argue that the Chinese dual-track liberalization allowed enterprises to reap the informational benefits from price liberalization while avoiding the disruption associated with the breakdown of the planning system. Despite the inefficiencies of only liberalizing part of the prices, some form of continued state control at the beginning of transition may avoid the output disruption and temporary fall in investment generated by a big-bang policy. Rozelle (1996) explains how the initial and abrupt liberalization of the fertilizer market in China in 1985 caused major disruptions in fertilizer supplies, leading the government to retake control of fertilizer sales in 1987. Five years later, during which time China's domestic marketing capacity developed, new fertilizer liberalization resulted in no disruption.

Macours and Swinnen (2000a) estimate that between 30 percent and 60 percent of average crop output decline in CEE countries was due to institutional disruptions. Based on a case study of the Slovakian sugar sector, Gow and Swinnen (1998) show that output and yields increased dramatically, both at the processing and at the farm level, after new (FDI-induced) contract enforcement mechanisms and solutions to input contracting were implemented. The solution to contract holdups in this case—as in other transition countries (McMillan, 1997)—comes from private rather than public enforcement.

In summary, both Russia and Central Europe were characterized by pre-reform subsidization of agriculture, relatively low labor intensity of farms and a small share of agriculture in the economy but differ in the pre-reform land ownership and the period under central planning. While both in Russia and Central Europe terms of trade declined in agriculture following price and trade liberalization due to pre-reform taxation of agriculture, the choice and implementation of privatization, land reform and overall liberalization policies differed substantially.

In Central Europe, land reform through restitution and physical distribution led to stronger individual property rights. Further, the more extensive and more radical liberalization of the general economy reduced obstacles for intersectoral labor mobility. In contrast, in Russia land ownership rights were allocated under the form of shares in the former collective and state farms, causing weak individual property rights and limited incentives for resource allocation improvements. Also, the dependence of individuals on farms for food security and social benefits, such as housing, further reduced mobility and the outflow of labor from agriculture. In combination with low overall liberalization and the lack of individual farming skills after several generations of Communist rule, labor mobility from farms and to other sectors is constrained. Hence surplus labor has not left agriculture and is trapped in large-scale farms that continue to be dominated by old management. The consequence is that with decreasing terms of trade, while GAO has declined to a similar extent as in Central Europe, ALP has fallen with GAO in Russia, while it increased strongly in Central Europe.

The third pattern, followed by China and Vietnam is characterized by growth in both output and productivity during transition. These countries started with very labor-intensive agriculture, which was taxed. Price and trade liberalization caused an improvement in the terms of trade. Institutional reforms included the distribution of clear and strong land use rights to farm workers and rural households, and a complete breakup of the collective and/or state farms into individual farms. Because of the high labor intensity (and low labor productivity) on the collective farms the shift to individual farming implied important benefits because of improved labor incentives and profit maximization, and low costs from fragmentation. The strong shift to individual farming was also stimulated by the low level of income in these TCs, where food security concerns played an important role: in all these TCs radical and widespread de-collectivization emerged to some extent spontaneous–as a reaction to a major crisis.

In combination these factors contributed to increases in GAO and ALP. However, the food security concerns, as well as the link between social benefits (such as housing) and economic sectors, increased intersectoral (and rural-urban) mobility costs, contributing to the slower growth of labor productivity than output. Institutional and organizational disruptions contributed to investment and output declines. They are argued to have been more important in Central Europe and Russia than in China with its more "gradual approach" to market liberalization. Several analyses show that these disruptions have caused important declines in output.

However, our analysis suggests that key determinants of output growth in China are (a) the terms of trade effect–which was importantly determined by the pre-reform taxation of agriculture–and (b) radical reforms in the allocation of land property rights and in the re-organization of agricultural production. In fact, Albania, the only European country with similar structural characteristics as China (and Vietnam), introduced radical market liberalization, causing strong disruptions in the exchange relationships. This has not prevented it from recording high growth rates in GAO (as in China and Vietnam). In fact, since the start of the reforms in 1991 and despite the chaos following the 1997 political upheaval, average annual GAO growth in Albania has been almost 10 percent (Cungu and Swinnen, 1999).

All this suggests that key determinants of agricultural growth during the first years of transition in China have also been initial conditions, radical land reform and farm restructuring. Hence, one should be careful and nuanced in using the "Chinese miracle" as an example to advocate gradual reforms in other transition countries.

Transition Dynamics: Lessons from Russia and Central Europe

During the first years of transition, output developments were significantly affected by initial conditions. However, reform policies–relative to initial conditions–grow in importance as the transition progresses. Figure 5 shows that while output continued declining in Russia, this trend was reversed in Central Europe: after the initial decline, output started recovering.

We observe in several Central European agricultural markets–and more so in the crop sector than in livestock production–that output development is U-shaped with three phases. There is an initial decline in output caused primarily by declining terms of trade and contract disruptions. It then bottoms out, as the terms of trade stabilize and their effect phases out, and later increases again as a result of increases in productivity. The latter phase is more significantly affected by reform policies than by initial conditions.

The initial decline in output is primarily caused by institutional disruptions, or "creative destruction."[4] The socialist system left a badly distorted system of input, output, and trade. The reorganization of this system, and the institutional changes associated with it, caused major disruptions and thereby declines in investment and output. While a variety of models have been developed to explain the mechanism–some focusing on information problems (Blanchard and Kremer, 1997), others on search costs (Roland and Verdier, 1999) and yet others on contract enforcement problems (Gow and Swinnen, 1998)–all agree that the organizational disruptions negatively affected output and investment during transition. Or, as Kornai's (2000: 4) put it more simply: "Correcting this structure called for creative destruction. Because destruction is rapid, whereas creation proceeds more slowly, the two processes led to a deep recession."

Figure 5. Changes in GDP since 1989

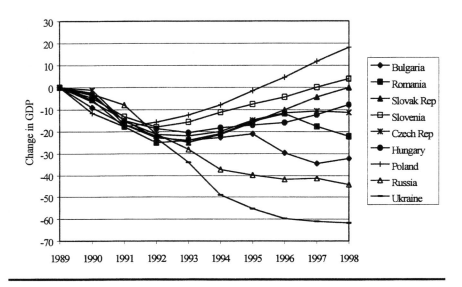

Source: OECD

This process is obvious from figure 5: output fell in all CEE and FSU countries with the disruptions during the initial transition years.

In order to have "creation" follow "destruction" one needs to implement basic reforms. While the output developments between 1989 and 1992 are quite similar, the trends clearly diverge afterwards. The reason behind these diverging patterns is differences in reform policies of the governments. Overall liberalization and sustained macroeconomic stabilization are essential elements for sustainable growth and have laid the basis for gradual institutional change in the more advanced transition countries. In the less advanced countries, stabilization has been jeopardized by the persistence of soft budget constraints (EBRD, 1999).[5]

While such reforms require a fundamental redefinition of the role of the state, they do not imply that the state should wither away. In Russia, however, the state has withered away in many important aspects (Schleifer, 1997), and has been unable to fulfill some key roles necessary for the development of a market economy, including establishing the rule of law, collecting taxes and establishing the basic conditions for macroeconomic stability. For example, estimates put the share of transactions which are carried out in Russia in the form of barter (mutual nonpayment) or with money substitutes at 75-85 percent (Bruszt, 2000).

The general reforms have strongly affected agricultural transition and performance, in particular with regard to creating stability, better access to capital and technology, and privatization. For example, the inflow of foreign investment and the associated inflow of technology, know-how and capital infusion in the agri-food chain have been most important in CEE countries. The progress of the general reforms, the macroeconomic situation, and the prospect of EU accession have created an environment more conducive to foreign investments.

Macroeconomic stabilization and general reform progress have improved access not only to foreign capital, technology, and know-how, but also access to domestic credit and capital sources for the farms. Credit markets have worked notoriously imperfect in CEE countries and the FSU, with disruptions due to privatization and overall restructuring causing major problems for farms, not only for investment purposes but even for working capital. These resulted in reductions in output; and the success of the recovery in some CEE countries is at least partially due to improvements in the general economic climate, which improved the working capital situation for the farms.

Another general reform with major impacts on agriculture is the privatization of companies involved in supplying inputs (fertilizer, pesticides, etc.) and credit to farms, and of food processing and distribution companies. Privatization procedures have differed significantly between countries. Kornai (2000) states that privatization strategies directed at selling of state companies, preferably to majority ownership structures, such as in Hungary, have been more successful than strategies based on some form of free distribution of property rights of state-owned companies, e.g. through vouchers.

The latter has mostly led to insider privatization in which managers have been able to collect a large share of the assets–as for example in the Czech Republic and more extremely in Russia–while the former has stimulated the emergence of many small enterprises and the inflow of capital, as for example in Hungary. This has certainly had a major positive impact on the performance of the entire agri-food sector in Hungary, also because much of the capital inflow came from foreign company investments.

While the initial decline in agriculture is affected by institutional disruptions and terms of trade effects, the recovery is driven by productivity increases (where the necessary reforms have been implemented). In CEE countries which implemented the necessary reforms, productivity increases have emerged in the second half of the 1990s. For example, figure 6 illustrates that yields have increased substantially in CEE.

Figure 6. Change in Yields in CEE*

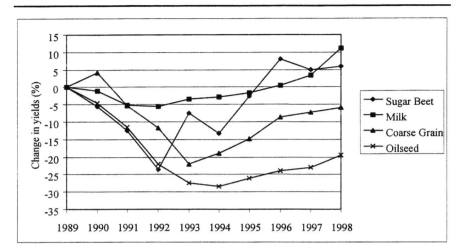

*CEE= average of Poland, the Czech Republic and Hungary

Furthermore, figure 7 illustrates–on the basis of data for the CEE sugar market–
how the increase in productivity has driven output recovery. While the initial
decline in sugar output is price driven (and through institutional disruptions [not
noted]) the recovery in the second half of the 1990s is largely productivity
driven (partly a result of institutional disruptions being overcome).

An essential ingredient in recovery and productivity increases is the
development of institutions for contract enforcement and access to capital. An
important source of increased productivity in CEE agriculture is the emergence
of new institutions for information, product exchange and contract enforcement.
Pre-transition systems were strongly vertically integrated. The central planner
provided the information and enforced contracts involving exchanges between
the various agents in the chain.

The removal of the central planning and control system, in the absence of
new institutions to enforce contracts, distribute information, and finance
intermediation caused serious disruptions throughout the economy (Gow and
Swinnen, 1998; Stiglitz, 1999).

New enforcement institutions have come in a variety of forms. Frequently,
the most successful ones have depended on private enforcement mechanisms
within the framework of specially designed contracts or institutional
arrangements. Increasingly contracts between private agents act as substitutes
for missing or imperfect public enforcement institutions (McMillan, 1997).

Successful institutions have offered enough flexibility to allow producers, suppliers, and buyers to adjust to the continuously changing environment during transition.

For example, while land-lease contracts initially often took the form of short (one-season) informal contracts, they have gradually evolved into more formal and longer-term contracts, reflecting reduced uncertainty and improved understanding of the market environment by both the owner of the land and the tenant. Leasing, not only of land, but also of equipment is another example of an institutional innovation adapted to transition as it mitigates farms' collateral problems in financing new equipment.

Vertical integration, especially with foreign direct investment, has played an important role in the re-emergence of the institutions of exchange. Vertical integration in various forms has improved access to capital, inputs, and technology for farms. Beyond supply of capital, agribusiness firms, in search of guaranteed and high quality raw materials (or product markets), have offered farms a number of arrangements to encourage greater production and marketing and to overcome constraints that have limited economic activity since the onset of transition (Gow et al., 2000).

Figure 7. Output, Relative Prices and Yields of Sugar Beet in CEE Countries

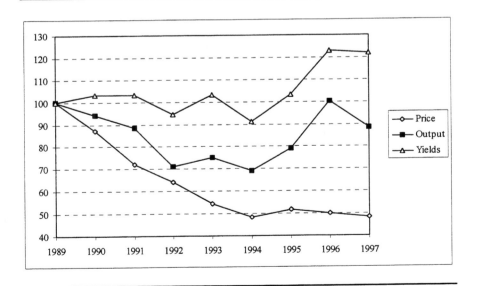

Source: Swinnen, Gow and Maviglia (2000).
* CEE countries: average for Poland, Hungary, the Czech Republic and Slovakia

For example, food processors have negotiated contracts with banks and input suppliers to provide farms with inputs that enable them to deliver high quality products to their company. Similarly, input supply firms have been involved with assisting farms to find guaranteed outlets for their products in order to stimulate demand. Foreign companies have played a leading role in this development (Foster, 1999).

Some Lessons from Rural Transition

1. Care should be taken in choosing what indicators are used to measure transition performance

If allocative efficiency is used instead of output as an indicator to measure success, it is less clear that the European agricultural transitions were such failures in comparison to those in China and Vietnam. If prices need to reflect the long-run scarcity values of outputs and inputs, then efficiency required that output prices were raised in East Asia, a move that would naturally lead to higher output. Likewise, when subsidies were removed, rational producers should use fewer inputs. This can be seen in the CEE countries and Russia where the ratio of output to input prices fell sharply, obviously leading to falling output in these countries.

2. There is no single optimal transition path

The optimal transition strategy needs to take into account institutional and political characteristics of each country. That said, however, the collective transition experiences do imply the following:

3. Any successful reform strategy needs to include some essential ingredients

In other words, ultimately successful transition requires a complete package of reforms. All countries that are growing steadily a decade or more after their initial reforms have managed (a) to create macroeconomic stability, (b) to reform property rights, (c) to create institutions that facilitate exchange, and (d) to develop an environment within which contracts can be enforced.

We clearly see the problems of not making progress in all areas. For example, when rights are not clear, as in Russia, producers have little incentive to farm efficiently or to invest, and restructuring is constrained. We see in other places that the creation of strong individual property rights is not sufficient. For example, in Poland in the initial years after reform, farmers had secure rights over their land. But, their inability to access inputs or to sell output prevented them from reaping the gains of specialization and improved labor effort. Both output and productivity growth performed poorly. In general, where both rights and markets came together we have seen productivity rise; where this has not happened, decline continued and/or subsistence farming proliferated.

4. *While all of the ingredients are ultimately needed, they do not need to come all at once, or in the same form. Successful institutions are adapted to local circumstances and are sufficiently flexible to accommodate changes during transition*

In China, reform without collapse was possible by introducing property rights reform first and gradually implementing policies that liberalized markets and facilitated decentralized exchange. This sequencing helped China grow rapidly in the initial years and steadily since. In CEE countries, after the initial politically-led disruptions, maturing property rights and the gradual emergence of markets and other ways of exchanging goods, services, and inputs have lead to productivity growth.

One of the most powerful lessons is that although all of the pieces of the reform package are needed, there is a lot of room for experimentation and variation in the form of the institutions that appear to provide incentives and facilitate exchange and contracting. First, in the case of property rights, incentives can come in many forms. At least during transition, full privatization in the initial period was not always needed.

Sometimes political economy realities limit the scope for privatization, such as in the case of land ownership in China, where only user and income rights were privatized–and then even imperfectly. However, the increase in the rights to the residual led to improvements in decision-making among farmers and resulted in major increases in output and productivity.

Second, regarding economic organization, there are many examples of hybrid forms, whereby the state-run agency or former collective has been able to continue to operate, and do so more efficiently since their members or managers have been granted clearer income, use, and transfer rights. For example, in China the state was able to use commercialized state input suppliers to create competitive fertilizer wholesale and retail markets (Park and Rozelle, 1998). Similarly, in the CEE countries, farming organizations (such as cooperative farms) which are never observed in Western economies, and which many experts had, *ex ante*, considered to be inefficient, have performed close to the efficiency level of family farms (Mathijs and Swinnen, 2001).

Successful institutions of exchange–nascent markets and forms of contracting–also have many hybrid characteristics. In fact, some of the most successful transitions have not gone straight from planning to decentralized market-based exchange. Markets, as it turns out, are emerging, but doing so quite slowly. China's experience demonstrates that, when politically feasible, partial reform in a sectoral sense (i.e., liberalizing some products but not necessarily all) and a two-tier pricing (i.e., a system of resource allocation half through planned transfers and half through the market) can end up creating markets.

These make the liberalization of the partially reformed sector successful, but such policies can also create a trading class that leads the push to expand the reforms and ultimately eliminate the need for planning.

Flexibility is needed because transition is so uncertain. Moreover, successful transition may trigger rapid growth, which itself will require institutions to adapt quickly. For example, in land markets, the initial focus should be on stimulating short-term land leasing, an institution much more adapted to transition circumstances. Later on, long-term leases and land sales should develop. In general nontraditional and flexible institutions have been more successful.

Finally, some more specific lessons regarding key aspects of agrarian reform:

5. *The nature of the land rights allocated in land reforms is more important than who gets them*

In the CEE countries land was either restituted to former owners, distributed to farm workers in delineated boundaries, or leased to new farms (in attendance of sale). In particular, the process of land restitution to former owners created major political debates and opposition, because it was argued that restitution would separate ownership from those using the land, with devastating consequences.

Looking back now, it appears that although these land reforms were complex and difficult to implement, they produced stronger and better defined property rights for the new landowners than in the land reforms in several FSU countries, such as Russia and Ukraine. In these countries, land was given to the users of the land, and distributed as paper shares or certificates to workers of the collectives and state farms. However, individuals cannot identify the piece of land that belongs to any given share, causing weak land rights for individuals and undermining their ability to withdraw land from the large farms. As a result, family farming is emerging only slowly, and large farms have little incentive to restructure (Lerman, 1999).

It appears that the transaction costs involved in land exchanges after clearly defined land rights are given to individual owners are, however substantial, still considerably less than those in accessing land when land rights are incomplete or not defined clearly. The first process at least has satisfied a basic condition for land exchange to develop, although often a lot remains to be done. In the second process, the basic conditions are fulfilled, notwithstanding that the land is formally given to those presumably most likely to use it.

6. *Farm restructuring and its effects yield a more complex picture than expected ex ante*

At the outset of transition, there were two extreme views. One held that collective and state farms were so inefficient that they would collapse and fall apart when government controls over the farm structures were removed. The other said that individual farming would not emerge because farm workers in CEE countries had no experience in running a farm business themselves.

The empirical evidence shows a large variation in developments. In some countries an almost complete shift to individual farming has taken place, while in others the opposite has happened, and most CEE countries show a mixed evolution. These differences are not accidental: they reflect differences in the incentives and costs of shifting to individual farming, caused both by policies and structural conditions. For example, the breakup of the former collective and state farms has been strongest in countries where the farms were least efficient and most labor intensive. This reduced the costs of production fragmentation and increased the gains of improved labor governance, and where government policies reduced constraints for individuals to start up their own farms (Mathijs and Swinnen, 1998). The shift was also higher in regions where at least some private farming survived during Communist rule (Rizov et al., 2001).

Although the share farmed by large corporate farms keeps falling gradually in most transition countries, it is a slow process and it is not obvious that they will disappear for quite a while. This is either because policies favor them or because institutional barriers constrain individual farming; or because they provide up- and downstream activities substituting for missing markets. In many countries a dual farm structure is emerging with a few very large-scale farms and many very small-scale individual farms (Sarris et al. 1999).

7. *There is scope for significant productivity improvement through better farm management and by hardening budget constraints*

Many studies show that the difference in efficiency between farms within a country are large and that improvements in management can therefore lead to significant overall productivity increases. However, policy is important. Where farms were forced to restructure and budgets were hardened, productivity increased strongly and the gap between different organizations diminished, while elsewhere efficiency actually has declined during transition (Mathijs and Swinnen, 2001; Sedik et al., 1999).

Notes

I thank Liesbeth Dries, Karen Macours, and Scott Rozelle for comments and assistance with this paper, and all my research collaborators of "ten years of analyzing rural transition" for their insights, critical comments, and the many pleasant moments. I am solely responsible for the views expressed in this paper.

1.   Our discussion here draws heavily on several empirical studies in which we estimated the impact of reform policies and initial conditions, and their "intermediate results," (i.e. changes in relative prices, farm restructuring, changes in property rights and overall economic liberalization), on performance, i.e. agricultural productivity and output. Two studies (Macours and Swinnen, 2000b, 2001) use aggregate data for fifteen transition countries; the third (Macours and Swinnen, 2000a) uses annual data on crop output for eight CEE countries.
2.   Table 1 summarizes the initial conditions and reform policies for the three "extreme" transition patterns. Details on initial conditions and reform policies for all transition countries are in Macours and Swinnen (2001).
3.   Only in former Yugoslavia, Poland, Laos and Myanmar was a majority of agricultural land managed by individual (family) farms.
4.   As explained above, in CEE and FSU agriculture, the negative output effect of institutional disruption is reinforced by declining terms of trade caused by price and trade liberalization and subsidy cuts.
5.   Several studies comparing economic performance of transition strategies in the FSU and CEE economies come to the conclusion that–taking into account differences in initial conditions and external factors–those countries which have reformed earliest and most radically are now doing best (Åslund et al., 1996; de Melo and Gelb, 1996; Fischer et al., 1996; Wyplosz, 2000).

Agrarian Reform in Post-Soviet States Revisited: Central Asia and Mongolia

Max Spoor

More than ten years after the breakup of the former Soviet Union in December 1991, in several of the successor states the agricultural and rural sector shows signs of stagnation and decay. Agrarian reforms have been very diversified, from very "cosmetic" in countries such as Turkmenistan, Uzbekistan, Belarus, and various provinces of the Russian Federation, to gradual in other parts, and even radical, as in Armenia, the Baltic states and Kyrgzystan. In Mongolia, which was always very much under the influence of the USSR, reforms have also been radical.

This chapter aims to analyze the reasons for this negative development, by comparing some of the experiences of land and institutional reform in four countries of the Central Asian region: Kazakhstan, Kyrgyzstan, Mongolia and Uzbekistan.[1] An analysis will be presented of the development of land privatization and farm restructuring in these post-Soviet States and its impact on the performance of the agricultural sector. While they represent various "colors" of the "transition palette," in all cases the institutional problems within the rural sector are quite severe. These are partly due to insufficient attention to them in the reforms, but also to the very problematic legacy of the Soviet system, in particular for the agricultural sector.

Privatization of land and other assets, and the restructuring of the previously dominant state farms (*sovkhozy*) and collective farms (*kolkhozy*) have been the focal point in agrarian strategies (Csaki and Lerman, 1994, 1996; Csaki, 2000; Mathijs and Swinnen, 1998; Wegren, 1998; Spoor and Visser, 2001). Reforms have shown a great diversity in form and implementation, and the outcomes in terms of current agrarian structures are very different indeed. However, there are common reasons behind the stagnation of agriculture during the final stages of the Soviet regime. Firstly, the large state and collective farms–while having been formed to benefit from economics of scale–suffered from low productivity and were highly inefficient, particularly in the use of capital resources. Technological innovation lagged behind, causing low crop yields and quality of production. Secondly, in the collective farms, free-rider behavior was dominant and the incomes (and food-intake) of the members or workers had to be complemented by the produce of the household plots. These had much higher land and labor productivity (partly by using subsidized inputs provided by the collective farm, as a form of "parasitical symbiosis").

Thirdly, these farm enterprises were taxed through the state-order system, which included obligatory procurement against low administered prices, providing strong disincentives to the farm enterprises, although the outflow of resources were compensated by the inflow of subsidized credit, public investment and services. Finally, apart from being production units, the *sovkhozy* and *kolkhozy* in the CEE and FSU countries (and Mongolia) had important social functions. These consisted of providing social and health services in rural areas, which was a complicating factor in the farm-restructuring process during the transition[2], as local government agencies could not take over this task.

As stated above, the agrarian reforms in the agricultural sector in Central and Eastern Europe and the former Soviet Union focused on privatization of assets, in particular land, and the restructuring of the existing state and collective farms. It has been shown that the reforms in the CEE and FSU countries were quite diverse in content and implementation. In a study of nine countries in the CEE region Matthijs and Swinnen (1996) noted that privatization took place as distribution to workers or members, restitution to former owners, sales of assets (with a variety of conditions attached) and leasing arrangements. The farm restructuring led to new enterprises, such as cooperatives, joint-stock companies, partnerships, associations of peasant farms, and to private farm and household enterprises. Sometimes these changes were cosmetic (ibid: 14), in other cases they were more profound and genuinely transformed the enterprises. In Russia, too, many differences can also be observed (Brooks and Lerman, 1994; Wegren, 1998).

The comparative study presented in this paper includes four post-Soviet States of the Central Asian region: Kazakhstan, Kyrgyzstan, Mongolia, and Uzbekistan. Most attention in studies on agrarian transition has been given to the CEE region and Russia itself, while these more peripheral post-Soviet States are relatively under-researched and therefore less well-known in the literature on transition. These countries show great diversity in terms of the sequencing and extent of reforms at the macro-level and *versus* the agrarian sector.

Analyzing Kyrgyzstan, often hailed as the showcase of reform in Central Asia, Delehanty and Rasmussen (1998) came to the conclusion that much of the transformation was initially cosmetic. Even after the new push in agrarian reforms during 1994-95, the private-farm sector developed only gradually, while other "reformed sectors" such as joint-stock companies, cooperatives and peasant associations still retained some of the features of–largely inefficient–Soviet management practices.

Kazakhstan has gone through a far-reaching process of farm restructuring, but most often without sufficient preparation, institutions and accompanying policies, which contributed to the current profound crisis of the sector. Mongolia has also chosen a road of rapid privatization, in particular within its crucial animal husbandry sector, and the break-up of the existing agricultural and livestock cooperatives, the *negdels*. However, the crop-producing farm sector practically collapsed in the first few years of transition, while market development in the vast rural areas, inhabited by nomadic herder households, is still highly problematic.

For Uzbekistan, Lerman et al. (1996) noted that a variety of land relations and forms of farm organization have developed in Uzbekistan, which is generally seen as one of the non-reformers. While the Uzbek government chose to keep most of the old agrarian structure intact, it did respond to emerging "land hunger" by distributing individual plots to more households or increasing the existing average (Spoor, 1995).

The chapter is divided into four parts. Following the introduction, part two presents a brief analysis of the macroeconomic development of the countries in the Central Asian region since 1991. Most macroeconomic strategies were based on the development of primary export sectors, without a balanced strategy that would also include the important agricultural sectors. This produced a context of crisis and development in the agricultural sector, while taking into account resource endowments, initial conditions of development and geographical location, the relative importance of the agricultural sector, and the impact of macroeconomic contraction.

Part three focuses on two interrelated aspects of the agrarian transition, the processes of land privatization and farm restructuring, and institutional reform that have taken place in the four countries. The agrarian reforms in Kazakhstan, Kyrgyzstan, Mongolia, and Uzbekistan are briefly reviewed, showing comparative developments and substantial differences. It will be shown that in spite of the slow process of privatization and the formation of only an incipient peasant farm sector, a wide variety of farm types and production arrangements have appeared.

In the final part some conclusions are drawn which underline the basic argument in this analysis: in these transitional processes there are no simple recipes nor ideal outcomes, but mainly complex dynamics and unexpected, and sometimes unintended results of transformation policies. Micro and macro efficiencies are developing in agricultural production, but much will depend on the formation of an accessible and competitive market environment in which these new (sometimes family-run) farm units can operate, and where the still dominant large-scale farms can become more productive and improve their technological level.

Institutional reform and transformation in this respect have been quite insufficient. Land markets, rural finance, extension services, communication, and transport will have to be improved, and political interference diminished, otherwise private farmers will not be able to survive or accumulate, and the large-scale farms will not have incentives to modernize.

Macroeconomic Development: Central Asian Region (1991-2000)

All the post-Soviet States have suffered from severe economic contraction in the past decade. The states in the Central Asian region are no exception to this rule. Sustained negative growth can be observed in all of them during most of the first half of the 1990s (see table 1).

Mongolia, with the smallest economy and population, resumed growth as early as 1994, with the help of substantial foreign aid. The other countries started their recovery in 1996. Kyrgyzstan passed through the deepest crisis, with GDP dropping to below 50 percent of the 1990 level. In Kazakhstan this was a little over 60 percent. In Uzbekistan and Mongolia, the contraction of the economy was relatively less severe.

During the Soviet era, the Central Asian republics and Mongolia (as part of the CMEA) benefited structurally from budgetary transfers from the "center" that provided investment resources for regional agricultural, industrial and mining infrastructure or social-sector institutions. Nevertheless, their development model reflected an increasingly one-sided inter-republican (and inter-CMEA) division of labor. Kyrgyzstan emerged as one of the Soviet Union's main wool producers, and a supplier of uranium, gold and mercury. Kazakhstan became a bulk grain producer, with expanded areas of cultivated land as a result of Khrushchev's virgin lands campaign in the 1950s, while simultaneously developing oil and gas production. Mongolia was the CMEA's main copper producer. Finally, Uzbekistan specialized in cotton, known as "white gold," and developed its gas sector (Spoor, 1995, 2000).

This division of labor also created dependency on mono-cultures (mainly cotton in some of the former Soviet Central Asian states), while the consequences of ruthless exploitation of natural resources with a general disregard of the environment remain a major long-term threat to public health and socioeconomic sustainability, such as in the Aral Sea basin (Spoor, 1998). Furthermore, some countries in Central Asia, such as Uzbekistan and Turkmenistan, imported more and more food, while most industrial (and to a lesser extent agricultural) inputs came from elsewhere. Many raw materials and primary agricultural products were "exported" to other republics of the USSR without any form of processing, while relatively little local processing capacity was built locally. This was also the case for Mongolia, despite it being an independent country. Industry was established with a total disregard of comparative advantage by simply subsidizing transport costs between the center and the periphery. Finally, as was mentioned above, during the Soviet period large-scale state and collective units dominated the agricultural sector, were heavily subsidized and worked under strict state procurement systems.

Table 1. Real GDP Growth of Mongolia and Central Asian States (1991-2000)

% Growth	1991	1992	1993	1994	1995	1996	1997	1998	1999	2000
Mongolia	-9.2	-9.5	-3.0	2.3	6.3	2.4	4.0	3.5	3.2	1.1
Kazakhstan	-13.0	-2.9	-9.2	-12.6	-8.2	0.5	1.7	-1.9	2.7	9.6
Kyrgyzstan	-5.0	-19.0	-16.0	-20.1	-5.4	7.1	9.9	2.1	3.7	5.1
Uzbekistan*	-0.5	-11.1	-2.3	-4.2	-0.9	1.6	2.5	4.4	4.1	1.5

Sources: EBRD (2001), *Transition Report Update* (London); EIU (2001), *Country Reports*, July, September, October 2001 (London); StatKom (2001), *Statisticheskii Spravochnik SNG v 2000 godu* (Moscow). NSO Mongolia (1999, 2001), UNDP (2000)

* StatKom (2001: 13) presents a higher estimate for 2000 in the case of Uzbekistan (4.2 percent, for the period January-September).

Because of the structural dependency that grew between the Soviet periphery and the center, such as in the Central Asian region, the disintegration of the Soviet Union had a dramatic impact on these economies. Commodity flows within the USSR and the CMEA had the character of planned transfers at the level of a central ministry or a *kombinat* (industrial complex), and markets (if one can speak of markets in this context) were purely captive. After 1991, the countries were forced to pay much more (sometimes at world market price level) for their imports, while traditional export markets for cotton, wool, gas, oil and meat were only partially replaced by hard-currency market outlets. Hard-currency payments within the CIS for exports from the Central Asian region are often delayed or even refused. The external shock caused by the disintegration of the Soviet Union particularly affected those post-Soviet states with sectors largely dependent on forward and backward linkages with the former Soviet economy, such as the case in industry.

Privatization of Land and Farm Restructuring

The privatization of land and other assets, in combination with the restructuring of the dominant sector of state and collective farms is generally seen as crucial to the reform of the agricultural sector in the FSU (Mathijs and Swinnen, 1996, 1998; Wegren, 1998, Csaki, 2000, Spoor and Visser, 2001). Quite premature (or even naïve) expectations in the early 1990s included the estimate that around 40 percent of the land in Russia would be farmed by private family farms by 1995 (World Bank, 1992; Spoor and Visser, 2001). However, the heirs of the *sovkhozy* and *kolkhozy* remained dominant, the private peasant farm sector stayed small, and private production came particularly from the household enterprises (or plots), which was all rather unexpected (see also Ellman in this volume). It has generally been recognized that the process of agrarian reform towards the formation of private farms remained very slow and complex (Csaki and Lerman, 1996; Spoor and Visser, 2001). In particular in Central Asia (except for Kyrgyzstan) and Mongolia, state ownership of land was maintained, and distribution of land to workers of *sovkhozy* and members of *kolkhozy* was in most cases only in the form of usufruct rights. There are substantial differences between countries with regard to inheritance, tradability and the length of the land leases.[3] Furthermore, changes in farm enterprises–like the formation of joint-stock companies, farmers' cooperatives and forms of partnerships (*tovarishchestvo*)–often represented nominal rather than real changes. This development reveals the existence of political and social forces that represent vested interests, but in some cases it also points to a certain reluctance among the farming population to embark upon private farming in view of often "missing" rural input, output and credit markets.

In the Central Asian region, land privatization has been a very gradual process, albeit with substantial differences between countries. Why has relatively little land been genuinely privatized (although the governments of the countries involved consider some of the above mentioned–mostly quite superficial–ownership transformations as "privatization")? There are a number of reasons for this. Firstly, there were initially insufficient incentives to break away from the remaining collective structures. New markets for inputs and outlets for agricultural production are emerging in a very slow and fragmented manner, while credit for private farmers is often not available. Furthermore, the social infrastructure of education and public health is still related to the old parastatal or collective structures. Secondly, the rural *nomenklatura* clung to power, or even hoped to increase it. Keeping the previous structures intact (albeit under another name) gave the *nomenklatura* better options to remain in social and political control of the rural areas (Spoor, 1999).

Nevertheless, when privatization of land does take place, it is also the former party elite that seems to get control over most of the best land. Newly established enterprises (joint-stock companies, peasant associations, cooperatives, etc.) are still closely tied to remaining large-scale state trading and processing companies (such as in Uzbekistan and partly in Kazakhstan), forcing them to keep their structure and previous forms of operation intact. Peasant farms–which are sometimes physically within the perimeters of the former *kolkhoz*–still depend on the farm manager of the latter for inputs and sales. Thirdly, agricultural production depends heavily on large-scale irrigation systems. There is a fear, particularly in Uzbekistan, that the breakup of the large production units into small peasant farms will lead to deterioration of the existing irrigation structures. Fourthly, governments are sensitive to the social and political consequences that land privatization might have. Therefore, although leasing of land (often with rights of inheritance and long periods of leasehold) has in many cases been the most advanced step on the road to privatization, most land is still owned by the state. The distribution of usufruct rights to farms on small plots of state-owned land by households is widespread, while the sub-contracting of collective land to households, forming "private" peasant farms (table 2) has emerged in response to popular demand for land. In Kazakhstan, in particular after 1995, large private farms with life-long usufruct rights have also been formed, while in Kyrgyzstan there is a tendency within the peasant farm sector to establish new forms of association (see also case study in Nooken, Djalal-Abad region, Spoor, 1999). In Mongolia land has traditionally been communal land property, founded on the nomadic tradition of the Mongolian herders, who have survived for centuries using customary rights of grazing areas and water resources. This is currently under debate, although most likely land privatization will be limited to arable land.

Agrarian reform–in terms of the formation of private family farms–shows actually quite different developments in the countries under study in this paper. In order to measure progress of agrarian reform one can use the composite "privatization index" (Spoor and Visser, 2001). The categorization ranges from non- (or minimally) to highly privatized agricultural economies (see figure 1).

Nevertheless, privatization in the agricultural sector, measured by the formation of private peasant farms (to be distinguished from household enterprises), has not yet advanced very much in the countries which are considered as the "reformers" (Kyrgyzstan and, to a lesser extent, Kazakhstan). Similarly it is not absent in a "non-reformer" (such as Uzbekistan). With the rapidly declining crop sector in Mongolia, one can only speak of private herders (and not peasant farms). In table 2, this country is left out, for lack of comparability.

Figure 1. Reform Paths according to a Privatization Index

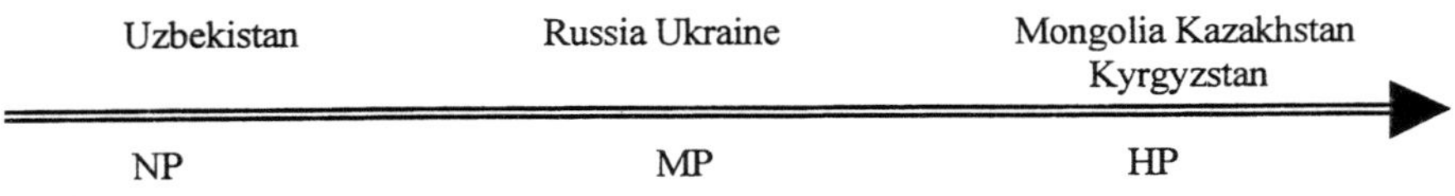

Uzbekistan	Russia Ukraine	Mongolia Kazakhstan Kyrgyzstan
NP	MP	HP

Source: Spoor and Visser (2001:892); For Mongolia, Spoor (1996).
Note: NP = Non- or limited privatization; MP = Medium privatized; HP = Highly privatized.

Actually, land reform has more often taken the shape of nominal or cosmetic changes, with state farms being transformed into joint-stock companies or cooperatives, and collectives into limited liability partnerships or leasehold companies. Such changes meant nothing more than exchanging the old name plate above the main gate for a new one. Nevertheless, land in the Central Asian region has been "privatized" in different ways, which also makes it difficult to assess what share of agricultural land is currently in private usufruct or *de jure* ownership.

As in the Soviet era, more land is in private use than is noted in official statistics. Previously, members of collective farms or workers on state farms had a small family plot, which produced a substantial part of the household cash income. In the post-1991 period additional land has been privatized in this manner, leading to an increase in the private household plots and *dacha*-gardens or orchards (that also already existed in the Soviet era), but more importantly, in the use of contracting schemes within the currently remaining collectives (Khan, 1996: 77). That is the main reason why a large part of agricultural production is considered to be of private origin after a decade of reform.

In Kyrgyzstan, the country that has reformed its agricultural sector most in comparison with the other former Central Asian states, private peasant farms under leasing arrangements have been formed since the mid-1990s. The length of the lease was extended during the reform, from forty-nine to ninety-nine years, although transferability was in practice still limited, because of fragmented markets for leasing rights. Private ownership was legalized by the end of the decade, but a five-year moratorium on land sales was instigated. By early 2002 experiments were underway in some regions to lift the restrictions on this ban. If one looks at the growth of private peasant farms, this is quite impressive. Their average size is, however, reducing and a closer look at table 2 also shows that by the end of the decade the total acreage of this sector had contracted substantially with regard to 1996, when the peasant farm sector was at its height in terms of acreage. One of the issues at hand was the rather hostile environment of markets, in particular in terms of inputs, credit and marketing of output.

Table 2. Number of Peasant Farms in Central Asian States (1992-2000)

Size=Ha	1992	1993	1994	1995	1996	1997	1998	1999	2000
Kazakhstan	3,300	9,300	16,300	22,500	30,800	42,500	51,300	58,400	67,300
Size	238	533	406	348	412	452	542	386	398
Kyrgyzstan	4,100	8,600	12,800	17,300	23,200	31,000	38,700	49,300	60,100
Size	25	44	67	43	63	48	25	20	17
Uzbekistan	1,900	5,900	7,500	14,200	18,100	18,800	21,400	23,000	31,100
Size	7	8	9	14	15	15	16	19	21

Source: StatKom SNG (1999); StatKom SNG (2001).

In Kazakhstan, agrarian reform was implemented much more half-heartedly. It took until the middle of the 1990s to implement a large-scale campaign to give "property titles" to the members of the large-scale agricultural enterprises. During fieldwork by the author in the area of Djambul (South Kazakhstan) in September 1997, it became clear that in many cases these "usufruct rights" were not much more than rights on paper. Unfortunately, the best land was allotted to the *kolkhoz* or *sovkhoz* management and many of the members and workers received land far from the administrative center of the enterprise, with no inputs, machinery or other forms of technology that they would need to produce. This non-transparent and easily manipulated land reform led to excesses in which land was "sold" for much less than its real value to speculators and traders (Spoor, 1999). Political interference remained strong at the provincial and district levels, in which the Soviet habit of planning (or rather: ordering) the production of certain crops and dominating markets with administrative methods, continued without any apparent change. Finally, markets were highly inefficient and fragmented, with enormous transaction costs. It was not excep-tional for a truck with grain from the north of Kazakhstan to be stopped many times en route by local officials, police officers or others and forced to pay "environmental tax" in kind before receiving permission to continue.

In Mongolia, privatization of all assets except land was undertaken in a very short period of time, during the early 1990s. The agricultural cooperatives (*negdel*) were eliminated, and the existing, very large stock of around twenty-five million animals (sheep, goats, cattle, horses, camels, and yaks) was privatized (Spoor, 1996). The de-collectivization resulted in disintegration of the crop sector, which had been heavily subsidized, including companies which had produced the fodder crops that provided a buffer stock of animal foodstuff for Mongolia's severe winters (Griffin et al. , 2001). In 1994 a new Land Law was approved by Parliament, establishing leasing rights for farms, although leaving untouched the vast pasture areas. While land registration was pushed forward in the latter part of the decade, a revised Land Law which would include the privatization of the common pasture grounds is the subject of fierce debate, especially after the MPRP (Mongolian People's Revolutionary Party) regained power in the elections of June 2000. Market development is the crucial missing link in Mongolia's otherwise radical reform path. In part this is forced by the geographical conditions in the country, which has the lowest population density in the world. The marketing of inputs and farm produce, in particular as the nomadic herders move with their herds over very large distances during the non-winter season, is complicated and costly.

Finally, Uzbekistan–the least reform-minded of the four countries–did manage to expand the sector of "private peasant farms." However, these are most often still within the boundaries of the large-scale enterprise, and their success or failure depends entirely on the relation between the "independent" farmer and the farm management (see above). As marketing channels are also still very much controlled by (former) state companies or regional authorities, these farmers have considerable difficulties keeping their heads above water. In the early 1990s the Uzbek government also focussed on expanding the number of household plots (and even increase their size somewhat) in a move to create more popular support (Spoor, 1993, 1995; Lerman, 1998). Large-scale enterprises, mostly under new names but the same in size and operation, still dominate Uzbek agriculture, although internally there is a myriad of forms of subcontracting and leasing that vary per region or even per company (see Kandiyoti in this volume). The Uzbek government is very reluctant to relinquish control over the sector that produces its main sources of foreign exchange and domestic accumulation, namely cotton. Combined with the major problem of water management (with large-scale surface irrigation systems), land reform and farm restructuring is slow (Lerman et al., 1996; Spoor, 1998).

The Impact of Reform on Agricultural Performance

A large part of the population in the Central Asian region is rural, such as in Uzbekistan and Kyrgyzstan, where the share is 62.6 and 65.3 percent respectively, even higher than at the beginning of the decade of reform. In Kazakhstan this share is currently 55.9 percent per cent, while in Mongolia (with predominantly nomadic herding in rural areas) it is 42.8 percent. This means that we are discussing countries that have dominant or significant rural populations, for which–in the absence of rural industries–agriculture (and services) basically provides the most important source of employment. Unfortunately, the importance of the agricultural sector in these countries (and in the transition countries at large) was not reflected in its place on the reform agenda of the 1990s.

On the eve of independence, agricultural production represented an important share of GDP, with sub-sectors like wheat (Kazakhstan), mutton and wool (Kyrgyzstan), hides, mutton, and cashmere (Mongolia), and cotton (Uzbekistan). The contraction of this sector was most dramatic, because of the inter-republican dependency in industry already noted above and its initial incapacity to compete in foreign (non-CIS) markets. By contrast, the agricultural sector was somewhat less affected during the first half of the 1990s, although grain production in Kazakhstan showed a strong negative trend, with large output declines and a diminishing share in GDP. In Kyrgyzstan share in GDP has grown, as there has been a strong recovery in agricultural production since 1995. In Mongolia, this is even more the case, while in Uzbekistan it fluctuated, with a gradual downward trend.

There are several factors behind this sectoral behavior. Firstly, agricultural production of cotton, grain, meat and wool formed part of nationally integrated production processes, depending only on some external (extra-republican or imported) inputs. Therefore the disintegration of the former USSR and the CMEA had a smaller direct impact on the agricultural sector of the Central Asian region. Secondly, it seems that although the terms of trade generally did not improve, as the costs of inputs (fertilizers and pesticides) went up much faster than output prices, the demand for high-value agricultural products (such as vegetables) grew, stabilizing incomes at least somewhat.

Table 3. Gross Agricultural Output in Central Asian States and Mongolia (1991-2000)

	1991	1992	1993	1994	1995	1996	1997	1998	1999	2000
Kazakhstan	89.0	84.3	76.5	66.9	61.4	61.7	62.7	61.6	62.7	..
Kyrgyzstan	92.1	79.3	67.0	53.5	50.7	54.2	59.6	60.9	63.1	..
Mongolia	92.6	87.1	83.4	89.8	94.1	96.0	110.3	109.4	112.7	92.2
Uzbekistan	99.5	88.5	86.5	81.9	81.2	92.6	86.9	90.6	94.7	..

Sources: StatKom SNG (2000); SSO (1995), NSO (1999, 2001).

Thirdly, agricultural commodities, in particular food staples, remained "marketable," with relatively little competition from imports. Fourthly, specifically for the important cotton sector, the revenues earned with hard currency exports provided finance for the import of spare parts, fertilizers and pesticides, which were previously transferred or bought at administrative prices. Nevertheless, the agricultural sectors in these countries also had substantial problems in recovering from the initial contractions (see table 3), in particular Kazakhstan with its dramatic decline in grain production and livestock. Mongolia recently suffered from the severe winter of 2000 (which was repeated in 2001), killing millions of heads of livestock (Griffin et al., 2001). More precisely, some of the key sub-sectors of agricultural and livestock production have done very badly, while others recovered relatively quickly. This can be seen in table 4. For example, crop production in Kazakhstan shows a large decrease in output, with the dominant grain sector recovering for only a few years, due to favorable weather. The livestock sector, which was supported by subsidized fodder crops and organized in large-scale units, also shows a strong contraction. Of course increase in slaughtered weight could also hide a decrease in the overall herd, but over the whole decade the trend is decreasing.

Kyrgyzstan recovered in the main grain crops and did extremely well in the expansion of potatoes, which are largely produced by private peasant farms. Mongolia combined a disastrous contraction in its crop sector (Spoor, 1996) with a rapid growth of the herd of sheep, goats, cattle, horses, camels and yaks after the privatization of livestock. However, the absence of marketing channels has forced herders to keep larger herds, and the decreasing share of breeding stock and ageing of the herds make this development hardly sustainable. The recent severe winters have decreased the number of animals substantially, and hence negatively affected the gross value added of the sector, which is largely determined by the livestock sub-sector (see also table 3).

Conclusions

In this chapter it has been argued that the post-Soviet states in the Central Asian region show various patterns of agrarian reform. We have limited the discussion to land reform, the formation of a private peasant sector, and the restructuring of large-scale enterprises, and some of its impact on performance of the sector. Kyrgyzstan and Mongolia seem to have progressed furthest in reforms, with the privatization of agricultural assets and land, at least in terms of leasehold or usufruct rights. However, Mongolia has enormous problems in the development of viable market institutions and structures, in particular for the vast rural areas inhabited by nomadic herders with private herds. In Kyrgyzstan more has been done in this respect, and the development of financial institutions (after initial debacles in this field in the mid-1990s), services and output channels have improved. This was already clear in the late-1990s (Spoor, 1999; reporting on field visits to the Kemin and Nooken districts in the east- and southeast of Kyrgyzstan).

Table 4. Main Agricultural Products of Mongolia & Central Asian States (1990-99)

(x 1,000 t.)	1990	1991	1992	1993	1994	1995	1996	1997	1998	1999
Grain (cleanweight)										
Mongolia	718	595	494	480	331	261	220	240	195	170
Kazakhstan	28,488	11,992	29,772	21,631	16,454	9,505	11,237	12,238	6,396	14,264
Kyrgyzstan	1,503	1,374	1,516	1,508	996[a]	913	1,329	1,734	1,619	1,630
Uzbekistan	1,899	1,908	2,257	2,142	2,467	3,215	3,562	3,776	4,148	4,331
Cotton										
Kazakhstan	324	291	252	200	208	223	183	198	162	249
Kyrgyzstan	81	63	52	42	54	75	73	62	78	87
Uzbekistan	5,058	4,646	4,128	4,234	3,938	3,934	3,350	3,641	3,206	3,600
Potatoes										
Mongolia	131	98	79	60	54	52	46	55	65	64
Kazakhstan	2,324	2,143	2,570	2,296	2,040	1,720	1,656	1,472	1,263	1,695
Kyrgyzstan	365	325	362	308	310	431	562	678	774	957
Uzbekistan	336	351	365	473	567	440	514	692	691	658
Meat (slaughtered weight)										
Mongolia	249	281	251	216	204	212	260	241	246	289
Kazakhstan	....	1,524	1,256	1312	1207	985	855	718	648	635
Kyrgyzstan	....	230	228	214	197	180	186	186	191	195
Uzbekistan	....	492	469	517	509	509	461	468	476	483

Sources: EIU (1995; 1999); World Bank (1994c); Spoor (1995); StatKom SNG (1996, 1998, 2000); National Statistical Office Mongolia (1994, 1999, 2001).
[a] In 1994 the grain situation (food and feed grains) had become so precarious that the Kyrgyz government had to make an urgent plea for EU food aid.

In Kazakhstan there is a profound crisis in the agricultural sector, in which private peasant farms have great difficulties in subsisting in a hostile environment of markets that are fragmented, often monopolistic and still showing strong political interference and rent-seeking behavior by the rural elite.

Finally in Uzbekistan, the country in which agrarian reform has been the least profound, the private peasant sector is slowly growing, but largely "under the wings" of the still dominant large-scale farms. The latter are changing in terms of their internal organization, but markets remain still very much influenced by the central government or regional administrations, whether directly or through parastatals.

In all the cases discussed here, institution building in the rural economy is the key to success, and–albeit with varying degrees–this aspect of agrarian reform has been largely insufficient. Private, public and mixed institutions that promote land markets (even when it concerns usufruct rights which are transferable), provide credit and accumulate savings, provide services, undertake applied research in improved technologies, govern efficiently the water supply and distribution and, finally, diminish transaction costs in commodity chains, and are essential in the eventual success of the newly formed "private" farms. In their absence they will have little chance of surviving, let alone of becoming a dynamic force that could lead to sustainable agricultural and rural development in these countries. Given that the rural populations are large and rural poverty and social exclusion are growing phenomena, resolving the "institutional gap" should receive absolute priority in the reform agenda.

Notes

1.   Kyrgyzstan, Kazakhstan, Tajikistan, Turkmenistan, and Uzbekistan are normally considered as forming part of former Soviet Central Asia. In the era of the USSR Kazakhstan was not considered to belong to what the Russians called "Middle Asia." Geographically (and culturally) Mongolia could be considered part of the "Central Asian region," and is considered as such here for the purpose of comparison of post-Soviet States in this region.
2.   In countries where large-scale agricultural units were indeed broken-up, the local administrative government agents were hardly capable of taking over the delivery of social services.
3.   Land Laws that would guarantee fully transferable and inheritable private property rights have been politically very sensitive issues. Most recently the new Land Law in Mongolia was returned by parliament, and is still being debated heatedly, in particular in relation to the pastures inhabited by nomadic families.

Farms and Factor Markets in Russia's Agriculture

Eugenia Serova and Irina Khramova

In the centrally planned economies the government dominated all sections of the agri-food chain. It established production targets, the required crop-mix for the collective (*kolkhozy*) and state (*sovkhozy*) farms, and linked producers and consumers, by fixing prices in the chain, supplying inputs, and subsidizing transport. The technical infrastructure needed for this massive intervention was in place. The reforms in all transition economies were accompanied by an almost immediate withdrawal of government from the agri-food distribution sphere. However, the appropriate market institutions did (and could) not emerge overnight. This lack of market institutions is one of the distinguishing features of the agricultural sector in transition economies.

Another problem is linked with price adjustments under imperfect competition in agri-food markets, originating from the former centrally planned economy. There are many buyers and sellers, and all of them are theoretically price-takers. However, imperfect competition on these markets has two major causes. Firstly, there are high entrance and exit barriers on factor markets. Entry to the sector is hampered by restricted investment resources and legal barriers, while unsuccessful producers cannot withdraw from the sector because the market for land transactions is still in an embryonic state. Secondly, sellers and buyers have almost no access to market information (and therefore there is no inductive learning), due to the lack of prior experience in markets and market information systems. This is linked to the first distinguishing feature mentioned above–the lack of market institutions. Operating on markets is a new experience for all actors and hence they have neither naïve nor Nerlovian (adaptive) price expectations. Buyers and sellers therefore tend to overreact to price adjustment process in transition, and price fluctuations can be unpredictable and violent. Furthermore, sellers do not always pursue price-maximizing objectives. Therefore, in this imperfect market environment price adjustment takes quite a different form than that described in the mainstream neoclassical literature. The lack of market information and of restraints on arbitrage provokes the monopoly power of local buyers in the agri-food chain and, therefore gives rise to monopsonistic pricing.

In almost all industrialized socialist countries, the government heavily subsidized food consumption. Market reforms have eliminated most of these subsidies and consequently–in combination with the overall contraction of the economy–consumer purchasing power has fallen, reducing demand for agri-food commodities. Foreign trade liberalization and the lack of a sound market infrastructure have also contributed to this fall in demand. Therefore, market reforms in post-socialist countries are inevitably accompanied by a decrease in agricultural and food industry output. Agricultural producers have mostly had to operate in a collapsing economy during periods of transition. However, it is known that agriculture shows an asymmetric aggregate supply curve. Due to a certain "asset fixity" in agricultural production, the supply response to falling prices can be less elastic than the response to rising prices.

Another consequence of collapsing agriculture in transition is the specific behavior of producers. During recession, agricultural producers seem to prioritize survival and risk-aversion. Farms tend to preserve their assets and personnel, despite the assumed profit-maximizing behavior in a short-run perspective (Ickes and Ryterman, 1994). This behavior also negatively affects the price adjustment process in agri-food markets during the transition.

Furthermore, transition economies are characterized by a low level of contract enforcement, and unclear property rights and legal frameworks. Together with the lack of marketing institutions, this causes high transaction costs for market actors. In the agri-food chain this is expressed in an inclination to vertical integration, which impedes market competition. Many economists have been concerned about the effect of vertical integration on markets (Tomek and Robinson, 1981). For transitional agriculture, this is especially worrisome, because it emerges in an underdeveloped market and can make adjustment and development of the problematic.

Finally, information asymmetry (Akerlof, 1970) is an essential problem in imperfect markets. In transitional agriculture this asymmetry is likely to be in favor of buyers: farmers are mostly separated from the sources of the information. If, however, mediation in the marketing of farm products is considered as a service provided by middlemen, they are the sellers of this service. The lack of information on the quality of this service then leads to high risks for buyers (in this case the farms). This can be an underlying reason for the inclination of farms to deal with old marketing institutions, rather than with new middlemen emerging in the agri-food chain.

In order to increase our understanding of the major transactions by farms in factor markets in Russia, we conducted a survey in April 2001 in three *oblasts* in the European part of Russia: Pskov, Tambov, and Rostov. The first seems marginal in an agricultural sense, with low productivity and yields. The other two have black soil and good climatic conditions for agricultural production. Rostov has the most liberal local agri-food policy, while Tambov's agri-food sector is more intensively regulated by local officials, as part of a more conservative policy of transition. The choice of regions was determined by previous studies we had conducted: the data from this new survey can therefore be compared with those from the previous ones.

The Russian agricultural sector consists of three main farm types: large-scale farms (the successors to the former collective (*kolkhozy*) and state farms (*sovkhozy*), newly established private farms, and households. The differences between these three types have been analyzed elsewhere (AFE-USAID, 1999). Our survey included only the first two types of farms (32 large-scale farms and 23 private farms in the three *oblasts*). While the survey gathered data on a multitude of transactions at the farm level, this article will analyze only two sets of inclusion in emerging factor markets, namely: (a) land, capital goods and inputs and (b) farm output.

Land Transactions

Land markets in Russia have been shown to be still in an embryonic stage of development. Analysis shows that the land transactions by the sampled farms in the period 1993-2000 mainly took the form of rent. Most of the legal entities have no land in ownership. Only one collective farm owned all its land in 1993, but it was reorganized a year later and all land was shared. Another farm is a state-owned enterprise, and land has been allocated to it for long-term use.

Land use increased in private farms, whilst it mainly decreased in large-scale farms. In the period mentioned, only three of the 23 private farms surveyed did not increase their land acreage (one even decreased its acreage). For the other 20 farms, acreage rose significantly. Among the 32 large-scale farms, only 10 increased their acreage, 7 kept it at the same level and 15 decreased it.

Farms can rent plots from individuals, legal entities and local governments. They can also rent land shares that have been distributed. The rent turnover is very important: of the 55 farms surveyed, 48 had rented farmland in the form of land shares or/and plots. The distribution of all farms by form of farmland rent was as follows: 19 rented only shares and 29 only plots; 21 rented both plots and shares. Farms owned a little over 5 percent of the land they used in the year 2000, and less than 5 percent in 1993. Around 95 percent of farmland was therefore rented.

All the large-scale farms rented farmland, except one in Rostov *oblast* (the state-owned farm mentioned above). Of the other 31 large-scale farms, 15 rented only land shares, while another 14 rented land from local authorities or even from other legal entities. It might be expected that large-scale farms which used only the land shares of their employees and pensioners would not expand their operations and acreage. Nevertheless, there is no obvious correlation between the growth of farm acreage and type of land renting.

Figure 1. Number of Changes of Acreage (1993-2000)

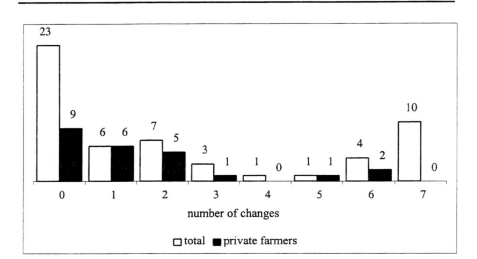

Source: AFE Farm Survey 2001

During the period covered, some large farms that rented only shares increased the number of rented shares, while others reduced the number of shares. More than one third of large-scale farms did not change their land use at all. The most interesting case of increased renting of land shares is when a farm attracts land shares from outside the farm enterprise, primarily from other large-scale farms. There were three such cases in the survey: two in Pskov and one in Tambov. Such increase of acreage can only mean that there is redistribution of land among large-scale farms: the most prosperous farms attract land from less successful farms.

In the survey 17 private farms rented land, in addition to their own farmland, while one used only rented land (land shares). Eleven of these farms attracted land shares, and 3 of these rent only land shares without renting land plots. Seven private farms rent only land plots, and no shares. Private farms rent plots mostly from the local authority. Only 3 farms rent plots from individuals and/or legal entities.

It is worthwhile noting how often land transactions occur, as it indicates the speed with which farms adjust to the changeable economic environment, and of land redistribution. In total 42 percent of the farms had not changed their acreage in the previous eight years. More than a third (35 percent) changed it three times or more (figure 1). Ten large-scale farms (mostly in Rostov) changed their acreage in operation every year. Interestingly, the acreage both decreased (which could be explained by the withdrawing of land shareholders from the 'mother farm') and increased. This upward trend has become more evident since 1999, when Russia's agriculture revived. Private farms mostly increased their acreage, although the number of changes in acreage is lower than for large-scale farms. This is explained by the fact that some of the farms were not set up until the end of the period covered.

In the sample there were several cases where farms rented out their land to individuals, other farms or to nonagricultural users. The size of rented plots did not exceed 500 hectares, and the rental period was one to five years. In all cases farms rented land out because it was not being utilized. However, as stated above, land transactions of this type were not widespread.

Only the farms in Rostov answered the question regarding the major limitations on farmland transactions. Nevertheless, the responses were quite interesting, indicating the main barriers to the development of a land market in Russia's agricultural sector. The distribution of answers is shown in figure 2.

Figure 2. Major Limitations on Land Transactions

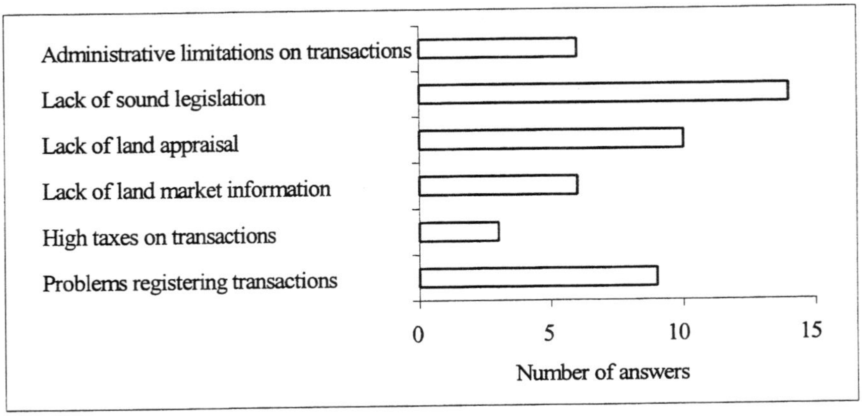

Source: AFE Farm Survey 2001

It shows that most respondents specify the lack of sound land legislation and of an appraisal system (which is also a consequence of lack of legislation). An equal number of large-scale and private farms specified this problem, but they differed on other obstacles: large farms more often complained about the complicated scheme of registration of land transactions, while private farms suffered from a lack of information on the land market. This seems understandable, as large-scale farms have to rent almost all their land from land shares, which demand a large number of individual contracts. Private farms seeking to increase farm acreage had no information on where land is available and who was willing to rent it. In three cases, high tax on land transactions was only indicated as a problem.

As these results on land transactions suggest, there is primarily a rental market developing. Land shares (a consequence of the non-physical distribution within state and collective farms) and physical land plots (owned by local administrations, private farms and households) are being rented out to large-scale farm enterprises and the much smaller private farms. Farms use the mechanism of renting land shares relatively intensively in adjusting to the changing economic environment, and this consequently affects land redistribution. Nevertheless, land transactions are substantially impeded by the lack of sound land legislation.

Input Transactions

As economic reforms have been introduced the agrarian sector has been confronted with increasingly stringent financial limitations, and many agricultural enterprises and farms have collapsed financially.

The basic causes of this agrarian crisis are primarily to be found in the Soviet legacy. First of all, relative prices in the agri-food chain were artificially biased in favor of agriculture, through subsidization of inputs, transport and capital. The price liberalization introduced by the Gaidar government in early 1992 resulted in a radical change in relative farm input-output price ratios, moving them closer to those on the world market. Since about 1994, relative price ratios have stabilized and no further sharp price disparities have been observed (figure 3).

Nevertheless, in the early years of transition, Russian farms were actually deprived of working capital. This could have been avoided by an effective credit system. However, at this initial stage of the reforms, such a system did not exist. Although the banking system had already been reformed, hyperinflation, high interest rates, the availability of only short-term loans and the shortage of collateral meant that credit for agriculture was very limited.

In addition, price liberalization also meant a sharp reduction in purchasing power and therefore in demand for agricultural products. Foreign trade, which was liberalized even earlier, also opened domestic markets for imported (and most often competitive) foodstuffs.

Figure 3. Changes in the Relative Prices in Agriculture (1991-99)

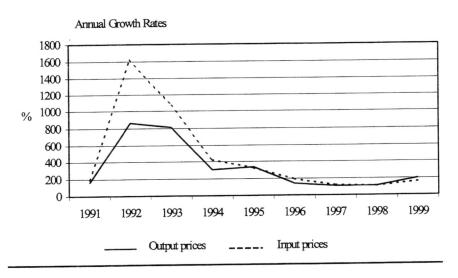

Source: Computed with data from Goskomstat (National Statistical Committee).

Furthermore, the government had withdrawn from the agri-food distribution chain in the early days of the reforms, before a market infrastructure capable of replacing the Soviet distribution system was in place. Imports began to displace domestic products, complicating the financial position of domestic farms even more. Structural reforms were badly organized and actually disoriented the managers of large-scale farms. Unprepared for the newly emerging economic conditions, the managers stuck to their old habits, to the detriment of farm development.

Land is under-valued, which is related to the slow development of land markets. Together with the absence of credit for working capital or investments, and the continuous stripping of capital assets, this has led to a serious de-capitalization of Russian farm enterprises. Since the early 1990s there has been a constant decrease in tractor and harvester inventories (table 4), and in mineral and organic fertilizer application rates (see below), which are important issues in an intensive agricultural production. The average harvested area per grain harvester in Russia increased from 152 hectares in 1990 to 214 hectares in 1999, and the arable area per tractor increased from 95 to 133 hectares during the same period. Inventories of agricultural machinery have steadily reduced during the past decade, though the reduction rate slowed down in 2000.

Figure 4. Inventories of Agricultural Machinery (1985-99)   **(x 1,000 units)**

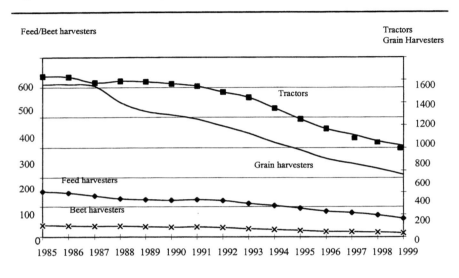

Source: Data from Goskomstat (National Statistical Committee).

The application of mineral fertilizers is on average at an extremely low level. It has been estimated that Russian agriculture should receive 8.5-10.7 million tons of fertilizers annually. However, only five percent of farms currently apply the necessary quantity of fertilizers.

As can be seen in figure 5, there has been a strong reduction in fertilizer use from nearly 90 kg/ha in late 1980s to less than 20 kg/ha in the late 1990s. A certain percentage of previous fertilizer use may have been inefficient, as no accurate economic calculations were made on a cost-benefit basis and, in the absence of sanctions, over-use occurred. However, the fall in use to very low levels has contributed to decreased yields in Russian agriculture.

The surveyed farms were also asked where and in what way they procured their main inputs and capital goods, such as fertilizers, plant protection chemicals, seeds, fodder, machinery and animals.

Figure 5. Fertilizer Application Rate 1981-99 (kg/ha)

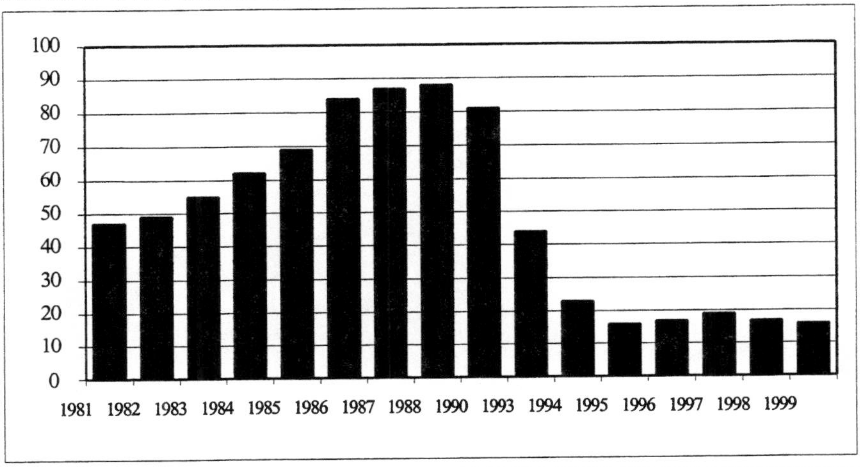

Source: Data from Goskomstat (National Statistical Committee).

The survey showed that both types of farms acquire chemicals and machinery from middlemen or (especially in the case of machinery) from manufacturing plants (see figure 6). For machinery it became clear that *Rosagrosnab* is the major middleman, a private enterprise which has developed–with extensive government support–into a quasi-monopolistic intermediary in this market.

However, since the crisis of 1998 farms have become more solvent and able to pay directly to the manufacturing plants, and purchases from the plants have been increasing. Not surprisingly, large-scale farms have better opportunities to buy directly from plants, as the latter prefer to deal with big customers rather than with small private farms. A relatively high percentage of 'other' channels for the acquisition of machinery have been covered by governmental leasing arrangements. The federal government and many regional governments run farm support programmes, in the form of "leasing." Some private farmers said that they acquired machinery according to the asset share withdrawn from the large-scale mother farm. However, this was a one-off method of acquiring assets.

While farms have to buy chemical inputs (fertilizers) from outside, they produce most of their seeds (figure 6). That means quite a significant deterioration in the level of technology applied. For instance, farms use their own grain to feed animals rather than buying food concentrates.

Figure 6. Channels of Acquisition of Major Purchased Inputs

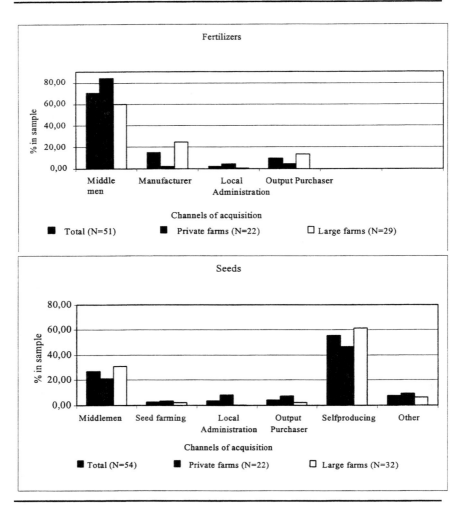

Source: AFE Farm Survey, 2001

As a consequence, the national output of this form of feed processing has grown manifold in recent years. The rate of feed conversion with such a fattening scheme is, however, extremely low.[1]

It should be noted that the purchasers of farm output also deliver a certain share of the inputs to the farms. There are various kinds of commodity-related credit. Part of that credit is provided in the framework of federal and/or regional commodity credits. Figure 6 shows that some of these deliveries occur within the framework of these programmes. However, some of these deliveries are indicators of vertical coordination in the agri-food chain. Processors and traders faced with a poorly developed market for raw materials seek to attach producers to them. Almost all inputs, except for animals, are delivered to farms by intermediaries. In accordance with economic theory such vertical integration in the food chain is a sign of market failure. For intermediaries, transaction costs on the raw materials market are higher than the expenses made in providing the farms with commodity credit.

Another important sign of market failure is the slow diffusion of cash transactions in obtaining inputs, as around 30-40 percent of transactions are conducted in cash. Like the national economy in general, in 2000 barter deals had fallen off significantly as a result of the 1998 crisis. Before the crisis, however, barter had been as popular as cash transactions. Barter deals are fraught with fraud and encourage tax evasion, indicative of the shadow economy in agriculture during a large part of the 1990s.

Private farms conduct cash deals much more often than large-scale farms. They have less access to governmental programmes, such as commodity credit and leasing arrangements. They tend to conduct few barter transactions since, unlike large-scale farms, they do not have a sufficiently large volume of products to trade. Secondly, barter ratios are normally less favorable for private farms and the managers of large-scale farms use barter for rent seeking.

Barter arrangements are not transparent for the shareholders of the farm and there is scope for fraud. Prior to the economic crisis of the late 1990s, mutual debt offsets were an important form of settlement between buyers and sellers in the market and there were even intermediaries promoting such arrangements. Agriculture was no exception but, after the crisis, mutual offsets were no longer applied to any significant extent.

The government leasing programmes led to a segmentation of input markets. Large-scale farms acquire less than 60 percent of their machinery via leasing programmes, preferring to buy on the free market. Twenty-nine of the farms in our survey (both private and large-scale) made use of leasing schemes in 2000. A total of 18 had acquired machinery via other channels. This implies that federal and regional leasing programmes together do not meet the farms' requirements.

The sampled farms were also asked what major problems they face in acquiring inputs. Their answers are shown in figure 7. The results show that the farms see their major problem as the high prices of inputs. As we have shown elsewhere (Serova and Khramova, 2000a), the average price of the main purchased inputs (fertilizers, tractors, and harvesters) significantly exceeds the average product of correspondent input.

Figure 7. Problems with the Acquisition of Inputs

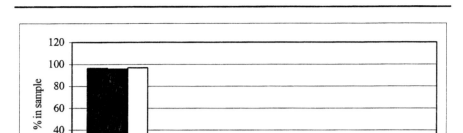

Source: AFE Farm Survey 2001.

In that study, we considered the average product of the factor (*AP*) as a proxy of the marginal product (though it would be more correct to assume that *AP* > *MP*). The price of the input was considered as a proxy of a marginal cost (*MC*). This substitution was necessary because of the absence of a satisfactory production function for Russian agriculture and the corresponding lack of marginal indicators. Therefore, from this simplified analysis one can conclude that prices are high indeed in comparison with productivity.

Finally, it is remarkable that around 20 percent of farms encountered opportunist behavior. This percentage was higher for private farms than for large-scale farms, which can partially be explained by the fact that the latter more frequently acquire their inputs through government schemes (leasing, commodity credit programmes), where officials serve as counterparts. The smaller private farms have less security in the market and are more often confronted with fraud. Among other problems mentioned most repeatedly were low quality of inputs and a lack of funds for purchasing (similar to high input prices).

Capital Transactions

We already stated above that farms lost much of their working capital at the very start of the reforms. During the macroeconomic contraction the farming sector was the least attractive for capital investments. This situation was aggravated by the lack of a sound agricultural credit system. Hence, agriculture has been in permanent financial crisis since 1992. Two attempts at massive debt restructuring for farms failed to stop indebtedness from rising steadily. By the end of the 1990s, the sector on average was making losses and the losses were increasing. After the severe economic crisis of 1998 the agricultural sector has recovered (partly because of favorable weather conditions), and has sustained growth rates. However, the enormous debt problem and the lack of profitability of a large majority of Russian farms are still unresolved.

Our AFE farm enterprise survey was implemented after the 1998 crisis and shows signs of a new situation regarding farm access to capital. Now, an absolute majority of farms rely on their own capital, without borrowing. Private farms are more reluctant to borrow than large-scale farms. Other sources of working capital–such as commodity credit, leasing and other government lending programs–are of secondary importance.

Large-scale farms have better access to such support programs than private farms, while subsidies are also given mostly to large-scale farms. On the other hand, private farms make more use of bank loans than large-scale farms. This is a somewhat surprising result, as it was long assumed that small producers in Russia have less access to formal financial institutions, because they cause higher transaction costs for banks. The survey indicates that this is not true. It is notable that bank loans occupy the same place as a source of farm working capital as loans from other lenders. The latter can come from farm product buyers, input providers and others. The formal banking sector in agriculture is still extremely underdeveloped, and farms therefore have to find their capital resources in other ways.

Through the farm survey we tried to clarify possible reasons why farms do not attract more capital from bank loans. Farm insolvency and a lack of banking networks in rural areas were not identified as important. The main issues were unacceptable interest rates and lending conditions, complicated banking procedures, and a lack of collateral acceptable to banks. All these problems are more important for private farms than for large-scale farms, which are bigger and have better trained financial staff (figure 8).

The current banking system is simply not suited to cater for agricultural borrowers. With a few exceptions, loans cannot be provided to the agricultural sector for periods shorter than nine months. The banks would prefer to work with the kind of collateral usual in the farming sector (trucks, cars and office equipment, but not agricultural machinery[2]). Banking procedures should be less sophisticated in rural areas, so that they are more user-friendly for less well-trained borrowers. The farms, however, complain about the complicated banking procedures. In the summer of 2000, the federal government launched a new credit support program for farms. This program not only subsidizes interest payments on bank loans, but also makes it attractive for commercial banks to lend to farms. Hopefully these measures will contribute to the development of a specialized farm credit system in Russia.

Figure 8. Problems with Getting Bank Loans for Farms

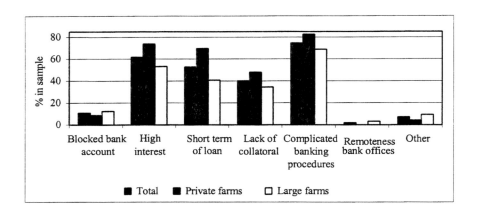

Source: AFE Farm Survey 2001

In summary, the financial state of the farms does not allow them to borrow from the banks. A majority of farms use their own capital and do not borrow. The bank network seems sufficient to serve the farms' needs but, according to the farms, is not adjusted to meet those needs. In particular the procedures to obtain loans are experienced as very bureaucratic.

Farm Output Transactions

The system of farm output marketing has changed significantly since the beginning of the reforms. In our survey we identified the main channels for marketing farm output. Since the sampled private farms predominantly market grain, we do not consider the marketing of other products below, as this would not be representative.

As far as grain marketing is concerned, the private and the large-scale farms differ significantly. The private farms sell two-thirds of their grain output to large and small mediators, while the large-scale farms market less than one third of their grain through this channel. Private farms do not deliver grain to the processing plants or local administration agents. As the private farms do not breed livestock their on-farm grain use is three times less than that of large-scale farms (9 percent as opposed to 27 percent). The private farms sell almost 9 percent of their grain output directly to households; for the large-scale farms this share is much lower. The latter use barter deals much more often than private farms.

Table 1. Marketing Channels of Selected Farm Products (Percentage of Total Sales in Volume, Large-Scale Farms)*

	Wheat			Grain			Milk			Meat		
	1995✦	1997▾	2000♦	1995✦	1997▾	2000♦	1995✦	1997▾	2000♦	1995✦	1997▾	2000♦
Processing plants	39	8.7	14.8	75	94.0	86.2	63	94.4	32.8			
Agents of regional administration	5	13.5	0	6	0	1.3	3	0	3.2			
Catering network	0	0	0	0	1.0	0	0	2.5	5.7			
Retail network	0	0	4.4	1	0	0.7	1	0	0			
City market	2	0.2	1.2	8.0	3.4	7.9	2.0	0	0.5			
Intermediaries	3	27.3	43.0	0	0	0.5	2.0	0	34.4			
Budget organizations	4	0	0	0	0	0.5	2.0	0	0.3			
Barter	16	24.6	12.6	0.0	0.7	0	4.0	1.3	1.9			
Payment-in-kind	4	8.4	11.6	1.0	0.2	0.5	1.0	0.1	6.2			
Dividends	0	5.6	5.0	0	0	0	0	0	0			
Retailing	9	1.0	4.8	2.0	0.3	2.5	15.0	1.6	15.2			
Other large-scale farms	3	10.7	2.2	0	0	0	1.0	0.1	0			
Other channels	1	0	0.4	1.0	0.2	0	2.0	0	0			
Total	100	100	100	100	100	100	100	100	100			

Source: Serova and Khramova (2000a); own farm survey.
*Without on-farm use of products.
✦Results of survey in Orel, Pskov, and Rostov oblasts (N = 82);
▾Results of Survey in Orel, Pskov, and Rostov oblasts (N = 48);
♦Results of survey in Pskov, Rostov, and Tambov oblasts (N = 32)

In 1995 and 1997 we implemented a large survey of the food chain in three *oblasts* (Orel, Pskov, and Rostov).[3] We have combined the results with those of our current survey to observe the dynamic process of market development. It should be remembered, however, that the surveys were done with different samples, in partially different regions and for different sets of products. However, some interesting conclusions can be drawn. The compiled results are presented in table 1.

The first obvious result is that the share of mediators in the marketing of farm output increased significantly, even in comparison with 1997. At the same time deliveries to conventional processing plants diminished, especially for meat. Direct retailing to households also increased. Farms seek the most appropriate channels of marketing and, less and less bound to the traditional channels, prefer those which bring prompt payment (better cash payment). As a consequence large-scale farms have become more independent in marketing and more flexible in the search for buyers. On the other hand, it has led to the emergence of an intermediary sector in the food chain.

For a long period grain was the major means for barter exchange, with farms acquiring almost all their inputs in exchange for grain and even paying taxes with grain. However, as table 1 shows, barter has strongly diminished.

Figure 9. Types of Transaction in the Marketing of Farm Output*

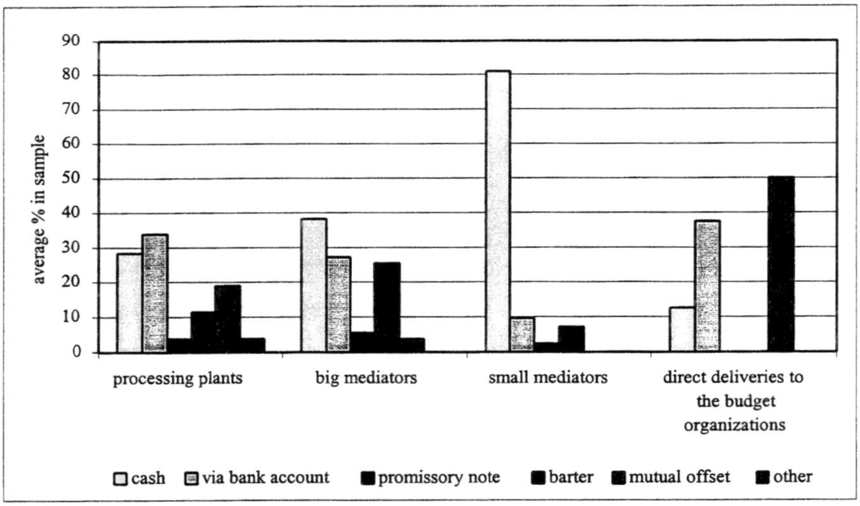

Source: AFE Farm Survey 2001

Figure 9 supports the above conclusion. It shows the distribution by type of transaction of some of the most important buyers of farm products. Mediators in farm products–both big and small–pay mostly in cash. The large mediators also provide commodity credit for their suppliers. These transactions were indicated in our farm survey as barter deals. Mutual debt offsets are typical for deliveries to the processing plants and the budget organizations.

Such deliveries can be considered as forced: faced with a shortage of money, farms must deliver their output in kind in return for a reduction of accumulated debts or other services. When their financial situation improves, it can be assumed that arrangements of this type will decrease. Cash deals will also disappear with the financial recovery of the economy in general and of agriculture in particular. There are already signs of this happening in the post-crisis period.

Limited domestic demand for agri-food products has been a major problem for marketing and even for the Russian agro-industrial economy as a whole. This assumption proved to be true after the 1998 economic crisis: import substitution stimulated the markets for domestic producers, and it became a turning point in development of the sector. In 1992, after the price liberalization reforms, the ruble had been devaluated to a much greater extent than in 1998, but the agri-food sector had been unable to take this opportunity: gross agricultural product contracted dramatically and agri-food imports sharply increased. One of the main reasons for this difference in supply response relates to the development of market infrastructure. In 1992, the state was withdrawing from the distribution sphere and trade was being liberalized, there was hardly any market infrastructure. So, in spite of a large gap between domestic and world prices, domestic producers could not access markets. The success after the devaluation of 1998 indicates that this time the market infrastructure and institutions were more developed and the sector could grasp the opportunity offered by the devaluation.

However, two other main problems show that the markets that have emerged are still underdeveloped. Price volatility is an indicator of a nonstable economy, fragmented markets and a lack of market information, with producers not yet having adjusted to the new conditions, expressed in extremist reactions by buyers and sellers.

There is a crucial difference in the answers of private and large-scale farms regarding the main bottlenecks in the marketing of farm output. From Figure 10, it can be seen that private farms consider the weak purchasing power of the population much more serious than the large-scale farms. This seems logical when you remember that private farms sell most of their output to households; their demand information is received at first hand, while the large-scale farms receive it via the mediation of their buyers. In addition, private farms are faced with more severe problems relating to contract fulfillment by their partners. They complain much more often about payment arrears and contract violation from the buyers' side. This shows not only that private farms have less market power than large-scale farms, but also that there is poor contract enforcement in agriculture as a whole.

Our survey was carried out in 2001, when the new Russian government had taken steps to reduce inter-regional trade barriers. However, during the 1990s, these barriers had been a heavy burden on agri-food markets, in particular in grain-producing areas. Only farms in Rostov–which was known for its tempo-rary grain export bans during the harvesting period–complained about trade barriers. Thirty-eight percent of farms in this *oblast* identified trade barriers as a problem, making them the third most important obstacle to farm output market-ing in Rostov, together with excessive licensing, after price volatility and weak purchasing power of the population.

Similarly, 22 percent of farms identified licensing and other barriers to market entrance as a problem. We have shown elsewhere that entrance barriers are quite important in the agri-food chain (Serova and Khramova, 2000b). They are, however, mostly applicable at the level of processing industries and wholesale or retail networks. Farms themselves do not feel these barriers, but they are affected by the limited demand for agri-food products.

Among "other" problems of marketing, the farms in our survey identified high transport costs and gasoline prices. As domestic Russian gasoline prices are much below the world and Russian export average, these complaints can be again considered as rather subjective. It would be fairer to include these complaints in the category of low purchasing power: low demand causes low prices for farm products, which then do not cover all expenses, including transportation costs.

Farm Services

With the collapse of the centrally planned economy, agriculture was confronted with a severe lack of traditional and new farm services, which have since emerged within the new market environment. All collective and state farms used to have their own specialists in agronomy, veterinary medicine, animal breeding and financial management. Those which have remained intact still retain such expertise within the enterprise. Newly established private farms, however, lacked such services. In addition, all farms need the market information, legal and extension services and management technology that are required by the new economic paradigm of the market. These services seem to be lacking most of all. Figure 10 shows the distribution of answers to which farm services the farms already receive and which they would like to receive. The first striking observa-tion is that most farms would like market information and legal services. Since 1992, the Ministry of Agriculture has been developing a market information system, while in Rostov, the Ministry has an office specialized in the provision of extension services to farms. In spite of these initiatives, the survey shows that farms are not getting the kind of information they desperately need.

Legal services are also very important for farms, which find themselves in a complicated economic and insecure legal environment. Most farms are separated from the centres of economic life, and very often their contract partners are better informed about current legislation, which weakens the farms' position on the markets. The farms are aware of this, but their financial state does not allow them to hire private lawyers. Hence, they seek public legal services.

The answers of private and large-scale farms differ significantly with regard to farm services. Since they traditionally have specialists on their staff, large-scale farms have access to veterinary and agronomy services and do not need to seek them externally. Private farms do not need veterinary services, because they do not have much animal husbandry. They do, however, regularly request agronomy services.

Private farms do not have access to sufficient extension services, product quality expertise or training, but also do not seem very interested in receiving them. Large-scale farms obtain slightly more of these types of service, and are also more interested in getting them in the future. Product quality expertise used to be attached to processing plants and procurement agencies.

Figure 10. Provided and Required Services for the Farm Sector

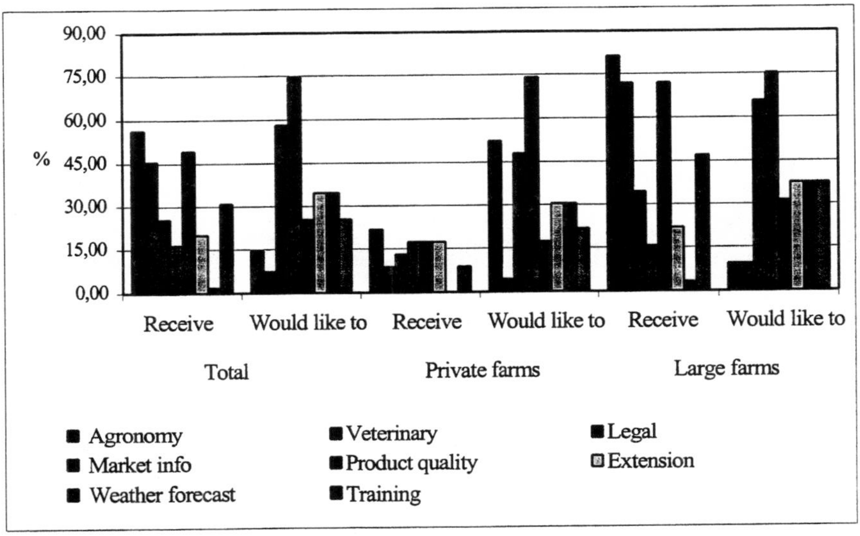

Source: AFE Farm Survey 2001

Inasmuch as the large-scale farms deliver their products to these conventional purchasers, they have access to this traditional system of product quality expertise. As we have seen in the previous section, private farms tend to avoid these conventional buyers and accordingly they have no access to this service. However, they do not seem to feel any necessity to receive it. The "other" services private farms would like to receive include tax and bookkeeping assistance, and training in computers. The large-scale farms did not express any interest in these services.

In general, the provision of farm services to farms, especially those required by the new market economy, is poor. Large-scale farms are in a better situation as regards acquiring traditional farm services, such as veterinary and agronomy services and product quality expertise. They are also more interested in extension, training and specialized weather forecasts. The private farms have less access to services, but seek essential ones, such as price information and legal services.

Conclusions

The analysis provided here is only to be considered as a preliminary stage in a more quantitative analysis of the transformation of farms, factor markets and institutions in Russian agriculture. Nevertheless, it does provide insights into the development of market institutions in Russian agriculture during the 1990s. Several general conclusions can be drawn from the survey:

1.   From the field data it can be shown that, after rapid restructuring of the farm sector and privatization in the downstream sector, agrarian reform is confronted with a huge institutional development problem. There is no clear governmental policy in overcoming this "institutional gap," and institutions tend to emerge spontaneously through trial and error.

2.   Institutional reform in the agri-food chain depends heavily on the macroeconomic environment. Thus, in a situation of financial instability and shortage of capital in the economy, a well-functioning banking structure in agriculture cannot be established. The transactions between farms and their counterparts are settled in irregular ways, e.g through barter, promissory notes or mutual debt reductions. The high unemployment in the economy as a whole includes even higher (and often hidden) unemployment in rural areas. This situation impedes the development of a well-functioning labor market in the rural economy. In the absence of macroeconomic stabilization, a major advance in institutional reform in agriculture should therefore not be expected.

3.   Land and labor legislation in particular lag behind the development of the corresponding markets. This leads to anomalous forms of transactions, and

impedes further development of the markets. Government policy in most cases creates obstacles for new institutional development. Instead of providing the conditions for emerging market institutions, it still often tends to perform some of the functions of the market itself. It was shown that, in input and capital markets, the government provides leasing services and credit. These seem to contribute to the monopsonistic power of some agents and market segmentation, and impede the emergence of private traders, leasing companies and a well-functioning rural banking system.

4.   Quite a lot has been achieved in the emergence of new marketing infra-structure, in which a set of new market agents appeared. During a large part of the 1990s agriculture was a collapsing sector, and the financial position of farm enterprises was deteriorating from year to year. Since the Russian crisis of 1998, there has been a slight recovery, and farms have begun to acquire capital goods. Agriculture showed substantial positive growth rates in the last two years of the decade. This helps the development of emerging market institutions, such as sales and leasing companies.

5.   Macroeconomic stabilization encourages the movement of capital from financial markets to the real sector, including certain branches of agriculture, especially the most dynamic. The better financial position of the farms also makes it possible for them to obtain bank credit. A specialized credit system is being established, but bureaucracy must be reduced and better access to loans guaranteed. Financial stabilization of the sector also leads to farm differentia-tion: some of the farms are becoming more prosperous, while others face bankruptcy. This development also calls for further development of the still embryonic factor markets in labor, inputs and land. The need for farm services is rapidly emerging, in the same sequence. Farms initially require services related to production and marketing. More recently, they have also felt the need for extension services, such as training, and more sophisticated services, including financial management and specialized weather forecasting.

Notes

The chapter is one of the outcomes of an international research project "Institutional Modernization, Market Adjustment and Organizational Evolution in Transitional Agriculture," financed by the Soros Foundation and led by Professor D. Terzive (Bulgaria). The survey in this paper was undertaken with the participation of A. Efimova (Pskov Agricultural Research Institute), S. Sazonov (Tambov Agricultural Union), A. Tarasov (Rostov Agricultural Research Institute), and V. Petrichenko (Grain Union of Russia). The authors thank T. Tikhonova, fellow of the Analytical Centre of Agri-food

Economics (AFE), for their technical assistance rendered, and the editor of this volume in the preparation of the final text of this chapter.

1.   Our study does not provide us with information on whether this method of production is a result of unskilled management, because the marginal product of industrial feed (mixed feed) is much less than its marginal cost.
2.   Use of farmland as collateral is prohibited in Russia by the 1998 Law on Mortgage (1998). In the autumn of 2000, a bill lifting this limitation was passed in the first reading by the State Duma, the Lower House of the Russian parliament.
3.   This research was part of a cooperation project between the Institute for Economy in Transition, the Centre of Economic Analysis (both Russian) and Kiel University.

Farm Restructuring, Property Rights, and Household Strategies in Rural Russia

Oane Visser

The majority of agricultural enterprises in Russia were privatized in the 1990s. The employees who became shareholders could opt to take out their share in land and start a private farm. However, like in the other large FSU states, most employees remained shareholders and the agricultural enterprises remained largely intact. The dominant expectation of a rapid growth in private family farms (expressed in World Bank, 1992) did not materialize (Spoor and Visser, 2001). This led some Western observers to conclude that hardly anything has changed within Russian agriculture (Brooks et al., 1996), but this, too, is not the case.

The massive, albeit rather formal, privatization process had already ended in the second half of the decade of reform, but the transformation of enterprises continued. When one goes beyond numerical indicators and takes a closer look at the farm level, it can be shown that incremental, but fundamental, changes are taking place (O'Brien et al., 2000). Property relations in most enterprises are not static–they change, mostly slowly but sometimes drastically. Contrary to the large-scale privatization in the early 1990s, which was largely a top-down process initiated (or more correctly pushed forward) by the state, the current changes in property relations originate much more at farm-level. Many of these changes are originating from the level of the household. As the social and economic role of the former *kolkhozy* and *sovkhozy* has dwindled, households have been forced to develop strategies to become more self-supportive.

The rural population in the less well-endowed Russian regions, located in the north and northwest of the country, was hit especially hard by the collapse of the centrally planned economy. The agricultural sector in these regions depended on federal budget transfers, which drastically diminished during the 1990s. As a consequence, the financial situation of agricultural enterprises in these regions sharply deteriorated, directly leading to falling income levels among the rural population. In these regions the question of enterprise reorganization and of household survival strategies is most acute. It is in one of these regions, Pskov *oblast*, that we investigated the reorganization of agricultural enterprises, the coping strategies of the farm employees and their households, and finally how the private initiative of the households influences further development of the agricultural enterprises.

The large-scale agricultural sector, consisting of the successors of the *kolk-hozy* and *sovkhozy*, is the main source of employment in the Russian country-side. Private peasant farming has emerged, but this sector is small both in terms of production and employment. Thus, as during the Soviet era, the income of the majority of the households depends on the agricultural enterprises. Although these enterprises have faced large drops in output and are ridden with financial problems, they have not cut their workforces drastically (which in itself also causes financial problems).[1]

Wages in the agricultural sector are very low; in the Pskov region they are just 560 rubles a month, which was about US $20 in 2001, while the official minimum wage for all economic sectors in Russia is 1513 rubles (*Pskovskaya Guberniya*, 22 Nov. 2001, 14). Wage arrears are chronic. However, like before, farm employees have their private "subsidiary" household plot, which provides them with most of the food they need.

We will show how the large-scale enterprises, which are formally persist-ing, are in fact disintegrating, largely as a consequence of the expansion of the household sector. We will investigate which changes in property relations within the agricultural enterprises made the expansion of the household sector possible. In doing so we will consider the amount of land which the employees received, as well as their access to the capital of the enterprise (tractors, machinery) and other enterprise resources (like fodder).

Furthermore, we will investigate what sets apart the small minority of suc-cessful enterprises which are not facing disintegration. Finally, we will examine the perspectives of the unprofitable and disintegrating enterprises. Is the process of disintegration likely to stop and is a return to centralized property and stability possible for such enterprises? Several scenarios for the development of unprofitable enterprises will be presented and discussed. This chapter starts with a short overview of the privatization process of the 1990s.

Privatization in Russian Agriculture

In contemporary Russia, three main types of agricultural producers are generally distinguished; first, the agricultural enterprises, which are the successors to the *kolkhozy* and *sovkhozy*, second, the newly established peasant farms and third, the household enterprises, based on the subsidiary household plot.

The privatization of the *kolkhozy* and *sovkhozy* started in 1992. The members of these enterprises had several options. The first and least drastic option was to remain a *kolkhoz* or *sovkhoz*. By the end of the first phase of farm reform, 1992-94, about one third of the collective farms had chosen to retain this status. The second option was to create a "closed" joint-stock company. This variant permits only farm members to own shares of the farm. The "closed type" variant was most popular, nearly half of the enterprises registered in this way. The third possibility was to reorganize by forming a joint-stock company or partnership of the "open type."

In this way, outsiders could also obtain shares in the enterprise, by buying them from the members. The government promoted this variant, as it was supposed to attract more investment to the crisis-ridden agricultural sector. However, only a minority of the enterprises reorganized in this way. The fourth and most drastic form was to disband the farm, and distribute land and property to the employees and pensioners in physical form. For chronically unprofitable farms this variant was obligatory. Apart from those which were forced to do so, very few enterprises chose to split up the collective.[2]

The privatization process gave farm members the opportunity to take out their share of land and start their own peasant farm. Other kinds of property, like machinery, were only distributed when an enterprise was disbanded. Nonfarm members could also start their own farm, by buying (or renting) land from a municipal land fund. During the first years of reform the number of peasant farms increased quickly, but in the mid-1990s, this growth had slowed down and the number of farms even declined by the end of the 1990s. Currently, there are about 280,000 farms in Russia, occupying only 6 percent of total agricultural land (Spoor and Visser, 2001). On average they use about 50 hectares of land, but in Pskov the farms are somewhat smaller.

Many factors prevented rural households from establishing private farms; the lack of all-round agricultural knowledge of the farm workers required to run their own farm, the unstable and risky economic environment, the uncooperativeness or even hostility of enterprise managers and village dwellers towards the farmers, etc. Furthermore, since the mid-1990s, declining state support made starting a farm even more difficult.

As a consequence, most farm workers stayed within the enterprises, and chose another strategy. They increased the private plots, the so-called "subsidiary household enterprises" they already had as *kolkhoz* or *sovkhoz* workers, as a less risky alternative to independent (peasant) farming. It is this main strategy of enlarged household production within the boundaries of the existing enterprises that we discuss here.

The Pskov Agricultural Enterprise Survey

This empirical analysis is based on survey data and ethnographical research. The survey included large-scale enterprises, peasant farms and household enterprises.[3] It was carried out in Pskov *oblast*, in northwest Russia, in the autumn of 2001. The survey consisted of two rounds. The first round took place in the Pskov district around the *oblast* centre, Pskov city, and included ten agricultural enterprises and ten peasant farms, and a somewhat smaller number of food factories and wholesale companies.[4]

At the large-scale enterprises, interviews were held with two or three specialists and members of the management. Furthermore, at each enterprise at least four employees were interviewed about their work on the large-scale enterprise and their household plots. At the peasant farms the farm head was the respondent. The second round had the same design but was carried out in Pechory, a district in the periphery of the Pskov region, on the border with Estonia.

More ethnographically oriented research was carried out in the Pskov and Moscow regions, during several field research periods in 2000 and 2001. It included semi-structured interviews with farms and agricultural enterprise in the Pskov region (in several other districts besides the survey districts), and interviews with different producers and processors in the Moscow region. In the last region also a short case study of a large-scale enterprise was carried out. Finally statistical data was collected in both regions at the regional and local level and government officials were interviewed.

The Increased Importance of Household Enterprises

In the past decade, agriculture in the Pskov region has been characterized by a sharper decline than in most other regions of Russia. The profitability of the enterprises declined quickly in the first half of the 1990s and continued until 1998. While in 1990 only one percent of the enterprises was unprofitable, in 1998 this had risen to 97 percent (Goskomstat Pskov, 2000: 19). A part of the enterprises disintegrated and 16 percent of the (377) enterprises that existed in 1990 have stopped functioning.[5] The agricultural land of the enterprises decreased by a third (Goskomstat Pskov, 2000: 19), because of the decreasing number of enterprises and the decline of land acreage of the enterprises that kept functioning. During the survey work I was told that areas of land now covered with low bushes and small trees used to be agricultural land a decade ago. Production in the enterprises has declined even more drastically than the amount of land. After a decade the former *kolkhozy* and *sovkhozy* produced about a quarter of what they did before (unpublished regional data). At the same time as the agricultural enterprises were declining, the household sector began to flourish.[6]

In all parts of Russia, the acreage held by household enterprises clearly increased since the start of the reforms, although they remain very small.[7] The size of these private plots nearly doubled during the first half of the 1990s, increasing from 0.2 hectares in 1991 to 0.36 hectares in 1995 (Goskomstat, 1999: 16). In the second half of the 1990s the size of the plots remained stable and only increased slightly in the latter years to 0.4 hectares in 1998. If we also include the various types of collective gardens and plots, the land per household increased from 0.34 in 1990 to 0.57 hectares in 1998. Nevertheless, compared with peasant farms (on average about 40 hectares large) and the former collective enterprises (several thousands of hectares large), they remained very small, although their share in the total production increased remarkably.

In Russia the household plots accounted for 5.4 percent of agricultural land in 1998 (Goskomstat, 1999: 45). Important differences exist in the *share* of private plots in total land between different regions. In the main agricultural provinces, located in the fertile black earth areas such as the Volga region and the Northern Caucasus, the share of the household plots reaches on average only 1.6 and 5.2 percent respectively (Goskomstat, 1999: 46). In the less 'endowed' areas in the north of European Russia the share of the plots amounts to around 15 percent. The household enterprises in the Pskov region own the highest share in land (18.4 percent).[8]

As a combined result of falling production in the collective sector and an increase in the household, the share of the latter in total production increased from 26 percent in 1990 to 57 percent in 1998 (Goskomstat, 1999: 18). For the Pskov region, by the middle of the 1990s the 130,000 rural households already produced 70 percent of food output. In the second half of the 1990s the share of the population in agricultural production in the region only increased slightly, amounting to 77 percent in 1999 (Goskomstat Pskov, 2000: 15).

What does a household enterprise look like? A rural household in the Pskov region, consisting generally of three to four persons, uses on average 0.75 hectares of land, on which it grows predominantly potatoes, the main staple food in Russia. More labor-intensive vegetables and fruits make up the rest of the plot. Sometimes rural households grow some fodder crops for their livestock. Households generally own about one cow, two pigs, some chickens and sometimes one or two goats or sheep. On average, Russian households own about one third of total livestock (Goskomstat, 1999: 108). However, some important differences exist in the size of plots (and number of livestock held), between households in successful and failing agricultural enterprises.

Property Relations and the Enlargement of the Household Enterprise

Several factors have been mentioned which made the option of private peasant farming neither feasible nor attractive for the majority of the rural population.

As their incomes depended more and more on their own household enterprises, the step towards establishing an independent farm would seem to become easier. In that case rural dwellers would receive more land, and they could spend all their time on their own farm, instead of working on the collective without receiving payment. The reason that most employees preferred to enlarge their small plots incrementally, while staying within the large-scale enterprise can only be understood when we take into account the Soviet legacy, in the form of the specific nature of the property relations between households and their enterprises, and the collective farm.

Before, the boundaries between the agricultural enterprises and the household enterprises were vague. Households could let their livestock graze on the collective meadows. Employees could use the enterprise's tractors to plough their plots and were supplied informally with fodder for their cows and pigs. *Kolchozy* often marketed the part of their produce that exceeded the planned amounts through the household enterprises to hide actual production figures and evade higher production quota in the future. In brief, there was a mutually beneficial symbiosis between the collective and the individual enterprises. Households could increase their food supply and save money for other expenditures by expanding their plot with subsidized inputs from the collective. The collective farm management, on the other hand, could stimulate its low-paid workers with these informal—in kind—transfers. Furthermore, the shadow economy of the households could be used flexibly to channel products back or forth as necessary in the game of plan fulfillment, in the best interests of the farm and its members (Humphrey, 1996).

At macro-level, the ideologically undesirable and therefore restricted private plots fulfilled several functions, which smoothed out some of the shortcomings of the planned economy. In periods of disappointing production in the collective sector, the rural households were given more freedom to provide extra production. Furthermore, the plots were a substitute for the unsatisfactory provision of food products through shops in the countryside and a compensation for the low wages in the agricultural sector.

During the 1980s, the restrictive policy of the 1960s and the somewhat more tolerant policy of the 1970s changed into a supportive one, which officially recognized the production potential of integrating the plots into the collective farms. Especially in livestock farming a tense symbiosis evolved between the household and the collective sector (Lerman, 1994: 530). Cattle from the collective farm were given to the households for fattening. A part of the cattle would be returned in autumn, and the *kolkhoz* would deliver the livestock to the state to fulfill production quota. In this division of labor the *kolkhoz* supplied young animals and the necessary fodder. The households provided labor and moderate buildings for the livestock. Starting in 1982, restrictions on livestock numbers were lifted for households which accepted cattle from the *kolkhoz* for fattening. In the mid-1980s this cooperation took the form of lease-contracts. Households could further expand their enterprises and were paid by the *kolkhoz* for the cattle or milk they delivered. As a result the households specialized more in livestock than the collective farms. *Kolchozy* derived 40 percent of their income from livestock, while the households earned 75 percent of their plot income from livestock. The share of the plot earnings in the total income of the households increased from 20 to 30 percent in this period (Lerman, 1994: 534).

During and after the privatization of the *kolkhozy*, the expansion of the household enterprises gained even more momentum. The official restrictions on private plot production were lifted and it became attractive, if not to say necessary, for farm employees to increase production. Wages in the agricultural sector, which were already low during communism, were not on par with the increase in other sectors, let alone with the rocketing prices of consumption articles. Furthermore wages were not paid for months on end and employees mostly received a large part of their wage in kind. The incentive for employees to increase their plots seems evident, but the increased incentive and the relaxing of the state policy alone cannot fully explain the remarkable growth of the household sector. The flourishing of the household enterprises was made possible by several developments.

First, as already mentioned, the size of the plots expanded. The state abolished the size limitations, enabling households to enlarge their land, unless the regional and local authorities or enterprises managed to maintain the restrictions. During privatization employees received the plots they already used during the communist period in ownership. Furthermore, most enterprises distributed somewhat larger fields for household use. These were the collective gardens and fields to which the members in general have usufruct rights. These fields (especially the potato fields) were enlarged to enable the employees to increase their food production in the midst of the mounting economic hardship of the 1990s. Finally, households could hire additional municipal land. Although, the household plots still remain small, they have increased–mostly twofold but in some cases ten to twenty times. The increase of the plots depends strongly on the state of the enterprise (see below).

Second, the access to resources of the large-scale farms mostly continued or increased. The process of integration (symbiosis) between the collective farm and the household enterprises that was stimulated during the 1980s, especially in the livestock sector, became stronger after privatization. Employees could buy fodder from the enterprise at cost price or even lower. They could use the equipment of the enterprise and sometimes also fuel. The large-scale enterprise became a provider of services and resources for the small-scale household sector. It prepared fodder and provided young animals for the households and provided transportation to market the livestock products from the small-scale sector. Furthermore, the large-scale farms opened shops and bakeries in which employees could buy products without money, the bill being deducted from their unpaid wages.

Illegal Outflow of Resources

Apart from the resources which the enterprise offered to its members, a semi-legal or illegal flow of goods towards the household sector already existed during communism. It was a public secret that farm employees obtained part of the inputs for their plots by stealing it from the collective farm. The Soviet journal *Krokodil* published cartoons about the shadow economy in the country-side, and people told me jokes about it from the Soviet period. The actual amount of the outflow of these resources is difficult to estimate, and can only be left to our imagination.

Articles in newspapers, conversations with people in the countryside and articles by agricultural researchers (Zeddies, 2001) all indicate that the stealing of enterprise resources (mostly by employees or other village dwellers) has become a widespread phenomenon since 1991. As employees were hardly paid, they pilfered the enterprise stores to survive. The agricultural sociologist Nikulin estimates that 12 percent of major resources (such as fodder) were stolen by employees on the farm he studied in the south of Russia.[9] During a stay at a Dutch-owned agricultural enterprise, I myself saw employees taking away and selling milk from the enterprise in the evening (Moscow region, summer 2000). Zeddies (2001: 481) estimated that theft of products and resources in the middle of the 1990s accounted for at maximum 5 percent for livestock products, but to about 20 percent for vegetables and potatoes.

Thus, the privatization of the *kolkhozy* and *sovkhozy,* making the employees shareholders, did not generally speaking result in them showing greater respect for enterprise property. The lack of private initiative in the form of peasant farming and the widespread support among the rural population for conservative policies opposing private ownership of land does not, however, testify to an *active* support for the maintenance of the large-scale farms. On the contrary, the erosion of discipline during the transition led to widespread stealing from farms that actually *broadened* the access of households to inputs. The heirs of the *kolkhozy* were first of all seen as prey, a fertile ground for informal activities. As a consequence, the dispersion and degradation of enterprise property acceler-ated. Thus the mutual beneficial cooperation between the collective farm and the household enterprises has become detrimental to the pre-existence of the first. According to Yelena Yakovlev, a renowned Russian agrarian journalist, nowadays 'the most widespread form of symbiosis is stealing a sack of grain from a collective farm' (*Izvestiya*, March 15, 2000, 1). Thus, the flourishing of private plots cannot be considered separately from the decline of the large-scale farms. Initially, the decline of the enterprises led to the enlargement of the private plots. With the expansion of the plots, they started to 'eat up' the collectives and triggered a further fall of the large-scale sector. Fadeeva (2000) speaks about the shift to a "parasitic symbiosis."

What measures did the enterprise management take to constrain this illegal outflow of resources? First of all, they introduced new practices or tightened up existing measures to protect stores and livestock farms from theft. Ninety percent of the enterprises interviewed now have locks on stores and guards at the entrance to the farm terrain. In more than half of the enterprises, these measures did not exist before the start of reforms. Furthermore, in 45 percent of the enterprises, specialists monitored the work to keep an eye on farm property, especially during the distribution of herbicides on the fields and the harvest period. At two farms, the farm employees used as guards were not considered sufficient to protect property and a private or state-owned security company was hired.

Observations at farm enterprises in the Pskov and Moscow region indicate that the measures to protect property are most strict in the enterprises which have made relatively large investments or have external investors. In the enterprises that were visited in the Moscow region, private security companies were only hired by enterprises with outside investments. In these enterprises security personnel in uniforms guarded the main buildings. Near the entrances of all the vegetable fields were signs warning visitors that it was private property and access was forbidden. In addition, an employee on horseback guarded the fields.

However, successful enterprises do not automatically always have a strong regime of protection. There must therefore be other factors which hinder the outflow of resources. Therefore we looked at the household activities in these enterprises in more detail.

Degradation *Versus* Stability in Large-Scale Enterprises

Despite all these measures, only in a small proportion of the enterprises is the management able or willing to stop the dispersion and degradation of property. The enterprises are mostly several thousands of hectares large and consist of several locations, so it is difficult to guard all their resources. However, some enterprises are able to keep their property and the enterprise together.

Some of the collective farms, which were successful during socialism, were able to avoid the steep decline in production that characterizes most other farms. These enterprises generally have a good location near the city, above average state of equipment and last but not least a strong and experienced director with a lot of business contacts. A typical example of such an enterprise is 'Pioneer,' an unreformed *kolkhoz* in the Pskov district. While surrounding enterprises have been confronted with sharp drops in production, equipment and workers, this *kolkhoz* has managed to keep production stable and make new investments. The director has been leading the *kolkhoz* for several decades, was a senator in the regional government, and has a good reputation within and outside the enterprise. His authority is undisputed. The stealing of resources also used to happen here in the early 1990s, but protection was increased and now some measures have even been relaxed, such as monitoring the fields by specialists. The most important factor for the preservation of the assets of the enterprise seems to be the small size of the household plots, enforced by a system combining stable, high wages with a strong labor regime.

Table 1 confirms that employees in successful enterprises have much smaller household enterprises than their colleagues in weak enterprises. The differences in the importance of the household enterprise, both in terms of the household plot size and livestock numbers, are striking. Household plots in enterprises that are on the verge of bankruptcy are eight times larger than the ones in the most profitable enterprises. Differences in livestock numbers are even larger.

Table 1. Financial and Productive Indicators of Large Farms and Household Enterprises

Characteristics of agricultural enterprises			household enterprises	
Financial state	No of Enterprises	Average Wage	Average Plot size, ha	Average No of cows
Medium/high profit	2	2,100	0.2	0.1
Low profit	4	1,220	0.5	0.8
Unprofitable	9	405	1.0	1.6
Near bankrupt	3	387	1.6	1.7

Source: Own survey in the Pskov, 2001.

To investigate why enterprises like Pioneer, as well as enterprises with less powerful leaders, manage to avoid household expansion and dispersion of property we take a closer look at the households within these agricultural enterprises.

Household Strategies: Boundaries to Growth

Wages in the agricultural sector are very low. Moreover, the wages are mostly not paid on time. In 1999, employees facing nonpayment had to wait for more than four months for their wages (Goskomstat Pskov, 2000). Since the financial crisis of 1998 the economic decline in agriculture has come to a halt and, as a result, the payment of wages is somewhat improving. In farms with wage arrears, the average delay decreased to about three months in 2000. However, this slight improvement does not yet seem to have brought a significant improvement in the lives of farm workers.

Are the farm employees able to compensate their low wages to some extent, with their private subsidiary plots? In the first part of the 1990s households drastically increased their private plot production, as we discussed earlier. The question arises whether they had the ability to increase private plot production further in recent years. This issue was addressed by the survey round in the suburban Pskov district, where all but one of the profitable enterprises (and all break-even enterprises) were located.[10] From the survey it appears that only a minority (of 30 percent) of the respondents further increased their own produce in the successful farms.

More than half of the workers were not able or willing to increase plot production further and kept household production at the same level. Ten percent even decreased their activities on the plot. Based on these findings no significant growth of the private plot sector is to be expected in the successful enterprises. The numbers of people willing to increase their private plot production in the coming years is even lower. Twenty percent plan to expand production, while ten percent expect a decline in private plot production.

By far the most important obstacle to the further increase of private production is the extra labor it would require. For 85 percent of the workers this is the main reason. In some families unemployed adults, children and pensioners carry out a large part of the work in the plot and garden (*ogorod*). However, in most of the households the work is done by the parents, who both work on the farm. In the summer and early autumn, working days at the large scale enterprises are long and this is precisely the period that the private plot requires most attention.

This means that during the 1990s, with the sharp increase in household production, the workload of the population increased enormously, unless the work at the large-scale enterprises became less intensive. According to the majority of the employees, this did not happen. On the contrary, they feel that the work at the former *kolkhozy* and *sovkhozy* has become more arduous.

In table 2 the interviewed agricultural enterprises are divided into four categories of profitability. It shows that the majority of the employees in successful farms stated that the intensity of labor on the enterprise has not decreased since 1991. More than half of the people have even experienced an increasing workload at the large-scale enterprise since 1991, and during the last five years. At medium to highly profitable enterprises all respondents indicated that farm work became more arduous. Unprofitable enterprises and especially enterprises on the verge of bankruptcy show the opposite pattern. Labor at the enterprise has become clearly less intensive since 1991. Since the financial crisis of 1998 the same trends have continued, although they are less pronounced. These findings strongly suggest that the expansion of household production at the successful enterprises is constrained by the much higher workload for the employees.

Table 2. Perceived Changes in Labor Intensity at Farm-level

	Since 1991			Since 1998		
Total (n=34)	More	Same	Less	More	Same	Less
Successful enterprises (n=12):	7	1	4	4	6	2
Medium/high profit	4	0	0	1	3	0
low profit	3	1	4	3	3	2
Failing enterprises (n=22):	2	7	13	2	17	3
Unprofitable	2	5	9	2	14	0
near bankrupt	0	2	4	0	3	3

Source: Own survey Pskov, 2001 (the ranking is based on enterprise accounts and interviews with specialists).

To explore this issue further, let us take a look at how many hours workers work on average at the enterprise. It appears that 70 percent of the employees have a normal, (official) working week of about 40 hours. Thirty percent stated that they spend at least one or two hours per day more on the enterprise, which means that they work 45 or 50 hours per week. Two workers even worked more than 50 hours (53 and 56).

Besides the work at the enterprise, employees have to spend time on their private plot to generate extra food and/or income. And it appears that they spend a considerable amount of time on their plots. On average, employees work 27 hours a week on their household enterprise. However, during the summer and harvest seasons, the work on the plot (and the work at the enterprises) demands even more time. This means that during the summer, the workers face an extreme workload. The average of 27 hours includes some employees who worked 17 hours a week, while others work even 35 hours a week on their private plot. Adding the work on the private plot to the farm work, employees work on average nearly 70 hours a week. It is thus far from surprising that they mention the workload as the main factor hindering the further growth of household production.

During the Soviet era, the limited size of the private plot was an obstacle for growth of private household production. In contemporary Russia the access to land is no longer an important obstacle to growth, certainly not in Pskov (except for some locations near large cities).

Another important obstacle to the growth of household plot production is the distance between the household residence and the private plot. Normally the central village of an agricultural enterprise, where the central office and the *dom kultura* (the social-cultural centre) are located, consists of two or three-story apartment buildings with no (or very small) gardens adjacent to them. For the people in the apartment buildings the time necessary to go to the gardens and plots is an additional burden, especially if we take into account that many rural dwellers do not own cars. Moreover, an average family uses different parcels of land which are not adjacent to each other; their private plot, their smaller *ogorod*, parts of collective gardens, and finally a parcel of land at most farms for potatoes. Hence, in fact the enterprise does not have to establish restrictions on household size. If the enterprise retains a strict labor regime, households cannot enlarge the plots very much.

Another very important factor is the lack of cheap inputs and fodder. This factor can of course be determined by management policy. A successful enterprise has restricted the volume of inputs and services destined to households, or has increased the prices. Even if households steal part of the resources, it means that the outflow of resources is restricted.

A Return to Centralized Property?

What happens in the majority of the enterprises? In most of the successors to the *kolkhozy* the size and value of the shared property has dropped drastically, in terms of machinery, livestock, and useable buildings. The interviews with nearby farmers generally gave the most straightforward and shocking information about this process of disintegration. In one former *kolkhoz*, the management tried to stop the decline in milk production by obtaining new cows through a lease construction. But the milkmaids neglected the new animals because of drunkenness and the new herd was soon troubled by disease. In the end the enterprise was forced to sell the cows to the meat factory, while the lease sum still had to be paid back.

What is the future of the unprofitable enterprises facing a process of disintegration? In principle, one could distinguish four scenarios. The first, and least probable, option is a shift to the model of the successful enterprises, namely: centralized property and rigid discipline in combination with small household enterprises. However, a number of recent developments in the agricultural sector offer new opportunities. In the last two or three years the fall in production has halted and the agricultural sector in Pskov and Russia in general shows indications of some recovery. The Russian grain harvest this year was the largest in more than 15 years. Furthermore, prices for several agricultural products are increasing as a result of the reduced import of food products from the West since the sharp devaluation of the ruble in August 1998 (*Pskovskaya Gubernaya*, 1 November 2001, 14). The increased prices could offer enterprises the possibility to become profitable and start an upward spiral. A hopeful sign is that the number of profitable enterprises in Pskov and other regions has increased over the last two years. However, for most enterprises which are not profitable this option will remain an unattainable ideal. When the Russian government designed a program for debt restructuring, providing possibilities for postponement of debts and chances to write off debts, the majority of unprofitable enterprises did not even apply. Fadeeva (2000) estimates that the number of enterprises that do not suffer from disintegration tendencies, in Russia as a whole, constitute 20 percent at most. In the Pskov region this percentage is even less than 10 percent. In the next sections, three other scenarios for unsuccessful farms will be discussed.

Shift to Peasant Farms

The second scenario is the opposite of the first; a split up in farms or associations of farms or most probably a mix of them, before all the property is worthless or has disappeared. This option was promoted already in the beginning of the 1990s by radical reformers. In this scenario only motivated people, who have a good relation with each other, can join in small units, which will probably lead to more responsibility among the members. However, several factors block this path.

First, the enterprise management is mostly afraid to lose its position. Furthermore, regional authorities do not see this as a viable option, because they consider it a purely negative development, a collapse of the agricultural enterprise, in their eyes the only serious producer. But most importantly, households are on the whole not interested in this option.

In the course of reform, the situation at most agricultural enterprises deteriorated. As production plummeted, enterprises were not able to pay their employees on time. Workers had to wait for months for their wages, and received most of their salary in kind (in agricultural products). It could be expected that the bad state of the large-scale farms would encourage workers to leave the enterprises. In Moldova, households at first stayed within the large-scale enterprises, but started to leave them more recently in large numbers as the situation became very harsh (Spoor and Visser, 2001).

The first reason why households are not interested in leaving the enterprise is that it has become very difficult to obtain credit to start a farm. During the first years of reform (1991-92) farms could still acquire loans at privileged interest rates of 2 to 8 percent through membership of the federal farmer's association. Because of the high inflation they could pay the loans back easily. Furthermore, they were exempted from taxation for the first five years. In the years that followed the interest rate on farmer loans increased sharply, rocketing to 280 percent in the mid-1990s. Also the interest rates on earlier loans were suddenly increased. Although this increase was partly compensated by inflation, it still meant a significant deterioration of the conditions for establishing and maintaining a farm. Furthermore, many farmers, who had used loans to build houses instead of making investments, were unable to pay back their loans on time and stopped functioning. Currently, the distribution of special farm credits through the farmer associations has virtually ended. For rural people who want to take out their share of land in the enterprise and start a farm, it is almost impossible to obtain credit through banks. As farmland, except for the small private plots, is not really private property but issued in unlimited periods of tenure, it means that it cannot be used as mortgage. Moreover, the value of land in a region with thousands of hectares of unused agricultural fields like Pskov is low. Only equipment can be used as mortgage, but this is precisely what starting farmers lack.

The second obstacle that hinders private farming is taxation. Once a household enterprise has registered as a farm it means that it is an official enterprise, and is subject to taxation. As the benefits of private farming, in the form of accessible credits, have virtually disappeared, registering as a farm only brings extra costs in the form of taxation. Thus rural people prefer to stay within the enterprises and maintain or extend their informal household enterprise. Moreover, farmers, who were exempted from taxation during the first five years of their existence, are re-registering their farms as household enterprises to avoid taxation. As a result, family farming becomes less and less transparent.

Thirdly, the shares of the employees in the privatized *kolkhozy* and *sovkhozy* sharply decreased in value during the last decade. Thus if they want to take out their share to start a farm it means that they receive less assets than starting farmers received in the early years. The share in land has remained the same, but it is no longer possible to receive a tractor, as was the case at the start of the reforms.

Contractual Symbiosis

The third scenario is a shift to 'contractual symbiosis.' It means that a social contract is established in which management and employees recognize the mutual dependency of household enterprises and the large-scale farms, and strive to create an efficient division of labor and property between the two sectors, which is beneficial to both. Concretely it means that large-scale farms specialize on providing fodder (a capital-intensive crop) and services, which require machinery like ploughing and finally the marketing of household products. Households specialize in labor-intensive production, especially livestock production. Farm management could decide to stimulate this cooperation and formalize it in contracts to avoid misuse of property.

In most of these enterprises the management not only took measures to protect centralized property, but decided that decentralizing property was the best (or only) way to protect property effectively (see also Fadeeva, 2000; Praust, 1998). Thus in some enterprises the moveable capital, e.g. tractors and combines, were handed over to some employees, usually the tractor drivers and mechanical engineers. These employees keep the equipment at their homes. This decentralization, which started in 1993, is an informal process. The tractor drivers acquire the use rights to the equipment and the responsibility for it, but do not buy it. In the border district of Pskov, we investigated that nine out of ten enterprises had handed over equipment to the households. This is a predominant tendency in the districts in the periphery of the region, where most of the enterprises are unprofitable. In the enterprises where the management tried to maintain the system of centralized use and storage of equipment "it led to a decline in the amount of machinery and a catastrophic bad state of the equipment" (Praust, 1998: 75).

As we mentioned, in the suburban Pskov district, where a lot of enterprises are profitable, or at least have a stable system of payment to their employees, the situation is different. Most enterprises kept their equipment under central management, without disastrous effects on the state of machinery. In this district pay is much better and consequently also the motivation and responsibility of the employees.

However, this kind of contractual symbiosis seems not to be widespread beyond the use of machinery. First of all this approach requires a complete reversal of the development that has occurred since the start of reforms. Relationships within the large-scale enterprises have become more and more informal. As the enterprises were not able to pay their employees a normal salary, let alone any dividend on their shares, they started to transfer other resources to them. Instead of their wage or payment based on their share, employees received extra hectares in land for their household enterprises or other resources like fodder and machinery.

To shift to a model of symbiotic cooperation, means that the *ad-hoc* distribution of resources, (when salaries cannot be paid or employees are in need), is replaced by a more structured cooperation (see also Fadeeva 2000). This creates a lot of additional work for the staff. A problem in most enterprises is that the level of education or the experience of the management is not high. The best specialists and managers have already left.

Furthermore, the unclear property rights enable the members of the management to retrieve resources from the farm themselves to an even greater extent than employees. During the first half of the 1990s, the directors, specialists and main lower-level specialists enlarged their private plots most of all (Efimova, 1997). The staff had the best opportunity to obtain resources either legally or illegally. In our survey the average size of plots of specialists and directors was more than 4 hectares, compared to 2.7 hectares for other employees. With regard to livestock, the numbers of cows and pigs were the same or slightly lower for specialists.

In the second half of the 1990s the private plot production, especially livestock, became less profitable. This was caused by decreased access to cheap fodder through the large-scale enterprises. The production prices of high quality, high-cost fodder like grain rose, partly caused by the rising prices for fuel, which constitutes an important part of production costs. Most agricultural enterprises were forced to diminish the share of production they allocated to the households, or they increased the prices at production cost-level (or even lower), to (still somewhat below) market prices.

Finally, parasitic symbiosis persists and blocks a change to a more balanced, contractual cooperation, because of the short-term interest of the employees. In their strive for daily survival the employees are interested in taking resources out of the enterprises as much as possible instead of being motivated to establish mutual-beneficial transfers between the large-scale enterprises and the households.

Uncontrolled Disintegration and Retreat into Self-Provisioning

In the enterprises where a process of uncontrolled disintegration is under way, little property will be left once they go bankrupt. Thus, the former employees will be left with their household enterprise and a few more additional resources with which to develop a viable peasant farm. The cases of enterprises where such a process has already occurred show that it is unlikely that profitable, commercial peasant farms will arise out of such collapsed enterprises. None of the fifteen most successful peasant farms in the Pskov district were located on the site of a former enterprise (unpublished regional statistics). Only on the site of an enterprise which was split up according to the second scenario (a controlled break-up) had three successful and relatively large peasant farms been located. In the case of uncontrolled integration, the people with most human capital left the place entirely instead of establishing a peasant farm.

Most educated and experienced people searched for work in other, more successful large-scale farms, in the agricultural departments of the district or elsewhere. Only those who did not have the opportunity to find a job elsewhere concentrated on small-scale farming, mostly by somewhat enlarging their household enterprise. As a rule households fell back to subsistence farming.

Conclusions

Property relations in most enterprises are not static but are changing, mostly slowly and sometimes drastically. The most remarkable change has been the enlargement of land and livestock owned by employees, leading to a flourishing household enterprise sector. The household enterprises are the main means of survival for the rural population in the context of the deteriorated economic situation on the large-scale farms. At the meso- and macro-level the households have become important food producers, especially in depressed regions like Pskov. However, the expansion of the household enterprises, which took place especially in the first of half of the 1990s, is a mixed blessing. It means an extra load for the rural population in terms of labor (only partly compensated by a decreased workload at the agricultural enterprises), and it has serious negative effects for the persistence of agricultural enterprises.

The problem is that the employees of an enterprise have in fact two socio-economic roles, which require different behavior and represent different interests: as an employee of the agricultural enterprise and as a semi-independent farmer. As semi-independent farmers it is rational to retrieve resources from the enterprise as much as possible and minimize the labor time at the large-scale farm. However, it means that they act as irresponsible employees by stealing farm resources and shirking their duties at the farm, leading to the neglect of cattle, equipment and other property. In brief, employees act as free riders caught into a "prisoner's dilemma." For an individual employee it is useless to refrain from free-rider behavior as long as others keep on taking away resources, because it does not lead to an improvement of the situation. As a consequence, all employees continue stealing from the common property. The result is that the common property slowly disappears. In the end all the members are worse off, because they miss the access to machinery and cheap fodder. As the roles of farmer and employee do not fall together for both workers and staff members, it is difficult to achieve collective action.

Instead of a continuing prisoner's dilemma leading to total uncontrolled disintegration, two other scenarios were discussed. First, the very unlikely return to a model of the traditional enterprise with centralized property. More realistic seems a split up into separate farms or associations of farms. Until now only six enterprises in Pskov have chosen this option. A large-scale shift to this model seems improbable for economic reasons (increased taxation and problems of division of property) as well as social-cultural and political reasons. Employees do not like the perspective of becoming independent farmers-entrepreneurs. Moreover, the management as a rule does not like this variant. They are afraid to lose their jobs, or see it as a *primitivization*, equally as bad as uncontrolled disintegration. They therefore try to prolong the life of the enterprises as long as possible. Moreover, regional authorities in most regions and certainly in Pskov, have more or less the same attitude and see enterprises as the only serious producers. Few officials see any sense in downsizing enterprises; on the contrary, they are still very much focused on the integration of enterprises and enlarging economies of scale.[11]

The scenario of contractual symbiosis seems the most prospective path in the current circumstances. It is less disruptive for the existing social and economic relations than the split up into peasant farms. Therefore it is more likely to receive support in the countryside. Furthermore, this model is less unknown to the rural population and the authorities than a division into separate farms, which has only been proposed by some liberal reformers, and lacking wider support. Contractual symbiosis on the contrary is more in line with the Russian agricultural context and history. Until Krushchev's second collectivization wave, household enterprises were also quite large and a tense and mutual beneficial cooperation between the two sectors existed. Over time the model of contractual symbiosis might evolve into a sector of larger independent private farms. At the moment the scenario of contractual symbiosis seems to offer the best prospects, although even this scenario will be difficult to achieve for large numbers of unprofitable enterprises in regions like Pskov.

Notes

1.   Employment at most of the enterprises declined but this was caused by the voluntary departure of workers, who sought other employment (e.g. in more successful enterprises) or started their own farms. Workers were only fired incidentally, and only for serious drunkenness or other breaches of the labor regime.
2.   Later on, a fifth method of reorganization was developed in the reform-oriented Nizhnii Novgorod region, supported by the World Bank. It envisaged the break-up of enterprises into smaller entities, cooperating on a contract base with each other, to improve efficiency by reducing size and creating "internal market relations." Outside this region only a small percentage of the Russian farms opted for this model, as it was too complex for enterprises to carry out by themselves and thus depended on active support from the regional administration.
3.   The survey was carried out with the help of A. A. Efimova and A. Efimova Jr. I am thankful for the broad knowledge of Pskovian agriculture they shared with me. In the Moscow region the research would not have been possible without the kind help provided by V. Koshelev of the Timiryasev Academy.
4.   The rounds in the Pskov region are part of a broader research project by the author, which will include a round in a region in southern Russia.
5.   According to official Goskomstat data, of the 377 enterprises that existed in the

beginning of the 1990s (Goskomstat Pskov 2000: 18) only 84 percent (311) are still functioning (*Pskovskaya Pravda*, 10 Oktober 2001, 311). If we compare the 400 enterprises which are registered with the 311 which are actually functioning, only 79 percent are functioning (unpublished regional data). The other enterprises are completely disintegrated and have split up into small family (peasant) farms or household enterprises.

6.   Although the share of the households in production increased sharply, the absolute increase was limited. In the beginning of the nineties household production increased by more than a third, but since the mid-nineties production has decreased. However, in part of the unprofitable enterprises, household production is still increasing.

7.   In some regions (in the black-earth regions of southern Russia (*Krasnodarskii Krai*), quite large household enterprises can be found, which own up to 30 pigs, but the number of such cases is small.

8.   Apart from some regions in the Ural and Siberia, which are mainly ethnic regions with a specific cultural and historical background.

9.   Personal communication with Dr. A. Nikulin in Moscow, summer 2001.

10.   Because all survey data from the Pechory district was not yet available we have only taken the group of farms in the Pskov district as a "sample" of successful enterprises.

11.   The authorities in the Novosokolnicheskii district in the Pskov region, for instance encourage (profitable and unprofitable) agricultural enterprises to unite. Three enterprises were combined to form an (at least in north Russian terms) gigantic enterprise with twenty-five thousand hectares of land.

Rural Households, Incomes, and Agricultural Diversification in Bulgaria

Diana Kopeva, Julia Doichinova, Sophia Davidova,
Matthew Gorton, Hannah Chaplin, and Dirk Bezemer

The debate on rural development in the Central and Eastern European region (CEE), and the Balkans in particular, has been characterized by a divergence between "optimists" and "pessimists." Pessimists have pointed to continuing problems of agricultural competitiveness, low incomes and underdeveloped rural infrastructure (Swinnen et al., 2001). This approach is pessimistic in the sense that it questions whether the associated countries can compete in terms of agricultural productivity and quality or attract significant levels of external capital to offset dependence on declining or low-income sectors. Optimists have argued that this assessment downplays the social capital of rural citizens, the level of pluri-activity and the degree of entrepreneurial spirit (Swain, 2000; Davis et al., 2000).

These writers, though not wishing to underestimate levels of poverty or difficulties of economic restructuring, draw attention to the capacities of individuals and local communities to adjust to economic restructuring and develop sustainable livelihoods. This debate however has suffered from a lack of comprehensive data on the range of rural incomes, household strategies and degree of dependence on agriculture. Based on primary data collected by the authors, this paper investigates the state and range of rural households in Bulgaria, paying particular attention to their incomes, degree of pluri-activity and the socioeconomic constraints to rural diversification.

Bulgaria's Rural Economy

During transition, economic output in both the agricultural and nonagricultural sectors of the Bulgarian economy declined significantly. Between 1991 and 1996, Bulgarian GDP contracted by an average of 2.5 percent per annum and economic problems reached a nadir in the latter half of 1996 and the first months of 1997. This period was characterized by a macroeconomic crisis with high inflation, rapid depreciation of the Bulgarian *Lev* and negative growth. While a degree of macroeconomic stability has returned since this crisis, the recorded levels of unemployment and poverty have risen.

During the communist period, Bulgaria was well known as a producer of grains, fruits, wines and livestock, and was a substantial exporter of certain goods. However, both volumes of arable and livestock production have declined heavily since 1990 (-50 percent). These falls in output have been the product of a leftward shift in both supply and demand (Kostov and Lingard, 2002). Serious problems that need to be overcome are the lack of output markets, land fragmentation, and the weak internal consumer demand, as well as farm-gate prices that are 50 to 70 percent lower than market ones. The insufficient development of road infrastructure, poor market information and the monopolistic possession or distribution of market information only strengthens the existence of subsistence farms. Two-thirds of the private farms are of this type – they do not produce for the market (Kopeva and Noev, 2001).

From a total of 1.8 million private farms in Bulgaria, 86 percent cultivate one hectare of land or less, and a mere one percent cultivate an area greater than 5 hectares (NSI, 1997). Around 5.1 million hectares (82 percent of Bulgaria's total agricultural land area) has been claimed for restored private ownership by the heirs of the former private owners (nearly 1.7 million in number) under the 1991 Farm Land Act (Davidova and Buckwell, 1997).

This return to small-scale agriculture has raised many concerns about the viability of rural incomes, especially given the relatively large proportion of the population that lives in the countryside and who are engaged in agriculture. By the end of the 1990s, 32 percent of the Bulgarian population lived in villages.[1] The rural population is in general older than in urban areas and a larger share of the population is of retirement age (Network, 2002).

Agriculture remains an important sector in the national economy, in terms of its contribution to both GDP and employment. Measured by its share of gross value-added, agriculture and forestry increased in importance in the second half of the 1990s, reaching a peak in 1997, before declining significantly. This pattern was caused by the contraction of the nonagricultural sector being greater than in farming during the early years of transition and in some cases agriculture acting as a buffer absorbing displaced labor from elsewhere (Kostov and Lingard, 2002). The unusual peak in agriculture's share of gross value-added in 1997 was caused by a combination of both the deep macroeconomic crisis and a successful harvest in 1997 which led to the gross agricultural output rising by 32.9 percent (EBRD, 2001).

According to employment statistics, in 1998, 26.3 percent of the labor force of Bulgaria was involved in agriculture (however, this share is based on the number of people and has not been translated into annual work units [AWU]).

As pointed out by OECD (2000), it is difficult to present an accurate picture of agricultural employment in rural Bulgaria. The above share of employment originates from a sample survey and there is no division by location. Enterprise statistics can help define the location of registered enterprises, but fail to give reliable information about agricultural employment, as most of the individual farms do not require legal registration. The demographic structure of those engaged in agriculture is very unfavorable. According to a Phare ACE survey conducted in 1998, the average age of farmers was 60.8 years (Kopeva, 1999).

The study of rural areas in Bulgaria is hampered by both the lack of a formal definition of rurality and the division used in national statistics based on the location of residence, villages or towns and cities. As a result, many small towns in predominantly rural areas are included in the urban group (OECD, 2000). However, as part of the EU's SAPARD program in Bulgaria, a National Agriculture and Rural Development Plan was developed and a working definition of rural areas has been applied. This includes municipalities with less than 30,000 inhabitants and a population density below 150 people per square kilometer. This is a broad definition, under which 229 out of 262 municipalities in Bulgaria can be classified as rural. Overall, according to this approach, 5,307 rural settlements, 81 percent of the territory and over 40 percent (3.6 million) of the population can be classed as rural (OECD, 2000).[2]

In the territory classified as rural, the average density of population is 40 people per square kilometer and the population of the working age is estimated to be 1.9 million (51.6 percent of the rural population). Educational levels are lower than the average for the country (OECD, 2000). According to OECD (2000), 34 percent of the Bulgarian rural areas can be considered less developed, i.e. have an income per capita under 30 percent of the national average and an average unemployment in two of the last three years exceeding by 50 percent the national average. These areas incorporate around one million people and around one fourth of the total territory in Bulgaria. There are large clusters of less developed rural areas in the northwest and northeast of the country.

Several previous studies on European countries show that diversification away from agriculture can play an important role in providing alternative employment opportunities and may alleviate rural poverty, for example Poppe (2002) and Benjamin (1994) on Western Europe, and Davis et al. (2000) and Chaplin et al. (2002) for the CEE. In general, the rationale for the promotion of diversification has been based on evidence of over-employment in agriculture and low returns to farming activities in the CEE (Swinnen et al., 2001).[3] Developing this previous research, the present study attempts to shed light on the degree of diversification of rural household incomes in Bulgaria and the role of nonfarm activities.

The Survey

The study is based on primary data collected by the authors at the household level. In order to incorporate the diversity of rural areas, a three-stage sampling procedure was adopted. First, regions and subregions were chosen based on a working definition of rural areas that distinguished between peri-urban and rural subregions, and then an identification of less favored areas (LFA) and more favored areas (MFA) was made in each rural and peri-urban subregion. This refers to the suitability of the area for agricultural production. The second stage involved the selection of a number of settlements in each subregion; and thirdly, a predetermined number of households within each settlement were selected. As there is no standardized definition of rurality in Bulgaria, the following criteria were adopted:

- A population density of less than 60 persons per square kilometer.
- The largest city in the municipality having no more than 30,000 inhabitants.
- The share of agriculture is at least 20 percent higher than the country average.
- The share of people engaged in agriculture is at least 20 percent higher than the country average.

About 170 municipalities correspond to two or more of these criteria. Based on this, two regions were selected, Plovdiv and Varna. Plovdiv is located in the central-south and Varna in the northeast of the country. They differ with regard to the importance of agriculture, share of employed persons in the primary sector, economic performance, and geographical and natural conditions. Two municipalities in each region were selected. In the Plovdiv region, Assenovgrad was chosen as a peri-urban subregion, and Suedinenie as a rural subregion. In Varna, the Provadija municipality was selected as a peri-urban subregion and Valchy dol as a rural subregion. These municipalities differ in terms of their accessibility, job creation potential, natural and agricultural conditions.

At the second sampling stage, settlements were selected in each sub-group. The third step was to choose households.[4] The overall target was to obtain a total sample of 120 households, 60 from each region, which were selected from villages in the LFA and MFA. Four types of households were of interest:

- Full-time farmers: all household members of working age work on the farm.
- Part-time farmers/self-employed households: at least one person with own business activity.
- Part-time farmers/wage earners household: at least one person with dependent activity, wage income.
- Full-time nonfarm activities: abandoned agriculture.

It was targeted to have equal shares of these categories in the sample. Within these predetermined quotas of 25 percent and taking into account locational characteristics, survey households were selected randomly. The sample was therefore not representative but structured, so as to capture different household types. Data collection took place in November 2001 through face-to-face interviews at the respondents' homes. Table 1 details the number of households by type in the selected regions and subregions. In the sample there are 34 households of full-time farmers and 32 households that abandoned agriculture. The rest have a mixture of agricultural and nonagricultural income sources.

Table 1. Sample households by type in the selected regions

Household type	Plovdiv Region		Varna region		
	Suedin-enie	Assenov-grad	Prova-dija	Valchi dol	Total
Full time agriculture	9	7	7	11	34
Part-time/Employed	12	2	7	5	26
Part-time/Self-Employed	2	12	7	7	28
Abandoned agriculture	9	7	9	7	32
Total	32	28	30	30	120

Background Information on Survey Regions and Subregions

This section provides background information on the two regions (Plovdiv and Varna) and the four subregions (Assenovgrad, Suedinenie, Provadija, and Valchi dol) included in the survey. Plovdiv is a larger region than Varna and registered a net inflow of population in 1997 (the year for which most recent data are available). The unemployment rate in 1999 was lower than the national average of 16 percent (EBRD, 2001). Agriculture accounts for nearly one fourth of gross value-added. In contrast, the Varna region is characterized by net out-migration and a higher unemployment rate. However, its location near the Black Sea and its tourist potential mean that it has attracted more direct foreign investment. Agriculture plays a less important role than in Plovdiv and accounts for 15 percent of the gross value-added.

The Assenovgrad municipality in the Plovdiv region is peri-urban and is situated in the southeast of the region. The municipality's population is concentrated in Assenovgrad (58,000 inhabitants) and six larger villages (between 1,000 and 2,000 inhabitants) situated in the plain, where over 96 percent of the total population live. Assenovgrad is comparatively densely populated and the urban population accounts for 80 percent of the total. The unemployment rate is lower than the country average and is similar to the average for the Plovdiv region. Regarding agricultural potential, the municipality is best suited for livestock. On the plain, cereals and sunflowers are cultivated. Farm structures include 20 producer cooperatives, a few farming associations and numerous individual farmers, operating predominantly small farms.

Suedinenie municipality, also in the Plovdiv region, is economically poorer and more agricultural than Assenovgrad. Situated in the Gornotrakiiskata lowland, three quarters of its territory is utilized for arable production and 90 percent of the population is involved in agriculture. The climate favors vegetable production, which accounts for most of the value-added in agriculture. As in Assenovgrad, the majority of farms are small-scale individual units. The unemployment rate is very high–nearly double the rate in Assenovgrad–but the infrastructure is of relatively good quality.

In the Varna region, the municipality of Provadija was defined as peri-urban and the municipality of Valchi dol as rural. The municipality of Provadija is dominated by Provadija town which is the administrative and economic centre, with 60 percent of the municipality population. There are twenty-four villages, three of which have more than 1,000 dwellers. The official unemployment rate is 33 percent, twice the national average. Two thirds of the unemployed have only primary education. Provadija municipality is a traditional agricultural region and is the granary of the Varna region, with maize, sunflower and barley production. There are twenty-three producer cooperatives, seven farming associations, and many individual farms.

The Valchi dol community is located in the northwest of the Varna region. Apart from Valchi dol town, the municipality encompasses twenty-two settlements, three of which are large. Unemployment in 2000 was 18 percent and has been rising in recent years although natural conditions are favorable for agriculture. The survey was implemented in selected villages in each of the four municipalities (subregions). The survey frame was such that the settlements were classified as "favorable" or "unfavorable" according to the conditions for agricultural production.

Methodology for Estimating Income

The estimation of total household income was of particular interest for the study. It was calculated to be as comprehensive as possible by including income from farming, nonfarm income, social payments, support payments to agriculture, interest from savings, remittances, other revenue mainly from rented assets and credit net of interest paid. Income from farming was defined as equivalent to profit (i.e. the difference between the total value of output and costs). The value of output is typically not equal to monetary revenues, since a part of agricultural output is consumed within the household or used to support the extended family in urban areas or as barter. Output was valued at average market prices in 2001. While these were not identical to prices actually received (due to regional price variations and differences between barter and cash sales), these prices provided a consistent measure for output valuation.

Cost information was not explicitly collected in the survey due to constraints related to the length of the questionnaire. In order to measure variable costs, production intensity was categorized on a five-point scale from "very low" to "very high," based on reported area and livestock numbers in relation to output. Using data from previous Bulgarian farm surveys, the quantities of inputs required for each product and each level of production intensity were estimated. Some synergies and trade-offs in production decisions were taken into account. Such synergies may include the availability of manure from livestock production for crop production, or the availability of fodder from crop production for use in livestock production. For these reasons the calculated ratios of variable costs to revenues were adjusted depending on the combination of products produced by the household. An adjustment was made for fixed costs but these were difficult to estimate accurately. However, as in small-scale, labor-intensive subsistence agriculture, fixed costs are usually very low relative to variable costs. This is unlikely to bias the results too much although agricultural incomes may be slightly overestimated.

Nonfarm income was calculated as the sum of income from wages and self-employment. Income from wages was based on the reported wages for first and second jobs, if relevant, and took into account the reported number of months worked per year. The annual number of working days was assumed to be 232 (or 1,856 hours). Income from self-employment was calculated on the basis of information provided by the respondents. In view of the fluctuations that such income is normally subject to, monthly income was taken either as reported or as the average of the best and worst months.

Social payments include various types of pensions (e.g. disability pensions, social pensions, state retirement pensions), child benefits, utility and transport subsidies for people below the poverty line or above a certain age, unemployment benefits, and payments under different programs for job opportunities. Other income components included support payments to agriculture. They appeared to be negligible in Bulgaria as only a few farming households benefited from farm subsidies. Remittances that households receive from household members living outside the region or abroad also appeared to be insignificant. The other revenue category also included any other unearned income not captured in the above categories, such as income from financial assets or from renting out assets. The most widespread component was income from renting out land. Credit received, minus interest payments, was also added to the annual income.

Overview of Findings

The total sample population of 120 households was comprised of 458 persons with an average of 3.8 people per household. In several households there are three generations living together. The mean age in the sample is 38.5 years and 53 percent are male, with regional differences: the mean age in the Plovdiv sub-sample is 42 years, while in Varna it is 35. Full-time farmers have the highest mean age (44.6 years). Part-time farmers, who have nonagricultural self-employed activities, have the lowest average age (34.9 years). This is in line with the general finding that households with younger heads are more willing to take the risk to diversify outside agriculture and have the capabilities to do so (Chaplin et al., 2000).

Regarding educational achievement, 30 percent of household members had only completed elementary school, 28.6 percent had completed both primary and secondary school, and 20 percent of household members had completed vocational school. Vocational schools give the same recognized level of education as secondary schools but with a greater specialization. Regionally, slightly higher educational achievement is registered in Valchi dol and Suedinenie (percent of people completing secondary school). This is related to the younger than average population in Valchi dol. Heads of household have achieved the highest level of education, followed by their spouses; two thirds and one half, respectively, have completed a secondary or vocational school. The lowest level of education is recorded in the generation of grandparents, who are in some cases are without formal education, though still literate.

Analyzing educational attainment by type of households, it appears that part-time farmers and those who had abandoned farming reported higher educational achievement, predominantly secondary school (over 30 percent of these households had completed secondary school) and over one in ten had university degrees. A large proportion of full-time farmers had only completed elementary school (42 percent). This is consistent with results from surveys in other CEE countries. According to a recent study of income and activity diversification in Poland, the Czech Republic and Hungary, the households that diversify outside agriculture have heads of household with a higher level of general education than nondiversifiers (Chaplin et al., 2002). A positive effect of general education on diversification has also been observed in previous studies outside of the CEE (Huffman, 1980; Woldehanna et al., 2000).

Agriculture, Access to Land and Other Occupations

Households in the sample have, in general, small farms. Only a fifth have more than 10 hectares and 45 percent occupy less than one hectare. Most households in the sample have access to land (78 percent); only among those households who abandoned farming was access to land rare (in a quarter of cases). Most of the land was acquired in the period after 1994. Only in five cases was land acquired before 1994, including three cases before the start of the reform process. Land was acquired by various methods, most frequently by inheritance as, during the restitution process, heirs of the original pre-collectivization owners acquired land. There are, however, differences in the methods of acquiring land between types of households. Full-time agricultural households bought 21 percent of their land, whilst the share of purchased land in part-time farming households is much smaller. Overall, more than 90 percent of those interviewed owned some land.

Because of the importance of different motivations and attitudes in the decision to diversify, farming households were also questioned on their objectives and plans. The two main objectives in farming appeared to be to maximize income and to secure a reasonable standard of living. The only exception is in the settlements with less favorable conditions for agriculture in Varna region, where respondents placed the highest weighting on providing for the next generation. Enjoying a rural lifestyle does not seem to be an important factor that keeps households in agriculture.

Households in the two regions also have different visions concerning the future of the farm and their role as farmers. More farmers in Varna prefer to stay in agriculture and even to expand; 22 percent of households in the Varna region foresee an expansion of their farm in the next five years. Most probably their plans are based on a more active land market in this part of the country and the efficiency of large-scale cereal production. Another 33 percent plan to keep the farm, whilst in Plovdiv this share is three times less or 10 percent. To sell their farm and to work outside agriculture was considered as preferable by 8 percent of households in Plovdiv, mainly part-time farmers, while no one in Varna contemplated such an option. Renting out the farm and finding off-farm employment is a preferred option for 10 percent of the households in the Plovdiv region, but for only 5 percent in Varna. These findings suggest, unsurprisingly, that production conditions play a significant role in the farmers' attitudes towards diversification. Most household members have only practical experience, rather than formal qualifications, in agriculture. A relatively small number of heads of households and children graduated from agricultural secondary schools, mainly in the Varna region.

Households that had abandoned agriculture stopped farming despite acquiring land through the land reform process. The most important reasons to abandon agriculture stated in both regions were the wish to concentrate on self-employment in a nonagricultural business, followed by the opportunity to start a more convenient and/or financially more rewarding job, and the possibility to ensure their family's standard of living. Land availability did not appear to be a key factor in this decision.

More than one third of the household members define the family farm as their main occupation. Again, there are substantial regional differences. In the Plovdiv region, which is more agricultural than Varna, around 50 percent of households indicate the family farm as the main occupation. In three of the four types of households the relative share of household members working on family farms is substantial, ranging from 40 percent for part-time farm households to 67 percent for the full-time agricultural households.

The second most important occupation is nonagricultural self-employment. Around 20 percent of respondents to the questions regarding occupation indicated that self-employment (having their own business) as the main occupation. In the households that abandoned agriculture, work in family businesses prevails in both regions. One third of the self-employed are engaged in agri-business activities and one fourth in trade. The share of agri-business is higher in Plovdiv as one may expect given its more agricultural character, whilst trade is more important in Varna, where there is more tourism. The share of households with self-employment as a secondary activity is low (6.6 percent). In general self-employment is full time and the respondents indicated that they worked more than nine hours per day for 11.7 months per year. The sample mean for monthly income from self-employment is 167 Euro with large monthly differences (e.g. a factor 2.5 between the best and the worst month).

The share of people with permanent off-farm work is rather small, around 10 percent. Despite the differences in unemployment rates between the two surveyed regions, regional differences in the importance of off-farm employment are minimal. Earnings from off-farm employment are quite low and this might explain the small percentage of household members diversifying in this way. On average, in the month preceding the survey they received 97 Euro. The lowest income level was recorded in households that abandoned agriculture (70 Euro). In addition, in order to partake in off-farm employment people have to travel an average of 41 kilometers to work. This suggests that employment may be found mainly in towns and raises a question of to what extent jobs can be generated in villages after the collapse of industries created in such settlements under central planning. This high figure for average distances to work highlights the importance of the physical infrastructure and particularly the frequency of public transport and the locational characteristics of households, namely the distance from a public transport stop.

Of all respondents to the questions concerning employment status, 10.7 percent saw themselves as unemployed. Thus, unemployment in this sample of rural and peri-urban areas appears to be lower than the regional and national unemployment rate. During transition, agriculture has been performing an important social function absorbing some of the labor released from industry. This has resulted in lower labor productivity and farm incomes, but on the other hand, it has provided a "safety net" for the rural population. Regional differences in unemployment rates are substantial; six percent of the surveyed people in the Plovdiv region considered themselves as unemployed, whereas in the Varna region this percentage was 16.1.

The average period of looking for a job is much longer in Varna than the average in the Plovdiv region. According to the types of household, it appears that households that abandoned agriculture find a job in a shorter period of time. This may suggest that members of these households are forced to accept poorer jobs as they cannot rely on farming as a safety net. This assertion is also supported by the lower monthly pay members of these households receive from off-farm employment. On the question of whether during unemployment or job search members of households provided paid services, 55 percent in the Plovdiv region responded positively, whilst in Varna all answers were negative. This may be one reason why in Plovdiv the period for job search is much longer than in Varna. While staying officially unemployed, in the former region, people gained some income and this may have made them more selective in choosing jobs. As for the main reasons for not looking for a job, respondents indicated they were retired, engaged in full-time education or pregnant.

The distribution of jobs by sector indicates that farming dominates, followed by the food industries and trade. The high frequency of farming, food processing and trade (often agri-food) might suggest that the rural population benefit from their skills within the food chain. This is related to the structure of pre-reform rural Bulgaria, where most of the people worked in collective and state farms, either dealing with agricultural production *per se*, or with upstream and downstream deliveries. Several farms also had processing units, at least at first stage processing, e.g. slaughter houses.

Finally, according to this survey, migration is not as important for rural households in Bulgaria as is often thought (Sarris, 2000).[5] Only eight of the 120 households registered absent members in the previous twelve months. The main reason for members being absent from the household was further study and internships. In the data set there was only one instance of migration for work.

Reasons, Constraints, and Attitudes toward Diversification

In order to assess the reasons for, and constraints to, diversification, respondents were asked to rank potential motivations on a five-point scale, where 1 was unimportant and 5 was very important. The most important reason given for diversification through self-employment was the desire to generate an additional cash income. The second most important reason given was to exploit an innovative product/identification of market opportunity, followed by the opportunity to generate income to invest in personal development and/or education of other household members. The lowest priorities were seen to be the lack of on-farm employment and regional unemployment. Clearly, income generation is the prevailing reason to engage in self-employment outside agriculture. When these statements are compared to findings concerning the *outcomes* of self-employment, it appears that the perception of the respondents is that they had achieved this objective.

In addition to income generation, households engaging in self-employment perceive that it provides better quality work than farming. Households were conscious of the risks of losing invested capital, but they did not place a high priority on this factor. The main impediments to diversification through self-employment as perceived by the sub-sample of households that did not engage in self-employment were too many competitors and insufficient availability of low cost credit. Little importance was attached to lack of time, absence of economic pressures or a preference for agricultural work. These answers reflect widespread agricultural over-employment and low incomes. They are also consistent with findings from Poland, the Czech Republic, and Hungary, where financial incentives, particularly low cost credit and seed money to start up non-agricultural businesses, were perceived as the most important devices for aiding diversification through self-employment (Chaplin et al., 2002). Overall, very few respondents thought that nonagricultural self-employment reflected low farming skills or attached a stigma to the creation of nonagricultural business.

For those who had diversified through nonfarm wage employment, the most important reasons for diversifying were to protect the household's standard of living and the prestige of off-farm work. Other reasons of some importance were the desire to generate income to invest on-farm or in local business and in personal development or education. The lack of on-farm employment was not seen as important. It is interesting that these farms, most of which are small, are apparently seen to be providing full-time employment.

The sub-sample of households which did not have off-farm employment were interviewed about the impediments they perceived to having an off-farm job. Apart from old age, other important factors relate to the generally unfavorable economic situation in the country. High regional unemployment, job insecurity, low and delayed wages are all signs that, although Bulgaria has managed to stabilize its macroeconomy, the labor market is not functioning well and wages are low. Despite rural development initiatives and the SAPARD program, it will be very difficult to improve the living conditions of the rural population while the whole economy stagnates.

Household Incomes

Based on the survey data, total household income was calculated as explained above. It should be underlined that farm income is sensitive to the methodology and assumptions applied.

Table 2. Household Income According to the Type of Household

Euro	Full-time Agric. (n=34) Mean	SD	Part-time & Employed (n=26) Mean	SD	Part-time & Self-Employed (n=28) Mean	SD	Abandoned Agric. (n=32) Mean	SD	All (n=120) Mean	SD
a. agricultural income	4,455	8,618	1,972	1,537	3,654	11,555	0	0	2,542	7,384
b. other farm income	113	404	0	1	82	388	0	0	51	286
c. total farm income (a+b)	4,567	8,603	1,972	1,536	3,736	11,541	0	0	2,593	7,386
d. wage income	271	1,378	1,085	572	44	232	263	557	392	911
e. self-employment income	0	0	0	0	1,829	2,004	2,269	2,449	1,032	1,890
f. non-farm income (d+e)	271	1,378	1,085	572	1,872	2,001	2,533	2,433	1,424	1,957
g. social payments	669	543	413	501	362	469	408	514	472	519
h. remittances	6	27	10	29	62	218	14	34	22	109
i. other income	35	152	18	95	0	0	88	428	37	239
j. credit received	83	439	269	753	847	3,866	80	452	301	1,927
k. interest paid	12	70	43	121	30	119	13	72	23	96
Annual income/household	5,619	9,648	3,725	1,912	6,850	15,604	3,109	2,396	4,826	9,248
Household size	3.3	1.6	3.7	1.2	4.2	1.2	4.2	1.3	3.8	1.4
Income per person	1,738	2,776	1,092	547	1,760	3,923	814	698	1,357	2,448
AWU in agriculture	2.30	1.27	1.92	1.09	1.88	1.11	0	0	2.05	1.17
AWU in self-employment	0	0	0	0	1.42	0.53	2.09	0.96	1.78	0.85
AWU in wage employment	1.50	0.71	1.04	0.20	1.00	0	1.75	1.16	1.22	0.63
Total AWU	2.39	1.27	2.96	1.15	3.33	1.36	2.53	1.09	2.77	1.26
Income/AWU	2,354	7,584	1,260	1,662	2,058	11,509	1,229	2,208	1,744	7,337

Note: AWU stands for annual work unit and equals 1,857 hours

Diana Kopeva et al.

Table 2 provides the detailed data on household income, income per person and per annual work unit (AWU) for the four types of households. Because of large variations in the income data, both means and standard deviations are reported. In Table 3, these data are summarized, with shares for farm, nonfarm non-earned income, and net loans received.

Table 3: Overview of Household Income by Household Type (Euro)

(%)	Full-time agriculture (n=34)	Part-time & Employed (n=26)	Part-time & Self-employed (n=28)	Abandoned agriculture (n=32)	All (n=120)
farm income	81.3	53.0	54.6	0.0	53.7
non-farm income	4.8	29.1	27.3	81.5	29.5
non-earned income	12.6	11.8	6.2	16.4	11.0
net loans received (1)	1.3	6.1	11.9	2.2	5.8
household income	100.0	100.0	100.0	100.0	100.0

Note: "Net loans received" is the difference between credit received and interest paid.

Income per person is on average 1,357 Euro (approximately 110 Euro/month), which reflects the generally low level of incomes in rural Bulgaria. Part-time/self-employed households and full-time agricultural households record the highest incomes per person. Households that abandoned agriculture record the lowest average incomes and the lowest level of paid average wages. Impoverishment, or the threat thereof, may well have been the main reason for these households to diversify, rather than the presence of new market opportunities.

Looking at income per AWU, the results appear at first to be surprising as full-time agricultural households register the highest income. This is not consistent with results from other CEE and EU countries which show that households with diversified sources of income in general garner a higher total income in comparison to those dependent only on farm incomes (Chaplin et al., 2002).

One possible explanation for the Bulgarian results is that the households that diversified or abandoned agriculture were pushed to do this, as their farms are smaller, and therefore their real income lower, in comparison to the households that stayed in agriculture. This might explain why they justify their diversification or exit from farming by the objectives to increase income or to secure a living for their families. The other important observation is that the standard deviation is very large, suggesting large differences within the sub-samples of household types.

As this research was partly inspired by the potential accession of Bulgaria to the EU, one of the main conclusions is about the striking difference in rural incomes with the current EU member states. According to Bulgarian standards, the current subsistent minimum to qualify for income support is 22.5 Euro per person a month (270 Euro per year). All rural households in the sample are above this minimum, but this should not divert policy attention away from the rural poverty existing by more conventional standards (Deaton, 1997).

Explaining Incomes and Diversification Choices

To evaluate the data in greater detail an attempt was made to analyze the relation between income quartiles and household characteristics. Table 4 indicates the mean score for households in each income quartile (1 the poorest, 4 richest). Overall, poorer households have a significantly younger head of household and cultivate the smallest areas of land. For example for income quartile 1, the average cultivated area is 2.1 hectares compared to a mean of 93.4 hectares for income quartile 4.

The means for the income quartiles 2 and 3 are 3.3 and 6.6 hectares respectively. The poor also own a relatively small share of the land they cultivate. The highest proportion of land owned is registered by income quartiles 2 and 3. The richest households only own just over one-third of the land they cultivate but they manage a far larger area. These large farms are characterized by significantly higher productivity. Interestingly, there appears to be little difference between the quartiles in the number of years of schooling for both men and women.

While the richest quartile does record the highest mean years of schooling for both men and women, the averages for the poorest quartile are greater than quartiles 2 and 3. There also appear to be few differences between the quartiles regarding average household size. Quartiles 2 and 3 have significantly higher scores for the level of infrastructure and are less remote. The richest income segment has the lowest mean index of infrastructure. This implies that infrastructure and remoteness is less of an issue where households have access to and cultivate large areas of land (quartile 4). Remoteness and low infrastructure are however relevant where the household has limited land available and needs off-farm activities to generate income.

Discriminant function analysis was used in an attempt to determine which variables discriminate between the income quartiles. Models were evaluated in terms of their ability to predict to which income quartile a case belongs. Forward stepwise analysis was applied, where variables are evaluated to determine which contribute most to the discrimination between groups. The stepwise procedure is guided by the respective F-values.

Table 4: Household Characteristics by Income Quartile

	Average Values					F-test
	Q1	Q2	Q3	Q4	All	
Age of head of household	41.9	52.4	53.8	50.6	49.6	4.626***
Men's total number of years' schooling	15.5	13.4	12.2	15.7	14.2	1.422
Women's total number of years' schooling	14.1	12.7	12.5	16.2	13.9	1.794
Active women as share of household members	48.8	52.0	51.4	51.9	51.0	0.149
Dependency ratio[a]	0.56	0.84	1.3	0.80	0.87	3.164**
Percentage of agricultural income in total household income	60.4	63.4	73.5	54.8	63.3	0.834
Land productivity[b]	38.6	51.0	99.2	41.7	58.5	2.646*
Labor productivity[c]	215.1	304.6	424.8	3035.7	971.2	2.486*
Total cultivated area (hectares)	2.1	3.3	6.6	93.4	25.5	5.536***
Percentage of total area owned	42.9	91.7	69.4	35.7	59.6	1.637
Infrastructure[d]	3.5	11.6	10.9	2.2	2.9	3.176**
Remoteness[e]	8.8	11.6	10.9	8.5	9.9	1.125
Household size (persons)	3.7	3.8	3.7	4.0	3.8	0.242

Notes: *Significant for $p < 10$ %; **Significant for $p < 5$ %; ***Significant for $p < 1$ %.
a.   The dependency ratio is defined as the ratio of the number of members younger than 16 years of age and older than 64 divided by the number of family members older than 16 and younger than 64.
b.   Labor productivity is defined as the ratio of net farm income to the total AWU of the household.
c.   Land productivity is defined as the ratio of net farm income to total land area cultivated.
d.   Infrastructure is the sum of the distance to various hard infrastructure units below 20 km of distance (hospital, post office, school, bank etc.) divided by the number of hard infrastructure units.
e.   Remoteness is the distance (km) to the next town plus the distance to the nearest bus station.

The F-value for a variable indicates its statistical significance in the discrimination between groups, that is, it is a measure of the extent to which a variable makes a unique contribution to the prediction of group membership. Using the stepwise method, two variables were retained in the model: total cultivated area and the age of head of household. Because the average age of the head of the households and the avarage cultivated area are both increasing with increasing income, one can conclude that households with more land and older heads of households are significantly more likely to be in higher income quartiles. The F-test values show that this relation is statistically significant.[6] A fuller evaluation of the model, however, indicated the presence of multi-collinearity. For example, several independent variables not included in the model are related with total cultivated area (e.g. labor productivity and land productivity).

Table 5. Classification matrix for Discriminant Function Model

Observed income quartile (%)	Predicted income quartile			
	Q1	Q2	Q3	Q4
Q1	66.7	0	33.3	0
Q2	41.4	0	58.6	0
Q3	26.7	0	73.3	0
Q4	33.3	0	40.0	26.7

Table 5 details the classification matrix for predicted and actual group membership based on the canonical discriminant functions. In this table, the rows are the observed income quartiles and the columns are the predicted income quartiles. When prediction is perfect, all cases will lie on the diagonal. The percentage of cases on the diagonal is the percentage of correct classifications: 42 percent in this case. This is better than chance, although modest. The model is reasonable at predicting membership of groups 1 and 3 but fails to predict any membership of group 2. Overall, there is evidence that land cultivation is related with higher incomes.

Factors that are associated with households' diversification status (full-time farming, part-time with wage employment, part-time with self-employment and abandoned farming) rather than their income level were explored using the same method. Below only the mean scores for each household type and F-tests are reported (table 6).

Households that abandoned farming were characterized by a lower average age of the head of the household. Their location also tended to be less remote. The table shows that full-time farms are not necessarily larger than other farms. Households which are engaged both in agriculture and self-employment derive on average about three-quarters of their total household income from agriculture while for households which combine agriculture with paid employment this is 92 percent. Agriculture is still the dominant source of income, even in part-time farms. There are few differences between the household types in terms of size, remoteness, and level of infrastructure.

Table 6. Household Characteristics by (hh) Type

	Farm	Wage Empl.	Self-Empl.	No-Farm	Mean	F-test
Age of head of hh	56.1	52.2	46.3	44.7	49.6	4.619***
School years of men in hh	12.2	14.5	14.9	15.1	14.2	0.863
School years of women in hh	11.6	13.9	14.8	15.0	13.9	1.580
Active women as % of hh members	56.2	49.7	48.6	49.4	51.0	0.764
Dependency ratio	1.0	0.69	0.77	0.90	0.87	0.913
Share of total hh income from Agric.	99.5	92.2	74.2	4.6	63.3	128.467***
Land productivity	72.1	101.4	67.9	9.4	58.5	5.485***
Labor productivity	1153.4	584.7	2448.5	28.7	971.2	1.419
Cultivated area (ha)	44.9	12.5	50.4	1.1	255.4	1.542
Percentage of total area owned	67.1	71.4	64.1	14.1	59.6	12.586***
Infrastructure	3.5	2.7	3.1	2.6	2.9	2.008
Remoteness	9.8	12.3	9.5	8.6	9.9	1.128
Household size	3.4	3.6	4.0	4.1	3.8	1.9

Note: *Significant for p <10 %; **Significant for p <5 %; ***Significant for p <1 %.

Conclusions

While nonagricultural activities have been thought to be important in the rural areas of the Balkans, there has been little previous research on Bulgaria. This study has sought to assess the economic activities of rural households in the country. Particular attention was paid to sources of income and the characteristics of households that engage in nonagricultural gainful activities. The relation of these characteristics to their portfolio of activities and their income levels, both monetary and in-kind, was explored. The findings can be summarized as follows.

Most rural households have access to land and in addition own land, but farms are generally small. The pattern of agricultural production influences regional attitudes towards renting land. Where there are economies to be captured from large-scale cereal and sunflower production, land rental markets have developed.

The decision to diversify appears motivated by a desire to earn extra income and to secure a decent standard of living, particularly where the agricultural assets owned by the family are meager. Low incomes constitute the main driving force for diversification, and households that diversify still register lower incomes per annual work unit than full-time farmers. This suggests that some households with smaller farms or farms located in less favorable agri-environmental conditions are pushed to move out of agriculture.

Developing a nonagricultural business is the preferred option for diversification by households in the sample. Wages are too low and job insecurity too high for them to prefer off-farm wage employment. The attitudes displayed to diversification are in general positive, although a number of households report a more reserved attitude, acknowledging the risks involved in moving outside their core agricultural activities. The Bulgarian data contradicts a persistent myth concerning the importance of income from migration and remittances. The level of migration is rather low and the most common reasons for a member to be absent from a household are studying and taking up internships.

Returning to the debate between optimists and pessimists about the future of rural areas in CEE countries, it seems that much of the Bulgarian evidence supports the optimist view. Notwithstanding the huge difficulties and low incomes in rural Bulgaria, there is potential for economic development. Members of households in the sample are reasonably educated, and are motivated to develop new enterprises. This is particularly true for full-time farmers and those part-time farmers who combine farming with non-agricultural self-employment. The main constraints to do this stem from the poor macroeconomic state of the country, low asset ownership and the underdeveloped labor market. Although rural development initiatives are badly needed, their effectiveness will be constrained while the whole economy stagnates.

While diversification is an option desired by many of the people in our sample, it should not be seen as an alternative to agricultural activities. Households that are engaged in agriculture full time are among the richest in the sample, and diversification appears mainly driven by the threat of (deeper) poverty rather than by the existence of economic opportunities that can compete with agricultural production in terms of profitability or labor productivity. Agriculture and nonagricultural activities are complementary rather than mutually exclusive options in the portfolio of rural economic activities. If both are well developed, a variety of rural households will be able to develop sustainable livelihoods.

Looking at the issue of rural poverty, if the Bulgarian very low subsistence minimum is applied, there is little poverty in rural and peri-urban areas. The unemployment rate in these areas is lower than the average regional or national rates. However, this should not divert the attention of policy-makers away from rural poverty. Agriculture has played an important social function during transition, absorbing people left unemployed by the collapse of industrial enterprises during the reform process. This resulted in lower labor productivity and over-employment in agriculture. The income gap with current EU member states is a strong challenge to policy-makers, as Bulgaria might join the EU as soon as 2007. Supporting the development of the rural agricultural and non-agricultural economy, and particularly the local economy in villages and not only in towns, is crucial for improving the income situation and retaining young and educated people to reside and work in rural areas.

Notes

This research was undertaken with support from the European Community's Phare ACE Programme (Project P98 1090 R). The content of the publication is the sole responsibility of the authors and it in no way represents the views of the Commission or its services.

1.   Bulgarian national statistics treat only villages as a rural residence and, therefore, there is a lack of information concerning the demographic and economic situation of towns in predominantly rural areas.
2.   However, according to the European Commission, the rural population is about 2.5 million (EC, 1998). This discrepancy reflects a lack of formal definition of rural areas.
3.   In the current EU Member States agricultural diversification has been promoted for similar reasons, although programs have had mixed success in encouraging farmers to pursue such strategies (Phillipson et al., 2001).
4.   A household is defined as a group of people who live together and, routinely share money, goods and resources for the household.
5.   For example Sarris writes "the motivation for [his] analysis is provided by the case of a small CEE country that is characterized by a relatively large agricultural sector and exportation of considerable amounts of labor to neighboring EU countries. Albania (and possibly Bulgaria) provides such a case" (2000: 172).
6.   The F-statistic indicates whether the independent variables can significantly discriminate between the groups.

Land Consolidation and Agricultural Services in Albania

Malcolm D. Childress

The land reform in Albania after 1990 has resulted in dramatic changes in the ways agricultural land is managed. Before the reform there were 550 state and collective farms with an average of 1,200 hectares in size. These farms covered approximately 18,000 fields, averaging 36 hectares and usually grouped into single contiguous enterprises. Privatization of agricultural land was based on equitable division by size and quality to the worker households of the former farm, resulting in the distribution of multiple small plots.

After the reform approximately 546,000 hectares were divided among 480,000 families with average farm size of 1.1 hectares, typically divided into two to five parcels. The total rural area, including pasture land that was not privatized and villages, covered 1.8 million hectares. Parcels average 0.25 hectares in size. Moreover, the fields which these families now operate are rarely contiguous, usually scattered across the landscape with varying qualities and accessibility. An estimated 5 percent of arable land is now consumed by paths and fences. One-way distance to all of a farmer's parcels averages four to five kilometers in Lushnja and five to seven kilometers in Vlora. In short, the farming landscape is highly fragmented.

This chapter discusses efforts to encourage consolidation of fragmented agricultural landholding in Albania, but argues that until such efforts are linked to improvements in the associated agricultural services environment they will have little effect. A private land market is developing slowly. Easing transaction obstacles and facilitating the association of agricultural enterprises for certain activities are partial steps towards consolidating land at operational scales large enough to take advantage of commercial opportunities. For land consolidation to be a successful strategy, however, farms consolidating plots need to make linkages to improved financial, infrastructure repair, input supply and marketing services. In this connection our experience with a land consolidation pilot project under preparation by the Ministry of Agriculture and Food (MOAF) is used to suggest ways that some of its potential pitfalls might be avoided.

With this fragmentation of landholding, it is difficult to obtain the full benefits from private capital investments made in agriculture. The state is also making investments in infrastructure, such as rehabilitating the irrigation system. The existing extreme fragmentation of land makes recovering that investment difficult, as returns on the fragmented holdings are too low. Fields which are far from the farmers' homes or which do not have easy means of access tend to be used less intensively and lack capital investments (30-40 percent of agricultural land area is estimated to be underutilized or abandoned). Agreements for shared operations, such as mechanization of an area, or common marketing of products, are infrequent.

Effects of land fragmentation can thus include less intensive use of land, diminished investments and decreased value, leading to lower production and higher costs. For example, agronomists estimate that mechanization costs are approximately 50 percent higher and labor costs even 70 percent higher with wheat production on fragmented landholdings in Albania, compared to consolidated 12 hectare blocks. These are the primary irrigation units in the field layout in Albania, which agronomists use as a reference point.

Agricultural land markets, which should ultimately provide the primary mechanism for widespread land consolidation and farm enlargement, are only just beginning to function in Albania. Legislation regulating land sales came into effect in 1998, and rural land registration is approximately 80 percent complete. Market imperfections, however, are inhibiting the ability of these incipient land markets to reduce fragmentation in the short or medium term. Imperfections stemming from inadequate information about land characteristics, problems of coordination among multiple market actors and high transaction costs comprise a set of land market constraints which prevent widespread use of land markets by rural residents to achieve more efficient use of their land. Related factor markets, referred to here as the agricultural services environment, are also poorly developed in most areas of the country and put a brake on land transactions, even when land market constraints can be overcome.

Inattention to resolving these imperfections in the short and medium term threatens to jeopardize the viability of several of the initiatives and investments being made in the agricultural sector by Albanian and international institutions (such as irrigation system rehabilitation). These investments assume that operational size of landholding will match the scale required for competitive use and distribution of inputs and outputs. Thus there is a disconnection between current landholding structure and the scale and scope of productivity which is being expected of it. Gaps in agricultural services are the central contributing factor to the persistence of this disconnection.

The government of Albania's policy paper on agriculture, the "Green Strategy," emphasizes land market mechanisms as an "activator" of greater efficiency in agricultural services, stating:

The activation of an agricultural land market remains a priority. The current land fragmentation, combined with the insecurity concerning property rights, makes it difficult to adopt the most economical and efficient strategies with regard to the use of performing mechanical means and other industrial inputs, and the marketing and distribution activities (MOAF, 1998).

Likewise, the World Bank's sectoral assessment of agricultural reforms focuses attention on land fragmentation and suggests that as "various forms of voluntary consolidation without administrative involvement are being observed in isolated instances; these forms of consolidation should be reviewed and possibly piloted, in particular in irrigated areas." (World Bank, 1999)

In this situation of high land fragmentation, and the presence of significant market imperfections, it is warranted to explore the options for overcoming these constraints on investments and production through some form of voluntary, market-led land consolidation[1]. The government of Albania is now attempting to do this through preparation of a pilot project under the Ministry of Agriculture and Food's Agricultural Services Project, financed through a World Bank loan. A wide variety of models of land consolidation have been implemented worldwide, but viable options for the current Albanian context can essentially be reduced to promotion of land market transactions which allow for exchanges, rentals, purchase/sales, and parcel reductions. It should also promote grouping or association of contiguous landholders for coordination of specific production and post-production activities. For either of these models to successfully lead to cost reductions, productivity improvements and increasing commercialization, however, they need to be closely linked to an improved agricultural services structure. Interviews with farmers show improving commercial opportunities in input and output markets are more likely to drive land consolidation than land consolidation itself is to drive new production patterns.

The proposed land market intervention by the MOAF to promote land markets will focus on brokering land market agreements among multiple landholders which lead to more consolidated holdings in a village area. It will subsidize transaction costs in these cases. It is a well-intentioned intervention that has the notable advantages of simplicity and low cost, addressing some of the specific land market imperfections. However, because the planned intervention does not explicitly link up with improvements in village-level availability of services, and eschews support for the promising experiences of land consolidation through coordinated production by local associations, its impact may be limited. The concern is that the project intervention will bring about small improvements in farm management, but not facilitate strong commercial expansion of the type sought in Albania's agricultural strategy.

Many landholders are interested in consolidation, but they resist making transactions because of perceived risks, costs and coordination difficulties under current conditions for input supply and output distribution. The Agricultural

Services Project Social Assessment reveals that 50 percent of the farmers view land consolidation as beneficial, and a near similar percentage is willing to consolidate land through some mechanism. A separate sample of farmers in Fier and Lushnja indicates that over 70 percent of respondents would endorse parcel exchanges for parcels of similar size and quality if transaction costs were lower (Wheeler and Lushaj, 1999). Given that interest is in fact so high, it is interesting that so little land consolidation is occurring.

As a form of operational land consolidation, small group coordination for some farming activities is also no longer out of bounds for Albanian farmers. In Lushnja a sample survey of farmers in 1999 revealed that 62 percent would prefer to work in a farm structure comprised of extended family (Wheeler and Lushaj, 1999). Another study revealed 41 percent of farmers in a sample in the lowland plains wished to organize into an association, but felt constrained by fragmentation of landholdings (Canco et al., 2000). Another research project found 59 percent of farmers in favor of small production groups as a way to overcome the negative effects of fragmentation (Lusho and Papa, 1995).

What is meant by grouping or association in this regard, it is important to note, is a voluntary, seasonal or medium-term agreement about coordination of the use of contiguous or closely spaced land parcels. This is seen among small groups of individual landholders (i.e. 2-20 individuals, typically members of the same extended family or neighbors), who explicitly maintain full ownership rights over their constituent parcels. This type of arrangement permits operational consolidation for activities in which there are economies of scale and timing, such as plowing and irrigation, without altering private land rights. Landowners are clearly not interested in contributing their land permanently to an enterprise or to create a new collective. Previous research, which revealed a negative perception of grouping arrangements, no longer reflects the reality of many rural residents. They are interested in arrangements with family or neighbors, which increase the efficiency of land use as long as their private land rights and capital contributions remain with the individual. Nevertheless, the substantial hypothetical interest in land consolidation is stopped by the real constraints to production on larger scales. Farmer opinions about the fragmentation problem have now been extensively documented and conclude:

> The primary result gleaned from the fieldwork and survey results is that farmers express a desire to consolidate their land holdings. This desire remains unfulfilled in view of issues of tenure security; a lack of an established and accepted system of exchange compensation; lack of infrastructure support to justify potential exchanges and the high costs of formalizing the process (Wheeler and Lushaj, 1999).

The author's fieldwork in 2000 in group meetings with 150 farmers in four communes revealed the same hypothetical interest in consolidation of landholdings. But land consolidation was strongly viewed as only one piece of desired strategy to reduce risk, increase productivity and improve value added to agricultural production through infrastructure, marketing, credit provision, and crop switching. Farmers expressed the view that the risks and costs of making land transactions (even with reduced transaction costs) are not worth it unless improved services, particularly in market access, simultaneously become available.

For these reasons it is important that proposed solutions to the land fragmentation issue link up with a larger vision of Albania's agricultural development. This vision calls for increasing integration of the rural sector in Albania with the country's own urban centers and integration with European markets. The institutions which have emerged during the last ten years are themselves too fragmented and inadequate for this to happen. New models of agricultural production and service provision, based on private associations and distribution/marketing networks appear as the most promising institutional basis for this integration to occur in Albania.

Subsistence Farmers in Albanian Agriculture

Agriculture is the most important sector of the Albanian economy. It accounts for 50-55 percent of GDP and 40 percent of total employment. The rural population is decreasing, from two million in 1989 to 1.8 million in 2001, but still accounts for 58 percent of the country's population (INSTAT, 2001). While urban sectors are expected to continue to grow rapidly, the centrality of agriculture in Albania's economy implies that rural socioeconomic development will remain a main driver of the country's well-being for at least the next decade. Indeed, the ways in which urban development will proceed are highly sensitive to the pace and depth of income growth and opportunity in the countryside.

Albania is following a two-tiered agricultural development strategy, which seeks to fulfill domestic food needs while also increasing integration of its production with the European market. Both tiers are necessary to integrate rural areas with the rest of the country and the region as a whole through trade, infrastructural improvements, improved communications, education and health. An overview of farm and sectoral characteristics is provided below. It motivates an understanding of how landholding and land consolidation fits into current farm operation and the agricultural services environment, relying primarily on the EU Phare ACE Programme 2000 Survey results published by Mathijs et al. (2001), which is the most recent comprehensive farm survey available.

Most Albanian agricultural production is carried out on subsistence farms. This farming is primarily oriented to food production for the household and community. In the plains 76 percent of the farms sell no more than 20 percent of their crop production. Only 5 percent of farms sell 80 percent or more. Albanian farms can thus be categorized as belonging to four types: subsistence, semi-subsistence, small commercial farms (partially capitalized with equipment and transportation), and associated forms of production. Extrapolating from survey data on percentage of production marketed, 80-90 percent of farms fall into the subsistence/semi-subsistence categories. While this farm structure provides livelihood for the rural population, growth prospects for Albania's rural communities, and the desired domestic and international market deepening depend mostly on the potential future development of more commercially-oriented agriculture currently practiced by only a tiny minority (Mathijs et al., 2001).

Household Income

Private farms represent the most important source of income for households in rural areas (44 percent). The second single most important source of income is remittances from emigrants (17 percent), followed by the combined contribution of salaries, pensions and social assistance (26 percent), and nonagricultural activities, such as trade (9 percent). The level of income is perceived as unsatisfactory for many households. Forty percent of families feel their income is not enough to buy the most important things they need in life. This group has monthly household earnings (production and cash income) of less than 20,000 lek (US $142). About 34 percent of families believe their income is satisfactory to meet their major needs. The remaining 26 percent believe their incomes meet all needs. The economic situation is worst for farms that do not have arable land or only 0.1 to 0.5 hectares. Only families with monthly income of 30,000 to 50,000 lek (US $212-354) believe they are in a good enough economic situation to meet their demands (Mathijs et al., 2001). For Albania as a whole, monthly household income from all sources averaged 16,620 lek (US $118) in 1998 (INSTAT, 2001).[2] The strong proportion of farm income in a context of low overall household income in rural areas means that on-farm improvements such as consolidation of parcels have a major role to play in enhancing incomes.

Prospects and Plans of Rural Households

Sixty percent of rural families are interested in expanding or intensifying agricultural activity. The most serious perceived obstacles to increasing their activity are inadequate funds (33 percent), inability to buy land to expand the farm (18 percent) and lack of credit (13 percent). Irrigation and low price of products are also factors. The remaining forty percent, which are not interested in expansion of agricultural production, believe that agriculture is not profitable. Over 50 percent of rural households are looking for off-farm wage employment. Employment abroad is viewed as the most favorable economic alternative if it were available (50 percent of households), although 30 percent believe agricultural or livestock production would be the most profitable option (Mathijs et al., 2001). These observations indicate that mechanisms like land consolidation, which improve productivity and permit farm expansion, are valuable to a majority of the population.

Emigration to urban areas and foreign destinations is a significant phenomenon in rural Albania. From 1989 to 2001 the rural population fell by 20 percent and the trend continues. Most internal migration is focused on Tirana (62 percent) and other major cities (INSTAT, 2001). A high proportion of internal migration is from the northeast districts to Tirana or other cities in the plains with northeastern districts, accounting for 37 percent of internal migrants since 1990 (INSTAT, 2001). From the point of view of landholding and farm operations, migration increases the available land per capita, and creates opportunities for land consolidation. If land administration institutions improve and migrants release their attachments to holding unused land as a "fallback" strategy, emigration will likely free up land resources for greater consolidation of operation holdings through the land market. Anecdotal evidence, however, suggests that this process requires education and experience. Leasing of migrants' land is still thinly developed, even among families, chiefly because of fears that ownership rights may be permanently lost if land is leased.

Poor Operation of Land Markets

In theory, efficient farm landholding patterns and sizes would be predicted to emerge over time from land market transactions, which adjust between the preferences and intensities of different landholders' needs and capacities. In practice, such land markets are constrained in Albania by a number of factors. These constraints are not due to inadequate legislation; all types of land transactions are legally supported and a formal registration system is operational in all districts. The constraints instead have to do with scarce information and coordination problems among potential buyers and sellers, high transactions costs, constraints in other markets which reduce the potential income stream from land, and perceptions of tenure insecurity.

Due to the way that privatization was carried out, farms have a similar structure across Albania. The privatization process was based on equity in the size and quality of parcels distributed to workers. This resulted in households receiving multiple small parcels of different quality in different locations. Average total land area per household was 0.89 hectares in the survey sample. This average is slightly higher in the plains areas (1.07 ha), and slightly lower in the mountainous zones (0.56 ha). Estimates vary on the amount of land uncultivated from 12 percent to 40 percent. The most frequently cited reason for leaving land uncultivated is lack of capital. Land quality and the distance to parcels are also frequently cited reasons for leaving land out of production. (Mathijs et al., 2001)

Table 2. Land Market Issues

Is there any agricultural land available in your area available for purchase?	(%)
Yes	25
No	75

How easy is it to buy agricultural land?	
Very easy	4
Relatively easy	11
Rather difficult	29
Very hard	33
Impossible	23

What are the most serious problems in buying land?	(%)
Difficult to find people willing to sell land	34
Legal procedures are too complicated	10
Difficult to find land which has clear titles	5
Hard to know if there are any potential conflicts over land to buy	3
Hard to find land free of disputes	6
Land is too expensive	23
Other reasons	19

What are the most serious problems in selling land?	(%)
Difficult to find people willing to buy land	47
Legal procedures are too complicated	10
Legal procedures take too long	1
I do not have clear titles for my land	6
There are conflicts over the land I wish to sell	1
Buyers fear that other people might claim this land	9
Price of land is too high	21
Other reasons	5

Source: ACE Survey Results, 2000 (Mathijs et al., 2001)

The ACE Survey study finds that farms in Albania average 2.84 parcels nationwide (Mathijs et al., 2001). Another study finds a range from 2.24 parcels to 6.5 depending on the *comuna* (Wheeler and Lushaj 1999). Most farms use one to two parcels (52 percent of farms), while 42 percent of farms use three to five parcels.

Insecurity and conflicting claims about land ownership are still an issue is Albania. The ACE survey found only 13 percent of farmers had a registered ownership certificate, although 73 percent had the original privatization certificate. The property registration system, however, records over 80 percent of rural properties as being officially registered. Claims of ex-owners and ancestral rights also complicate landholding and inhibit land transactions.

Although the full range of lease, purchase/sale and mortgage transactions are legally and institutionally supported, perceptions of the ability to transact land are negative as the survey responses in Table 2 reveal. These results suggest that a combination of coordination problems between potential buyers and sellers, price considerations and complicated legal procedures are holding back land market transactions. Perception of high land prices may be due to the fact that an asking price for land capitalizes the full potential value of a parcel under its most productive use. As many potential buyers cannot use the land optimally because of gaps in the agricultural services environment, a gap is opened between asking price and their ability to pay. The fact that many households view landholding as an insurance policy may also increase sellers' reservation price and lead to disequilibrium between demand and supply. The average price of one hectare of desirable irrigated farmland in the plains was around 600,000 lek (US $4,000) in 2000 according to local informants.

Inefficient Agricultural Services Environment

The fragmented landholding structure and its subsistence orientation cannot easily change to higher value production patterns without improvement in the agricultural services environment, that is, the related markets and public allocation mechanisms for inputs (including water), and for distributing production. This section describes the status of the agricultural services environment, showing that it is not yet adequately integrated with production units.

Because less than 20 percent of rain falls during April-September, irrigation plays a major role in making land productive in Albania. About 430,000 hectares of land have some irrigation infrastructure installed. Most of this infrastructure deteriorated during the 1980s, however, and by 1993 only 80,000 hectares were actually irrigated. Since 1993 irrigation rehabilitation projects have rehabilitated 75,000 hectares in seven priority districts. One hundred and eighty Water User Associations (WUAs) have been established and are in charge of operation and maintenance and collecting tariffs for the secondary and tertiary systems. Only about 20 percent of these WUAs are operating without problems, however, and outside of the priority irrigation rehabilitation areas little has been done to reverse the deterioration of infrastructure (Kodderitzsch, 1999).

Seeds are a key determinant of plant potential and product quality. Farmer-produced seed is currently the main source of about 90 percent of seeds used. Farmer-produced seeds are poor quality, often contaminated with weeds and prone to diseases in wheat, maize and beans. Attempts are being made to support a private seed supply system based on a liberalized regulatory regime that permits access to imported seed material.

In fertilizer supply, a network of private sector agents called the Albanian Fertilizer and Agri-Input Dealers Association (AFADA) imports most of the material being used. But credit constraints to both dealers and farmers have limited the amount of fertilizer which can be distributed. As a result, less than a third of crops receive minimum nitrogen and phosphate needs, and little potassium is applied, leading to soil degradation. Animal feeds suffer from the same constraints (Kodderitzsch, 1999).

Albanian agriculture relies both on farm machinery from the socialist period, as well as some 5,000 mechanized vehicles imported during the 1990s through a variety of programs. About 60 percent of farms utilize mechanization, while 22 percent use animal traction and 18 percent rely on manual labor (Mathijs et al., 2001).

Extension information, plant protection and animal health assistance are provided by the Ministry of Agriculture and Food through a staff of 1,400 with presence at the commune level. Although this network comprises 70 percent of the Ministry's budget, it is inadequate to meet the needs of the large number of new private farmers with only one agent for every 720 farmers. The AFADA dealers have filled in some of the gaps, providing information and demonstrations to farmers in their areas. But there remains a shortage of information on appropriate technologies which are affordable to farmers and applicable on small-scale operations. Adaptive, on-farm research is mostly absent (Kodderitzsch, 1999).

The Ministry of Agriculture and Food's Green Strategy (1999) identifies weak marketing infrastructure (collection, storage, sorting, packaging, transportation) and supporting institutional mechanisms as two of the main constraints to increasing incomes of private farmers. Producers now face high marketing costs as most sell their production themselves in nearby markets. There is difficulty in reliably bulking up orders of sufficient quantity at standard quality grades to meet the demands of bulk processors and importers (although there are promising experiences in eggs, dairy and beans). Processing, packaging and labeling are also thinly developed, resulting in loss of market share for domestic products in Tirana and inhibiting export development. Agricultural trade policy, it should be noted, is relatively open, with a four-line schedule of *ad valorem* tariffs (0, 7, 25 and 40 percent) depending on the degree of processing of the import. Albania's main imports are wheat, sugar and oils (80 percent from EU countries). Its main exports are medicinal plants, tobacco, and fish.

Most Albanian farms rely on their own resources to finance operations. After the liquidation of the Rural Commercial Bank and merger with the National Commercial Bank in 1997, the rural sector has been left short of essential financial services, especially agricultural production credit, and credit of input supply and processing. The credit gap is expected to continue for some time. Currently the only sort of credit provision in rural areas is provided by the Albanian Development Fund (ADF) and its village outlets. The ADF has been very successful with providing and collecting small loans (average US $500) in a type of solidarity group lending. But this type of advanced micro-credit does not permit larger-scale commercial expansions.

Taking these input supply, finance and distribution issues as a complex, it is obvious that the existing agricultural services environment in Albania serves farm producers poorly and contributes to the predominance of farm decision-making which emphasizes subsistence, is not well integrated with markets, and inhibits entrepreneurial activity.

Land Consolidation and Land Market Imperfections

Given the nature of the land fragmentation problem, and its role in constraining improvements in productivity and competitiveness, a pilot project in land consolidation in Albanian is under preparation by the Ministry of Agriculture as part of the World Bank-financed Agricultural Services Project. The pilot project is expected to become operational during 2002 in four communes. While land transactions and a small set of group farming experiences are beginning to take place, the scale and scope of these experiences remains quite small, and many are occurring outside of formal channels (which weakens the property registration system and ultimately the security of land rights). The pilot project will attempt to build on these scattered experiences.

Traditional methods of consolidation involving lengthy negotiations and state-sponsored compensation payments, complex re-mapping of parcel borders and adjustment of infrastructure are regarded as expensive and inappropriate in the current Albanian context. The approach which is proposed to be piloted in Albania is participatory, demand-driven and market-led, and is believed to be both a cheaper methodology for arriving at operationally consolidated land-holdings which display efficiencies in production and post-production, and to be more socially acceptable to landholders. The demand-driven, market-led approach, to be taken in the pilot project, is intended to be based on similar principles which have been enunciated by the Land Tenure Service of the FAO (FAO, 1999):

- Land consolidation has to be participatory, democratic and community driven.
- It is founded on the principle of assisting the community to define new uses of its resources and then reorganize its spatial components (parcels) accordingly.

- The focus is on rural livelihood rather than on primary production of food staples.

The end result is community renewal, that is, sustainable economic and political development of the whole community.

Monitoring and evaluating these assumptions and principles will be an important aspect of the pilot project. This is particularly so because the project as currently conceived is intentionally narrow in approach. It will focus on market transactions among farmers in a village "consolidation zone" by providing information on parcel location, size, soil quality and availability and offering the incentive of subsidized transactions for brokering multiple-actor transactions which meet criteria of increasing contiguous parcel areas. The pilot project as currently formulated will not promote any association-led activity such as field coordination and does not explicitly connect service institutions with the farmers interested in land consolidation. These are potential pitfalls which may prevent the pilot project from being as successful as it could be.

The types of transactions which will be promoted and subsidized are parcel exchange, leasing, purchase/sale and creation of easements.

Parcel Exchange

The exchange of parcels of land between landowners within a specified location may have the advantage of consolidating farm holdings and promoting more efficient use of land. Due to the homogeneity of soil type in some zones of the pilot districts, in theory land could be easily exchanged without an elaborate system of compensation. This observation is especially true of parcels carved out of the same cooperative field and belonging to the same extended family or *fis*.[3] Results from Wheeler and Lushaj (1999) indicate that 82 percent of farmers in a plains district believed a system of land exchange within the village would help to increase production. The same survey indicated that most existing exchanges are not registered in the Immovable Property Registration System (IPRS).

Informal discussions with farmers and *comuna* agronomists indicate that they fully understood the theoretical benefits to land consolidation through parcel exchange. Unfortunately in practice the majority of farmers are reluctant to exchange parcels for the following reasons:

- The *cost of the legal process of exchange*. The Wheeler and Lushaj survey found that approximately 32 percent of the respondents stated that a large constraint to parcel exchange is that it is too expensive to register the exchange in the IPRS system. Wheeler and Lushaj quote an interview with the head of the IPRS office of the district of Lushnja which revealed that there have been around 30 cases of land parcel exchanges in his village since the registration offices have been opened. Of these only 10 cases had been officially registered.

About 20 cases were exchanged unofficially through verbal agreements between farmers. The main reasons cited for not registering parcel exchange are the high transaction costs in terms of both money and time. According to the Civil Code of Albania a land exchange is defined as a land transaction and thus requires the same process for purposes of registration within the IPRS.

The MAF pilot project proposes to solve this issue by either a) directly subsidizing the transaction costs through financial arrangements with municipal authorities, the IPRS, notaries and topographers for transactions meeting project criteria; or b) by obtaining a governmental decree which specifies that transactions leading to consolidation in specific areas during the project will be exempted from transfer taxes registration fees.

• The *heterogeneity of soil quality*. Farmers are very reluctant to exchange unequal land parcels even if it were possible that a system of compensation could be instituted. The small survey found that 75.5 percent of respondents were willing to exchange parcels under the condition of identical size and quality of the parcels to be exchanged. The pilot project will use soil maps and soil samples to provide objective criteria for proposing exchanges among heterogeneous parcels.

Facilitation by an agricultural specialist, provision of parcel index maps and soil maps to classify parcels will help to solve the problems associated in creating exchanges. Compensations for quality differentials will not be paid for by the pilot project, but will be the responsibility of private parties to manage. It should be noted that transaction procedures are especially costly for exchanges. Current regulations require that both parties pay a private valuer to appraise each of the parcel, that both parties separately register the transaction, and that both parties pay a transfer tax. If the transfer tax is not exempted, it is likely that exchanges will be re-cast as "sales," and the transfer tax evaded by understatement of the sales price.

Rental

The results of the survey by Canco et al. (2000) indicate that of rural residents who intend or desire to move to cities (from 40-60 percent of all residents), an average of 52 percent do not want to risk selling their land but would be interested in renting it. Because rural to urban migration continues to be high, it is expected that this supply of land for rental will continue to exist on a widespread basis. The potential lessors may be divided into two groups: those who intend to move to urban areas, and part-time farmers. Tenants (lessees) will be those farmers who see their future in the countryside. Rental of land is occurring on a widespread basis in the pilot project *comunas*, but is mostly short-term rental of one season or one year, and mostly between family or clan members. In all the pilot project *comunas* some land areas were defined as being uncultivated because the owner had left for the city or left the country and had not rented or sold the land parcel. Facilitation of further rental could therefore increase farmers' operational holding, and in some cases, consolidate contiguous holdings.

Purchase or Sale

This type of land transaction is beginning to be more common in Albania. Canco et al. (2000) indicate that only 12 percent of a sample of farmers are interested in buying or selling, but the survey is based on data from 1995. A modest number of purchase and sales transactions are occurring in the pilot *comunas*, and a small number of registered transactions in each district. Nevertheless purchase/sale transactions appear to be discouraged by the cost of formal transfer, uncertainty about land values and strong feelings in some areas about ancestral rights to land. These considerations indicate that public information, transaction cost reductions and facilitation of transactions could lead to economically beneficial purchase/sale transactions.

Easements

The creation of easements is another modality through which fragmented and noncontiguous parcels may become linked through land market transactions. This is particularly true where current access pathways are nonexistent or too small to permit the entry of machinery. This option has not been systematically studied and is very locally specific. It should be included in the menu of options for achieving market-led land consolidation. By facilitating these types of market transaction, the pilot land consolidation components are likely to achieve some valuable consolidation of operational landholdings, especially where exchanges and rentals are already beginning to become common, or in specific fields where homogenous strips can be traded. But without explicit connection to improved services, farmers will have little incentive to overcome the uncertainty involved in land transactions, or to predictably plan on the cash flow from agriculture necessary to undertake the investment for purchase or lease of new landholdings.

The Emerging Role of Groups and Associations

Another promising area for simultaneously achieving cost reductions through increased operational size and a structure for crop distribution is through the coordination of agricultural activity by a small group or association of producers. Some farmers are now deciding to work together in order to reap the benefits of economies of scale on one or more of the activities involved in the crop production process. Arrangements of this kind are highly varied, ranging from a verbal agreement between two brothers who jointly work their land to large associations engaged in multiple processes from production to grading and distribution. Between these two extremes are a variety of farm groups that may define themselves formally or informally and may have very different motives for existence. Some groups choose to consolidate activities such as plowing and land fertilization to economize on the number of trips or passes that a piece of agricultural machinery will require. Others involve specific consolidation of contiguous landholdings to grow a crop on a larger scale for bulk delivery. These arrangements have the advantage of reaping the benefits of physical land consolidation without requiring any change of ownership.

During the immediate post-privatization phase, farmer attitudes towards coordination and association were negative, due to perceptions that such arrangements would repeat aspects of the collective farm system. Now perceptions have changed. Coordination of activities and formation of associations are being increasingly seen as economical and mutually beneficial by farmers. The basis for these arrangements is usually the extended family, which may mean a whole village in certain cases.

Activity Consolidation

When farmers plant different crops on the same ex-cooperative field, they have difficulty in using tractors and other machinery as well as irrigation, drainage, and transport systems. In order to minimize these negative consequences of individual farming, some farmers have agreed to plant the same crop on adjoining parcels. The motivation for this is to reap economies of scale in certain activities of production such as plowing or harvesting. Lusho and Papa (1995) found evidence that production results were better when farmers plow and plant their land at the same time than when they perform these tasks at different times. Activity consolidation is occurring on a sporadic basis in villages in pilot projects target areas in Lushnja, Fier, Mat, and Korca.

Agricultural Production Groups

The organization of farmers into agricultural production groups may mitigate more of the negative effects of land fragmentation than individual farming can. In a study of five "production groups" in Lushnja, Lusho, and Papa (1995: 20) found that the primary advantage expressed by respondents was the consolidation of their fragmented holdings and the reformation of ex-cooperative fields. Other advantages cited were: increased levels of mechanization, less loss of land, preservation of existing infrastructure (irrigation and drainage systems), and more efficient coordination of agricultural tasks (plowing and planting). Another advantage was the increased possibility of placing products on the market. They further expressed that an average size of 30-50 hectares is optimal for an agricultural production group. In other areas, where fields are laid out in 12 hectare parcels divided by canals and drainage works, this size is regarded as natural for group coordination of activity.

Interviews with agronomists and farmers nevertheless indicate residual negative attitudes toward large associations and cooperatives. Evidence from the Wheeler and Lushaj survey show that 72 percent of respondents believe that the best type of organization for joint production is either the direct nuclear family alone or the extended family. Only 14 percent thought that a large association would be the better form of organization. From the total Wheeler and Lushaj study sample, 51 percent said that they thought farmers in their village were willing to farm together in an association of some kind. Many farmers and village elders state that the only way they could be convinced to work in an association larger than the immediate family is if they could be assured of the sale of their produce. Interviews with potential group-association farmers revealed that both market access and investment constraints are inhibiting the formation of commercially-oriented production groups.

It seems that by not finding ways to assist activity consolidation and formations of producer associations (through educational mechanisms, provision of credits and facilitation of input supply, production technology and marketing services) that the MOAF's pilot land consolidation project is missing one of the main areas of meaningful land consolidation. Apparently MOAF and the World Bank are still concerned that such types of arrangements will be subject to the incentive and management problems of old-style cooperatives and collective farms.

This is unfortunate as farmers have clearly moved to an appreciation of smaller, flexible organizational forms in which incentives for productivity maximization are shared by all participants and management is accountable. These types of arrangements also appear to be better suited for integrating production with the emerging service environment, because they permit greater economies of scale in input supply, credit provision, machinery use, and distribution than almost any single operator farm can manage.

Risks for Efficient Land Consolidation

While the pilot project will appear to be oriented to resolve some of the major constraints to land consolidation, while avoiding others, there are additional factors which may thwart efforts to continue land consolidation as a proactive policy beyond the pilot project.

Continuing Fragmentation

IPRS data on transactions do not present a clear picture of continuing fragmentation because several categories of transaction are reported together (sale, exchange, subdivision). Nevertheless, it is obvious from interviews with registrars and landholders that fragmentation continues to occur through inheritance and family transactions (typically a father gives one or more sons land parcels). Some of these transactions leave existing parcels intact, while others create further subdivision of parcels. In addition, home-building is contributing to additional fragmentation in some areas. It is not likely that this dynamic can be directly halted given family structures and traditions. There are, however, countervailing interventions and trends which, in combination with the consolidation activity, could slow and limit further fragmentation.

Land taxation based on land's market value is a policy which could contribute to limiting fragmentation. A value-based land tax would help to encourage consolidation by giving landowners an incentive to rent out or sell parcels which they were not using productively. Rural land taxation is currently under discussion by the Albanian government. Another option associated with land taxation could be to establish a higher tax rate for parcels or farms which fall beneath a minimum size. However, experience has shown that policies mandating minimum parcel sizes are not fraught with problems. People simply subdivide land informally. In addition, it is quite difficult to make external determinations of minimal viable holdings given the different mixtures of off-farm and agricultural activity that different households have.

Notaries Are a State-Sanctioned Monopoly

Transaction costs are driven up by excessive notary fees in Albania. Law 7829, On Notary (1 June, 1994) governs the notary profession. A notary is a private professional appointed and licensed by the Ministry of Justice. All notaries are lawyers. Notarial fees are also determined by the Ministry in consultation with the Association of Notaries. Fees are uniform across the country and there is thus no competitive pricing for notarial services. There are approximately 200 notaries in Albania. Maintenance of the state-sanctioned monopoly raises transaction costs and times. If any qualified individual could perform notarial services and set prices according to the market, transaction costs for conveyancing would fall dramatically.

Association Formation Is Legally Complex

The creation of an association is governed by the Articles 39-53 of the Civil Code. An association is a nonprofit entity set up according to its Charter, which must include the name and purpose of the association, head office and location of activity, membership and dues, meetings, voting and termination of the association. An association must be registered in the District Court where the head office is located before it becomes a legal entity. It is barred from doing business until it is registered although it can perform initial organization activities, such as establishing the Charter and managing board. One problem noted from USAID projects that have helped set up farmer's associations is the fact that Article 39 of the Civil Code states that associations are nonprofit entities. Thus, the associations are technically breaking the law when they charge their members for services and inputs.

Complications in Agricultural Land Transactions

The provisions on ownership and other rights of the agricultural family are incomplete and ambiguous. Agricultural land is owned by "the family" with one member, usually the eldest male, designated as the Head of Family to represent the family in property transactions. However, there is no clear definition of who belongs in the family/unit. Although the Civil Code states an agricultural family is composed of persons related by blood, marriage, stepson relations or those who are otherwise admitted as family members, this broad definition allows a potentially large number of people to claim legal rights in the property. It is also unclear what the status is for family members who are students, work abroad or work at other jobs.

Also, since the definition states the family farm belongs to its "members" and is composed of "persons," both men and women are vested with property rights. This contradicts the traditional practice of agricultural families embodied in the *Kanun* whereby land is handed down to males only. The *Kanun* sets out specific rules and procedures for family life and has been adhered to by rural Albanians for centuries, especially in the North. According to the *Kanun*, property is administered by males but the entire family contributes to and benefits from the agricultural economy. Once a female marries, she moves in with her in-laws and no longer has rights in her birth family's property. Thus, inheritance issues are potentially caught between the traditional practice embodied in the *Kanun* and new laws that vest females with property rights.

Ex-Owners

Albanian law recognizes that pre-communist owners of agricultural lands have certain rights. A satisfactory solution to compensating the ex-owners heirs for those rights has not yet been established. This lack of clarity throws uncertainty over land transactions in many areas, even though legal privatization and registration is complete.

Conclusion

As in other countries in Southeastern Europe, the fragmentation of Albania's agricultural land is recognized by farmers and policy-makers as an inefficient allocation of land for productive uses, especially for commercially-oriented farming. How this allocation can be changed depends on the decisions of producer households operating within a "decision space" which is shaped by the availability and cost of a gamut of agricultural services.

The MOAF's pilot project in land consolidation will test the hypothesis that overcoming a narrow set of land market imperfections can catalyze land consolidation and lead to improvements in productivity and marketed surplus. The analysis of this paper argues that this set of measures is insufficient in itself to foster consolidation of land at the scale required for substantial alterations in cost structure, crop selection and marketed surplus, given the underdeveloped agricultural services environment. Programs such as the pilot project in land consolidation are more likely to be successful if they attempt to resolve land market imperfections in conjunction with imperfections in associated markets. Pilot projects seem especially well suited to mobilize suppliers, credit providers and distribution infrastructure in a spatially defined area where land market transactions and innovative land uses can simultaneously adapt to changing opportunities and prices in related markets. It will be instructive to monitor the progress of this three-year pilot program.

Both new land market transactions and new forms of coordinated production and distribution through family-led activity coordination and/or formation of associations are ways to achieve the functional benefits of land consolidation. But all of these land consolidation activities are much more likely to be a response and improved agricultural services environment than to be a stimulus for the creation of such an environment. The sequencing of interrelated reforms play an important role for their overall sectoral success. Albania's nominal creation of flexible land markets may be ahead of the creation of flexible input supply and output markets. The sooner these can be brought together, the sooner goals of improved rural incomes and greater integration of agricultural markets may be achieved.

Notes

1. Large scale, state-backed land consolidation approaches are not considered politically and economically feasible in Albania at this time. This contrasts to approaches to land consolidation being carried out in Armenia and Hungary for example.
2. Mathijs et al. (2001) use income category estimates (0-20,000 lek; 20,001-30,000 lek etc. while INSTAT uses a point estimate of the average (16,620)). The Mathijs' numbers say that 40 percent of households report income less than 20,000 lek, but not

how much less. That categorical estimate is consistent with an overall national average of 16,620 lek/month, especially as poor farmers are one of the main demographic groups which contribute to that average. But to be more precise, it might be better to use INSTAT's measure of monthly household income in towns with fewer than 10,000 people. In this stratum monthly household income is 14,250 lek (US $101).

3.   The term *fis* refers to people related by blood and of the same clan.

Pathways of Farm Restructuring in Uzbekistan: Pressures and Outcomes

Deniz Kandiyoti

Agrarian reform in countries undergoing post-socialist transitions has involved remarkably diverse processes. These have ranged from the reconstitution of private land ownership rights in Central and Eastern Europe to various forms of enterprise restructuring in the former Soviet Union. The European republics of the FSU have exhibited a different configuration of transition to the market than the Central Asian republics which are more heavily reliant on agriculture and primary extraction (Lerman, 1998). Central Asian governments have themselves adopted different types of land reform legislation with varying degrees of state monopoly over agricultural land and central controls over production decisions (Spoor, 1995).

The aim of this chapter is to analyze the complex set of factors that condition local pathways of reform by focusing on the case of Uzbekistan.[1] The initial stages of transition were, here as elsewhere, accompanied by economic recession, rising unemployment and greater reliance on the domestic economy for self-provisioning and on informal self-help networks to palliate increasing pressures on existing safety nets. In Uzbekistan, the initial decline in GDP was tempered by the fact that the country produces a major export crop, cotton, that could find alternative markets. The agricultural sector has acted as a 'shock absorber' providing livelihoods for an ever greater number of people, albeit on a shrinking resource base.[2] The large rural labor surplus of Uzbekistan, the low levels of rural wages compared to the rest of the Soviet Union, and low levels of labor mobility were already widely documented before the breakup of the Soviet Union (Craumer, 1992; Lubin, 1984; Khan and Dhai, 1979).

Against this background, the pace and content of agrarian reform in Uzbekistan is being shaped by a complex set of factors. The first section of this paper examines several contradictory pressures that influence policy outcomes. I shall argue (following Stark, 1992) that the constraints (and resources) of policy-makers are not simply financial and material but also political as they entail historically conditioned patterns of mediation between state and society that differ qualitatively from country to country. In Uzbekistan, serious consideration must be given to the particular place occupied by agriculture in the political economy of the country and the types of internal accommodations that evolved during both the Soviet and post-independence periods. After independence, the agrarian reform agenda of international donor agencies and increasing pressure on land as a source of self-provisioning for households have added further complications. The second section examines the effects of these pressures on the agrarian reform process itself and on land legislation in particular. The third section utilizes enterprise level data to discuss the outcomes of two different patterns of farm restructuring; the shift from collective enterprises to joint-stock companies (*shirkat*) and the dismantlement of bankrupt collective enterprises reorganized into Farmers' Associations.

Conflicting Priorities: Legacies of the Past, Exigencies of the Present

The integration of Uzbekistan into the Soviet Union as a raw material producer, (accounting for two-thirds of all cotton produced in the Union) has had enduring consequences. There is an extensive literature on both the ecological effects of cotton monoculture in Uzbekistan and on the elements of coercion imposed on the workforce and the general population to meet Plan targets (Carley, 1989; Gleason, 1991; Rumer, 1989; Spoor, 1993, Thurman, 1999). What is equally significant is the particular dynamic this extractive economy set up between Moscow and Tashkent during the Soviet period, and between government elites and regional mangers after independence in 1991.

Cotton production mediated the links between Moscow, republic-level elites, regional elites and their local constituencies. Moscow relied on republican leaders, who relied upon regional leaders who, in turn, relied upon district leaders and farm chairmen to ensure that the cotton plan was fulfilled. It was on this basis that republican leaders in Uzbekistan could demand added financial transfers from Moscow. As the center increased its demands in the form of more and more unrealistic Plan targets, the local Party bosses curried favor with Moscow by passing these pressures on to the districts. However, there was more to this dynamic than meets the eye. It involved a process of subversion and resistance on the part of republican elites in the face of unrealistic Plan targets, but also a process of accommodation on the part of the centre whereby political loyalty was traded for a substantial degree of latitude in internal dealings. The anticorruption drive and the purges that followed the "cotton scandal" in 1987 not only revealed the nature of the dealings involved but unsettled the compromises that had been struck in the long period under Brezhnev, provoking nationalist stirrings.[3]

This centre-periphery dynamic has survived in modified form after the breakup of the Soviet Union and the emergence of Uzbekistan as an independent state in 1991. It is now played out between the Tashkent elite that retains control over cotton deliveries and exports and the provincial and district governors who have to fulfil the cotton procurement quotas set by the state. Although provincial governors (*hokims*) have a degree of discretion, they are direct appointees of the center and their political longevity depends on their ability to meet production targets. The give-and-take necessary to ensure the loyalty of regional bosses, by providing them with the wherewithal to extend patronage to their own constituencies, has been one of the driving forces behind domestic politics.

The social contract of the Soviet period has progressively been exposed to new sources of strain. During the early years of independence some prerogative to manage part of the cotton output was given to provincial (*oblast*) leaders which brought them closer to political inner circles. However, in time, the established patronage networks were disrupted and relations between center and periphery reconfigured. Between 1993 and 1996 regional bosses were increasingly deprived of their share of cotton export revenue to consolidate central governments' monopoly over all exports. This occurred against a background of decline in cotton export earnings linked to a fall in international cotton prices since 1995, as well as a decline in cotton production itself of about 20 percent since 1991 (World Bank, 1999).

At present, the latitude of collective enterprises in decision-making regarding sowing policies is very restricted. Compulsory quotas for the distribution of crop acreages have been adopted by governmental decree and passed down to the provincial, district and farm levels.[4] Some commentators note that the interests of the state elite, regional bosses and managers of farm enterprises may now be on a divergent path (Roy, 1999; Ilkhamov, 2000). It is in managers' interest to shift resources from the official register to the much less accountable petty commodity economy. This leads to a process of concealed erosion of the basis of the export economy and creates grounds for conflict between central and regional elites. This conflict sometimes erupts into the public arena with the not infrequent dismissal of governors charged with corruption and inefficiency.

What further complicates the range of pressures under which the government of Uzbekistan has to operate is the fact that international agencies are also involved in setting the agrarian reform agenda, insisting on privatization and structural reform. Some of the measures adopted to meet these reform objectives, however limited, have expanded the latitude of some local players in evading the tight central control aimed to link them into the production of the export commodity.

The broad agrarian reform agenda of international donor and lending agencies revolves around the achievement of four main goals; a) macroeconomic stability b) progress in structural reforms (privatization) c) the establishment of secure and tradable property rights and d) market determined exchange and interest rates. What is being proposed, more specifically, is the removal of barriers to farmers' incentives by eliminating the massive price distortions for cotton and wheat and instituting mechanisms that could stimulate efficient and environmentally sound methods of irrigation (Herman, 1999).

The pricing issue is recognized as crucial. After independence the terms of trade for agriculture deteriorated drastically. Uzbekistan was cut off from the budgetary grant it received from the USSR and the government was forced to find new sources of revenue. Extraction of surplus from agriculture by driving a wedge between the procurement price and the export price of cotton was a readily available alternative. By 1994, the procurement price for cotton in real terms was a fraction of what it was in 1990. Also in terms of investment share the agricultural sector lags behind. While the sector accounts for about 25 percent of GDP, it receives less than 7 percent of total investment (IMF, 1998).

Currently, agriculture is being squeezed through a system of low output and high input prices. Prices for cotton and wheat are subject to a mandatory system of production quotas and state orders[5] complemented by rationing of inputs, water and equipment and financed with "centralized credits" by government controlled banks. Prices are set as a result of negotiations between the producers and government-controlled product processing associations, which are monopsonistic buyers. These are well below world market prices.[6]

Producers also have to contend with late payment for their deliveries, which further erodes their returns due to high inflation. Input prices, on the other hand, have been subject to large increases. Meanwhile, direct subsidies to producers have also been sharply reduced and *de facto* subsidies now consist of free use of the irrigation system and debt relief and rescheduling.

This combination of suppressed output prices, monopolistic prices for inputs and reduced subsidies has meant that the internal terms of trade have moved strongly against agriculture. The agricultural sector is estimated to have lost 65 percent of its purchasing power since 1990. Various calculations of the indirect tax imposed on agriculture have been offered.[7]

While the reform measures advocated by international organizations have, so far, had a relatively negligible impact, some policy changes initiated by the government of Uzbekistan have had more significant consequences. The break-up of the Soviet Union meant that the trading links with other republics were disrupted leading to a shortfall in grain, and shortages of flour became apparent in many parts of the country. The response of the government was to expand the acreage of land devoted to wheat production substantially [8] and to increase the size of private plots that the population is entitled to. With production of an estimated 3.7 million tons of wheat in 1998–six times the 1991 level–Uzbekistan has largely achieved the goal of drastically reducing grain imports. Household plots now comprise about three million holdings encompassing 10 percent of arable land (World Bank, 1999), a substantial enlargement of the acreage devoted to private use. This latter measure was also, in part, a palliative for the fact that public employers were chronically in arrears of wages and that households were becoming increasingly reliant on self-provisioning and the sale of their private produce for survival. However, the decline in cotton revenue has had negative consequences for foreign currency earnings, deepening the crisis in public finance and aggravating the tensions between Tashkent and the regions.

Halting Steps: Agrarian Reform Policy and Legislation

The contradictory pressures discussed above are reflected in the vagaries of the agrarian reform process itself. Since 1990 there have been some fifty-five laws, decrees and resolutions passed including revisions to laws related to land reform. Several commentators have pointed to inconsistencies between the various legislative acts. The legislation on land and farm restructuring has been oscillating between increasing access to private land, in line with populist pressures and the structural reform agenda of international donors, and counter-measures to tighten and restrict private access to land in response to the imperative of retaining control over the production of cotton.

The official rationale against outright privatization included concerns over land speculation and the creation of absentee landlords and the fact that cultivation in Uzbekistan is totally dependent on irrigation delivered by a state-run system. However, the possible disruption of deliveries of cotton, the leading export crop providing the main revenue base of the state, is certainly one of the features of agriculture in Uzbekistan that makes it harder to break away from the structures set up under the command economy.

On the one hand, the state has a stake in the maintenance of existing export revenues and in keeping control over them. On the other hand, the insolvency of the collective farming sector, the cost of continuing subsidies, the growing land hunger of a population that has increasingly fallen back on self-subsistence and the impetus to step up the pace of market reform emanating from international donors create pressures in the direction of expanding private access to land. Land reform legislation thus reflects a bundle of contradictory priorities and objectives.

New legislation in the immediate aftermath of independence allocated more private land to households for their own use.[9] However, the creation of an "independent" farming sector got off to a difficult start. Initially, "leased" peasant farms were created within the framework of collective enterprises. These were typically allocated marginally productive fields from land reserves. Their contracts were transacted with collective farm managers and their produce sold to the collectives at their own prices (which were even lower than state procurement prices). As collectives got into deeper financial problems they started to be in chronic arrears of payments to farmers who could not get the money for the crops they produced.[10]

The decree of 18 March 1997 separated independent farms from collective enterprises by granting them independent legal status, the right to hold their own bank accounts and to enter into transactions with buyers of crops and suppliers of inputs in their own right. Accession to the status of independent farmer involved a number of administrative hurdles (presentation of a petition and business plan, first to the collective farm management, then at the district level) but was not tied to formal criteria for eligibility based on minimum sizes of land holdings or herds.

New legislation, passed in April 1998, introduced new criteria that are de-signed to tighten access to the status of independent farmer and to make a distinction between owners of smallholdings (now called *dekhan* or *dehqan* peasant farmers) and independent farmers (now called *fermer khojaligi*). The main intent of the April 1998 Law appears to be the introduction of a distinction between a smallholding sector subject to a size "ceiling," on which the state makes no demands aside from land tax, and a "commercial" sector which has more latitude for expansion in terms of acquiring land and nonfamily laborers but which is tied into the state procurement through a system of contracts.

The leasehold contracts (*shartname*) stipulate the size of acreage to be allo-cated to specified crops and what proportion of the crop is subject to state deliveries. This represents an attempt to pass on the risks of production to independent farmers whilst maintaining the state procurement system of certain strategic crops such as cotton and wheat. This is a major bone of contention with the international donor community, which would like to see access to private enterprises (if not to the land on which the enterprises operate) accompanied by the legally defined power to make decisions about the use of the property, within a framework of long-term security of land tenure, and without interference.

In addition to meeting minimum landholding and herd size requirements, specified by the April 1998 Law, aspiring independent farmers now have to pass an examination and obtain a farmer's certificate (*attestatsia* or attestation). This is justified on the grounds that people who have inadequate knowledge about agronomy should not be allocated land since they would be unlikely to achieve the yields specified by their contracts. This examination is quite formal, conducted by a panel of administrators and experts at the district level and based, in principle, on universal criteria of competence and knowledge. In practice, former collective farm administrators and those who are well con-nected seem to have a definite competitive edge.

Local Dilemmas: The *Dekhan*, the Farmer and the Manager

Despite the gradual nature of the changes in land tenure patterns, the share of the individual sector (household plots and peasant farms) in agricultural production has increased substantially (from 28 percent in 1990 to 41 percent in 1994 and 53 percent in 1997). The production of meat and milk has shifted almost entirely to the household sector.[11] The apparent dynamism of this sector should not, however, make us lose sight of the rigidity of what Ilkhamov (1998) has described as a three-tiered rural economy. This structure consists of collective enterprises (now called *shirkat*), still occupying the major part of irrigated, arable land, a thin layer of independent farms (called "farmers" under the 1998 Law), and a mass of collective farm employees who cultivate smallholdings (or "dekhan farmers" under the 1998 Law). In practice, decisions concerning land allocation still reside with enterprise managers (except, as shall be seen later, in cases where collectives have been dismantled altogether) who have to adjudicate among different categories of claimants such as rank and file *shirkat* workers pressing their statutory rights to personal subsidiary plots and aspiring independent farmers who may apply for leases of up to fifty years.

This process of allocation is taking place in a context where the importance of land in sustaining livelihoods has increased significantly. Whereas informal incomes deriving from private cultivation and trading activities existed under the Soviet system as additional incomes (Grossman, 1989), Humphrey (1998) notes that they have now moved to centre stage as the arena where new survival strategies are enacted in the post-Soviet republics. Uzbekistan now presents the spectacle of a country where schoolteachers, local administrators, doctors and agricultural workers are all vying with each other to get a toehold in agricultural land, a result of the collapse of public sector wages and of retrenchment in the services and rural industries. In the Ferghana valley, where population density is very high, land hunger is particularly acute. Rural households have responded by adopting a mixed portfolio of activities, allocated along age and gender lines, depending on local conditions for employment and cultivation. A combination of salaries and wages, which may be paid in cash or in kind, self-provisioning and sale or barter of produce from personal plots or animals, income from trading and other informal activities, and benefits and entitlements (such as pensions and maternity benefit) currently characterize rural livelihoods (Kandiyoti, 1998). As a result, reliance on household and subsidiary plots for self-subsistence and on off-farm and nonfarm informal activities has increased substantially.

The simultaneous attempt by enterprise managers to provide smallholders with a subsistence base whilst developing and diversifying leasehold markets in land represents a precarious balancing act that can hardly be sustained in the long run. Given the shortage of available land, the presence of different categories of claimants within the same territory sets up a zero-sum game among them. Thus, land leased to independent farmers on a long-term basis can only be compensated for by reducing allocations made to households by collective enterprises (or by altogether refraining from allocating land to new families). The alternative would represent an out and out loss of the collectives' own productive capability. In the shake-out accompanying this process the weakest players, namely collective farm workers who rely on their small plots, are likely to be the losers. Yet, the only hold enterprise managers have over their unpaid workforce is through the access they give them to small personal plots, free pasture for their animals on *shirkat* land and the use of cotton stalks after the harvest for heating and fodder. Their inability to honor what *shirkat* workers consider as their basic entitlements constitutes a source of serious disaffection. These dilemmas, which were freely acknowledged by the farm managers interviewed, are being played out in various ways in the context of different types of restructured farming enterprises which are discussed in greater detail below.

Uncertain Futures: The *Shirkat* and the Farmers' Association

The most common path of enterprise restructuring in Uzbekistan is the trans-formation of former *kolkhoz* and *sovkhoz* into joint-stock companies (JSCs) or *shirkats*. Under this model, the assets of the enterprise are evaluated and the total share value (or some portion of it) is distributed to collective farm members on the basis of salary, length of service and other assessments of labor input. The organization of production remains essentially unchanged and continues to rely on family leaseholds. The shift from work brigades to family leaseholds (*oila pudrati* or *arenda* in Russian) was the product of the Union-wide reforms adopted during the *perestroika* period. This system was modelled on the Chinese household responsibility system. However, it did not grant farmers the decision-taking freedom that was a key element in China's agrarian success in the 1980s (Pomfret, 2000). Producers remain tied into the state procurement system through contracts specifying the kind and quantity of crops they are expected to grow. A more recent change is the introduction of a new system of management making each production unit a separate accounting unit responsible for its losses and profits.

A pattern that is less common is the complete liquidation of former collective enterprises and the reallocation of the land to independent farmers. In this case, what is at stake is not the distribution of shares but of actual land parcels. This requires additional decisions concerning which individuals will exercise legal rights over which land parcels. There is a program of "sanation" (*sanat-siya*) of agricultural enterprises, which entered its second round in 1999-2000.

"Sanation" consists of a two-year pre-bankruptcy process, which aims to re-establish the creditworthiness and economic viability of an enterprise. The main instruments are external management, debt restructuring, sale of unnecessary assets and stocks, strengthening financial controls, laying off surplus workforce and cleaning inter-farm irrigation and drainage structures. After the sanation period, enterprises that are able to improve their performance are being restructured into *shirkats,* while those showing no sign of improvement are liquidated and transformed into associations of private and *dehkan* farmers. As of January 2001, a total of 213 enterprises nationwide were under sanation and 74 enterprises had been restructured into Associations of Private and *Dekhan* Farmers. Both the scope of this programme and the number of liquidated collective enterprises is likely to grow.

The first pathway may be illustrated by the case of Ok Bugday[12] in Khorezm which became a joint-stock company in 1999. This collective owns 2,740 ha of cultivable land about 60 percent of which is allocated to growing cotton, followed by rice (15 percent), sugar beet (11 percent) and wheat (7 percent) as the main crops. The remainder is sown to feed crops and vegetables. This land is cultivated by 1,800 family leaseholders (*oila pudratchisi* or *pudratchi*).[13] Family leaseholds were introduced here in 1985. This was intended to increase the sense of responsibility of the workers by allocating them the same plots year after year as family units. The shift to the *shirkat* brought about two further changes: a) the distribution of shares to members of the collective and b) the redefinition of family leaseholds as separate accounting units. The distribution of shares and the costing of returns on production at the household level are intended to further increase the sense of ownership and responsibility of *shirkat* members.

All those who have worked for the *kolkhoz* for more than two years (including pensioners) were eligible to receive shares. The criteria for the size of shares were based on length of service and salary level. A total of 3,500 shares were distributed; of these 800 were given to pensioners, 270 to technicians, tractor drivers and other technical personnel and the rest allocated to current workers in family brigades. The *paychik* (shareholders) have the right to pass on these shares to their heirs. The benefits accruing from shareholding are, at present, hypothetical rather than substantive since the enterprise is in arrears of debt payments to various input providers and unable to pay its members regular wages, let alone dividends. Shareholding also brings with it the possibility of having to shoulder the debts of the collective if it were to go into liquidation.

The transition from work brigades to family leases and more recently to the *shirkat* have entailed a progressive retrenchment of labor. In the process of turning into an association of shareholders, the *shirkat* had to shed a further 425 brigade members who are now unemployed (almost 20 percent of the total workforce of 2,250). Of these, 65 percent are women. The effect of retrenchment is the casualization of agricultural labor whereby fewer workers are formally "on the books," meaning that they lose the social benefits attached to being members of an enterprise.

In terms of the organization of production itself, however, the shift to *shirkat* status does not appear to have introduced significant changes. The procurement quotas for each crop are still allocated to different brigades, which divide the land among family leaseholders.[14] A significant departure from the past is that brigades are no longer the unit responsible for production. They only work on common maintenance tasks like cleaning and repairing water canals. The responsibility for meeting production targets rests, with each family-leasehold, which now constitutes a separate accounting unit. Every leaseholder enters into a separate contract with the *shirkat,* which is transacted yearly, specifying the acreage of land they lease and how much they will produce and receive in payment. Each family-leasehold is provided with a notebook and chequebook where they record all the expenses they have incurred for inputs. At the end of the year, when they settle accounts the costs of inputs that are owed to the *shirkat* and the salary costs of the technical services provided are deducted from the amount owed to the leaseholder according to contract stipulations. In the case of a leaseholder who has produced six tons of cotton fetching approximately 300,000 sum, more than half will go towards expenditures covered by the *shirkat* as advances for inputs. Furthermore, about 40,000 sum will be deducted towards the salary costs of the *shirkat* administrative staff (bookkeepers, water services and agronomists).[15] The net return will be of around 70,000 sum which constitutes about 25 percent of the amount on the contract.

Direct producers are thus disadvantaged in three different ways; they sell their cotton at low delivery prices, they pay for their inputs through noncash advances which price these commodities at a higher level than their cash value in the *bazaar* and they support an administrative staff of overseers and technical personnel. Given the fact that they are also deprived of cash earnings as wages, they are heavily reliant on their private subsidiary plots.

Furthermore, this new structure of production appears to be particularly onerous for the *shirkat* administration, a fact that was freely acknowledged during interviews. It now has to issue 1,800 separate yearly contracts and keep track of the expenses of all the leaseholders through the new chequebook system (one copy of these records is kept by the lessee and another submitted to *shirkat* bookkeepers). This internal accounting process may seem to imply that a system of sanctions will apply to those who are in permanent debt to the *shirkat* or who systematically fail to fulfil the terms of their contracts. However, the question of whether the manager has the right to revoke leases or to stop issuing new leases elicited the admission that a large number of leaseholders were already indebted to the enterprise, not least because they received in kind loans to conduct life cycle ceremonies such as weddings, circumcision feasts or funerals.

This admission goes to the heart of the social contract between the *kolhozdji* (collective workers) and their management. The ties that still bind workers to the collectives are a combination of a lack of alternatives and forms of paternalistic protection. The latter are coming under increasing strain as the resources of collective enterprises dry up. Apart from keeping their workbooks registered in the *shirkat* for the purposes of pensions and social benefits, members of the collective receive a number of incentives. They can use the cotton stalks (*xozapaya*) from the harvested fields as cooking fuel and animal fodder, they use *shirkat* land to graze their private animals,[16] and they have the right to sell cotton oil from any excess production of cotton or sugar from their sugar beet. Family brigades are also allowed to plant carrots, beans or other fast-growing crops on *shirkat* land after the wheat harvest for their own use, on a leasehold or share-cropping basis. Most importantly, the access of households to private subsidiary plots is mediated by membership in the collective enterprise, and *shirakat* workers are entitled to larger plots than the general population. These mutual arrangements have led some observers to argue that the cotton export-sector is dependent upon a stagnating smallholder economy on which it draws for its manpower needs, while the latter is parasitic upon the hidden benefits just described.

However, these arrangements become subject to more serious strains in cases where the crop mix permits the fuller development of competitive leasehold markets. Such is the case of Eski Kishlak in the Andijan province, which was transformed into a closed joint-stock company (JSC) in 1999. The process of distribution of shares, the organization of production through contracts with family leaseholders and the chequebook system for accounting follow the principles described above in relation to the Ok Bugday *shirkat*, with minor differences.[17] But there have been significant changes in cropping patterns in Eski Kishlak. The drive for self-sufficiency in grain since independence has meant that part of the acreage previously allocated to feed crops and cotton is now planted to wheat. Until 1992, there was hardly any wheat cultivation in Eski Kishlak. In 1997, *shirkat* land was allocated to cotton (1,429 ha), wheat (429 ha), rice (10 ha) orchards (8 ha) and other crops (90 ha).[18] By 2000, this balance had changed in favor of wheat (1,050 ha), with more than a doubling of the acreage in three years.

These shifts in cropping patterns have had a more profound impact on land tenure and labor deployment than farm restructuring per se. Unlike cotton, wheat makes it possible to plant other crops after the harvest in June. Those who can afford it have started leasing land from the *shirkat* at competitive prices to grow rice after the wheat harvest. There has also been a shift from *devzire* to *ak shali* (white rice) which has much higher yields (almost double) and fetches a similar price. Whereas previously local variety *devzire* rice was planted in early spring, now a second crop of white rice is planted after the wheat harvest in

July. This crop is ready for harvest in September. There is a visible increase in the supply of casual agricultural labor (*mardigor*) as a result of both growing unemployment and of changing cropping patterns, which have produced a substantial increase in labor intensive operations. This is taking place against the background of a gradual process of polarization and growing inequality in access to land. Those who have the means are in a position to lease land for cash, thus enlarging their holdings at the expense of claimants from among rank and file *shirkat* workers. It is therefore not simply a question of population pressure on land (which undoubtedly exists) but also the fact that access is now taking place in the newly commodified context of a land lease market. Before the expansion of wheat cultivation in Eski Kishlak, the amount of common land that could be redistributed for personal use was quite limited since the cotton crop cycle does not allow replanting after harvest. Additional household land consisted of house plots, *tamorka* land and leased nonirrigated land. With the increased acreage of wheat, the quantity of common land that can be reallocated to household use has, in fact, increased in absolute terms. The *shirkat* workers who receive no remuneration (except for a limited quantity of foodstuffs) feel they are entitled to a share of that land and feel bitter about being fobbed off with tiny parcels of bad land while wealthier villagers are able to help themselves to choice parcels. This is a context, therefore, where the combination of high population pressure, loss of nonagricultural employment, changes in cropping patterns and rapid commodification of land have eroded the social contract between farm managers and their workforce and are creating a source of deep discontent.

An even more volatile and uncertain future awaits the members of enterprises that have embarked on the second path of farm restructuring, namely the outright liquidation of the collective enterprise. This is apparent in the case of Yengi Kishlak Farmers' Association (*farmer birlashmasi*) in Khorezm. When the Yengi Kishlak *kolkhoz* was declared bankrupt in 1999 a Liquidation Committee was set up by the district *hokimiyat*. This Committee sold all the assets of the collective to pay off its debts, totalling 130 million sum, which were taken over by those former members of the collective who became the new farmers.[19]

The land of the collective was made available to prospective farmers by advertisement and applications were sought from members of the former collective. One hundred and fifty-three people applied. An examination was organized by a committee of fourteen experts, headed by the deputy governor of the province (in line with the provisions of the 1998 Land Law) as a result of which 53 new farms were created. There are now a total of 65 farms, including twelve that had been formed prior to the break-up of the collective. One is a livestock farm, 11 are fruit farms on orchard land and 56 are mixed cotton and grain (rice and wheat) farms.

The existing demarcations of land lots were kept intact and land parcels were allocated to prospective farmers by lottery to avoid disagreements over size and quality. The parcels range from a maximum of 97,7 ha to 1 ha. Moreover, the enterprises designated as "farms" are not homogenous entities. They range from single household operations (as in the case of 11 households that cultivate orchards) to groups of family leaseholders cultivating the same parcel. On larger tracts of cotton and rice fields there may be anything up to 15 or more family leaseholders (*oila pudratchisi*), an important point to which we shall return.

Whereas previously independent farmers were allocated land by applying to the collective farm and seeking approval of its General Meeting, these new farmers had their allocations directly ratified by the Land Registry. In principle, they have leases ranging between a minimum of 10 and a maximum of 50 years.[20] Each year a new contract is transacted between these farmers and the district branches of government controlled product-processing associations. They have state orders (*goszakaz*) for different crops and have to deliver 50 percent of their wheat and rice and 100 percent of the cotton. They may receive credit at a discretionary rate of 15 percent and have a tax holiday for two years.

Before the breakup of the collective, *kolkhoz* land was cultivated by 550 family-leaseholds (*oila pudrati*). The management entered into contracts with the various buyers and providers of inputs on behalf of the whole enterprise. Now that each farmer transacts his/her own contract directly with input providers and with the buyers of crops, they also receive their production advances directly from the buyers, in accordance to the terms of their contracts.

However, the former family leaseholders are still working on the same land. The new farmers have to draw up yearly work contracts with them (*mihnat shartnamesi*), undertaking to pay a monthly salary for their work (*ish hakki*) depending on the acreage that they cultivate. In principle, the farmers have the legal right not to renew these contracts but the prospect of evicting fellow members of the collective who have cultivated the same family leaseholds for many years must present a thorny dilemma. There is some anecdotal evidence about people "changing places" to be with their relatives and of new farmers inviting members of their wider kin group to work on their farms. However, it is too early yet to draw any inferences from such information.

In total 62 percent of the new farmers are members of the technical/administrative cadres of the former collective, with only 38 percent rank and file *kolkhoz* workers whose primary occupation is agriculture. In keeping with this profile, 32 percent of the farmers have university-level education, 29 percent technical/vocational education and 38 percent only a secondary school education. This amounts to a high proportion of farmers (61 percent) with tertiary level schooling.

Interviews with various provincial and district-level administrators concerning the rationale for "examinations" in the selection of farmers consistently stressed the technical nature of the job and the requirement of appropriate professional skills. Entitlement to land was unambiguously presented as a technocratic prerogative. My initial interpretation of this administrative discourse was that it represented an attempt to underscore the meritocratic basis of the decisions taken, presenting them as devoid of favoritism or preferential treatment. The data from Yengi Kishlak suggests that more pressing concerns may also be at work. The redeployment of former technical cadres made redundant by the breakup of the collective clearly constitutes a top priority. It must also be recognized that these cadres possess "social capital" accrued from their experience with collective farming; their ability to enter into transactions with input providers and marketing boards in their own right is higher than that of rank and file members of the collective.

It would be highly pertinent to compare the profiles of independent farmers who applied for land allocations on an individual, voluntary basis to the "new" farmers of liquidated enterprises. Although there is no systematic data on this, it is possible to infer that the "early" farmers were individuals in a position to initiate and carry through the complicated bureaucratic steps involved in receiving an allocation. This required, among other things, adequate knowledge of the application procedures and good relations with district authorities who have the final say. Not surprisingly, members of collective farms who are in the higher administrative echelons are best placed to clear the necessary hurdles. Paradoxically, the fact that many aspiring farmers were still in employment as managerial or technical cadres may inadvertently have increased the number of "registered" women farmers. Since only "full-time" farmers are legally entitled to receive land, men holding such posts resorted to registering their wives as the titular head of their farming enterprise. In contrast, the redundant cadres of Yengi Kishlak had no choice but to register themselves as farmers or seek an exit option by finding work elsewhere. This exit option is more and more elusive in a context of deepening unemployment where agricultural enterprises are everywhere shedding employees.

The farming option, moreover, brings with it new problems and risks which may be best illustrated through the case of a typical new farm. This 26 ha farm already has six family leaseholders working on it. They each cultivate the same mix of crops, 2.5 ha of cotton and 2 ha of paddy, with one family also raising silkworm. These "sitting tenants" have now become incorporated into the new farm as workers, with one of their former enterprise colleagues as their new boss. Six individuals who are the heads of their family leaseholds have signed work contracts (*mihnat shartnamesi*) with the new farmer, and only they are entitled to receive a salary (*ish hakki*), although they acknowledge that they actually work as entire families, with at least three or four people contributing to production. The permanent contract holders are meant to receive 2,000 sum per month for 1 ha of cotton or rice land cultivated. The farmer acknowledged that there were serious problems in keeping up with such payments despite the fact that household resources, such as animals and the proceeds of the family smallholding were used to capitalize the enterprise. Questions concerning the economic feasibility of the farm elicited considerable unease. Similar sentiments were echoed by other new farmers. One of them exclaimed: "We sold 88,000 sum worth of animals. We were dreaming of a plot of 4-5 hectares. Instead we drew a plot of 37 ha. What misfortune!"

Although it may seem surprising that anyone should bemoan receiving a large parcel of land, the conditions under which these allocations were made make this reaction quite understandable. Although the land now "belongs" to individual farmers on long leases, the conditions under which production decisions are made have not changed. The farmers are still tied into the unprofitable procurement system. Apart from meeting the terms of their delivery contracts, they now have the additional burden of having to pay their own workforce and remaining solvent all at once. This means, in effect, that both the social costs of production and the risks involved have been passed on to them. In a relatively short period many may face the dilemma of having to evict most of their workforce or face bankruptcy. Setting up as farmers has meant, in many cases, having to dig into private household reserves by selling animals or using *tamorka* crops to capitalize their enterprise. Since they do not have the option of diversifying into more profitable crops, they can only attempt to cut their costs.

Writing in the very different context of reconstitution of private landowner-ship rights in Eastern Europe, Verdery (2003, forthcoming) argues that land in Transylvania is being devalued and turned into a negative asset through privatization by covertly assigning risks and obligations to new owners. She argues that de-collectivization is about making land a carrier of liabilities, giving people land rights to produce owners who will take on the debts for the costs of machinery, inputs, irrigation and repairs and eventually liability to tax. In Uzbekistan where the rights of ownership are, in fact, reduced to lease-holding under binding contractual conditions that leave little room for maneuvre, the new farmer is faced with pure liability.

The gradual phasing out of an overblown and unproductive rural workforce is a stated government objective, accompanied with the parallel promise of the growth of rural industry and services that will absorb excess labor. However, the currently depressed state of the agricultural sector discourages the growth of services and industry, creating a vicious cycle of growing unemployment and poverty. Under these conditions, land reform of the type represented by Yengi Kishlak can become a disempowering experience, hence the reticence of many new farmers. They are, in fact, managers with severely limited rights to ownership or control.

Those who appear to be doing somewhat better are not the "new" farmers but those who are able to lease land against cash payments to grow crops that are not subject to procurement quotas. Most enterprises have some land reserves. In Yengi Kishlak, there were 58 ha left over from the land distributed to 65 farmers. Of these, 16 ha were allocated as private subsidiary plots and 42 ha were kept in reserve for future construction projects. This land was leased out to some households against payment of a fixed amount per hectare. Apart from having to pay tax, these leaseholders are not obliged to grow crops that are subject to procurement quotas and can sell their produce on the open market. However, the ability to lease land in this fashion implies that a household has either enough spare cash or sufficient animal wealth and labor power to finance such a venture. One such household reported having sold their animals and leased an apricot orchard of 0.4 ha for 200,000 sum. They also leased 2 ha of land to grow melons and watermelons for 300,000 sum for one year.

They try to cut their costs by substituting their own labor and that of their broader kin group to machinery and paid help, and they use natural fertilizer where they can and buy the rest in the *bazaar* which is cheaper. They have to pay tax for land and water and will only be liable to tax on their profit after two years. Relative prosperity in this case depends on occupying niches that enable producers to evade procurement obligations.

Conclusion

The pace of agrarian reform in Uzbekistan has been slow compared to both its neighbors in Central Asia and to other countries undergoing market transitions in the FSU. The continued reliance on cotton as the major export crop and the stake the state retains in the maintenance of existing export revenues has made a shift away from the institutional structures of the former command economy a halting and difficult process. On the other hand, the insolvency of the collective farming sector, the cost of continuing subsidies, the growing land hunger of a population that has increasingly fallen back on self-subsistence and the impetus to step up the pace of market reform emanating from international donors creates pressures in the direction of expanding private access to land.

As a result, agrarian reform legislation between 1990 and 1998 reflects a set of contradictory priorities and objectives. However, an exclusive focus on legal rights, reflected in changing codes, does very little to elucidate processes of transformation in social entitlements and access to land in rural Uzbekistan. As Hann (1998: 7) reminds us, the focus on formal legal codes "must be broadened to include the institutional and cultural contexts in which such codes operate."

An understanding of changing entitlements must necessarily take account of the type of social contract represented by the Soviet farming system. In line with the more general principle of "labor decommodification" operative in Soviet labor markets (Standing, 1996), wages of collective workers were always low but compensated for by a bundle of social benefits channelled through membership of enterprises, including access to a plot for household use. These formal benefits were complemented by more informal mechanisms of paternalistic responsibility vis-à-vis workers, such as helping them to defray the costs of life-cycle ceremonies or assisting those stricken by disease or personal tragedy.

The crisis in public finance that followed the breakup of the Soviet Union had significant repercussions on the agricultural sector. Rural Uzbekistan underwent a dual process of demonetization and reagrarianization as workers stopped receiving wages and those displaced from nonfarm occupations due to retrenchment in rural industry and services also started falling back on land. The simultaneous objectives of the maintenance of cotton revenues and the provision of a basic level of self-subsistence for workers acted to consolidate the division between a stagnating smallholder sector and the export sector, the two being mutually dependent upon one another.

The general effects discussed above are mediated at the local level by different paths of farm restructuring in regions with distinct ecological and demographic features. Neither macroeconomic policies, nor agrarian reform legislation constitute an adequate guide to the micro-dynamics of change in access and entitlement occasioned by the restructuring of enterprises. Two paths of restructuring were examined above: the transformation of *kolkhoz* and *sovkhoz* into joint-stock shareholding companies or *shirkat*, and the liquidation of collective enterprises in favor of associations of independent farms.

It is clear in all cases that the attempt to provide *shirkat* workers with a subsistence base, whilst developing leasehold markets in land creates tensions and contradictions. Land leased to independent farmers and tenants on a short or longer-term basis reduces the pool out of which allocations can be made to households. This has meant that the claims of *shirkat* workers to additional plots may be marginalized in favor of those who have the means to pay. The fact that this is taking place in a period of contraction rather than expansion of nonfarm employment, which might have created avenues for diversification, fuels intense land hunger. It must be pointed out, however, that this situation is the product of a very specific conjuncture. It reflects a point in time when labor retrenchment and growing inequalities in access to land are not attenuated by significant mechanisms of rural out-migration, receipts of migrant remittances and diversification into nonfarm activities or viable forms of self-employment. If these alternatives were to materialize, they may provide a degree of relief from what appears to be a deteriorating set of circumstances. The agrarian reform process in Uzbekistan, however partial, is creating consequences, which add increasing urgency to the search of alternative livelihoods in rural areas.

Notes

1.   This case study forms part of an UNRISD project on Agrarian Reform, Gender and Land Rights, a comparative study on Brazil, South Africa and Uzbekistan. The fieldwork was carried out between March 2000-2001 in the provinces of Andijan and Khorezm.

2.   Between 1989 and 1994 employment in agriculture grew at an annual compound rate of 4.6 percent while agricultural output declined by 3.8 percent. (Khan, 1996). It must be noted here that only 10 percent of the territory of Uzbekistan is habitable land and that the rural population, over 60 percent of the total, is concentrated on 4.5 million hectares of irrigated arable land in oases and along rivers. The amount of arable land per rural resident (0.37 ha) is low compared to other FSU republics (2 ha per person in Ukraine and 0.75 in densely populated Moldova).

3.   The posthumous disgrace of Rashidov, first Secretary of the Uzbek Communist Party, and the imprisonment of some 2,600 officials in 1987 for their part in the "cotton scandal" (also referred to as the "Uzbek affair") followed when it became apparent that payments were being made for fictitious cotton deliveries. At the heart of this episode were allegations that Uzbek officials, at all levels of the republic, had been defrauding the central government through an elaborate system of bribe taking and padding reports. The state allegedly paid more than one billion roubles in 1978-83 for cotton that was never produced, based on an inflation of cotton output by as much as 4.5 million tons.

This purge led to an upsurge of nationalist feeling. People were less concerned about corruption, especially if it had the effect of diverting funds into Uzbekistan, and more about the persecution of Uzbek cadres (Pomfret, 1995). Karimov issued a decree on December 25, 1991 pardoning most of those convicted in the "cotton scandal". In the nationalist atmosphere of political independence, this was a means of signalling that this affair had been a symbol of foreign intervention. For a more detailed account of the purges and reactions to them see Fierman (1997).

4.   Decree of the Cabinet of Ministers, No. 317, 24 June 1997.

5.   Wheat is subject to a two-tiered pricing system: 25 percent at the state order price and 25 percent at a higher administered price (the "negotiated" price). In fact, this amounts to 50 percent since the additional negotiated price, is in practice, mandatory. The state order for cotton is 30 percent of planned production. Producers who meet production targets, in principle, have the right to sell the residual 70 percent to the state marketing board for a higher price. However, producers who do not meet their production targets do not have the right to sell any cotton at the higher price. For this reason, actual state procurement is much higher than the formal state order since ambitious production targets are frequently not met.

6.   By way of comparison, Chinese farmers received the full international price at the farm gate–US $ 1,590 per ton in 1998–in contrast to US $775 per ton received by Uzbek producers. With prices at 60-65 percent of international levels and the condition that foreign exchange must be surrendered at the official rate, cotton producers in Uzbekistan are clearly disadvantaged (World Bank, 1999).

7.   Herman (1999) estimates that a large indirect tax equivalent to US $200-US $400 is charged annually per hectare of irrigated land. Trushin (1998) offered the following estimates for 1995; subsidies amounting to 608 million dollars, an outward flow of between 1,098 and 1,223 million US $, a net resultant outflow from agriculture of between 499 to 615 million US $. This represents between 2.3 to 2.9 percent of GDP or 8-10 percent of GDP produced by the agricultural sector. Khan's (1996) estimate was of a similar order, namely over 10 percent of the value of GDP originating in agriculture.

8.   Government objectives to pursue wheat self-sufficiency had a major impact on cropping patterns since independence. Between 1990-96 there was a reduction in the areas sown to cotton (from 44 to 35 percent) and forage (from 25 to 13 percent) while the share of arable land allocated to cereals increased (from 24 to 41 percent). However, the drop in forage crops caused a decline in animal husbandry and a critical shortage of feed and the substitution of cereal for cotton lowered the returns from agriculture. Land used for cotton produces 1.2 to 3 times more added value per hectare than land sown to wheat (Trushin, 1998).

9.   According to one estimate the amount of land for personal plots increased from 110,000 ha before independence to 630,000 ha in 1994 (362,840 ha of which was cropland). However, these legal norms are subject to local availability. In high population density areas, new families may not receive an allocation or their plots may be well below the legally allowed norm.

10. A TACIS (1996) report on the Bulungur district of Samarkand cites this factor as one of the main reasons for the failure of many independent farms and the decline in their numbers between 1991 and 1995. Between 1993 and 1995, 1,646 peasant farms had failed (800 of these in 1995 alone).

11. This was in part related to an acute shortage of feed crops that has worsened with the conversion of land planted with barley and lucerne to wheat (the aggregate feed available in 1997 was about one-third of 1991).

12. The names of the enterprises are pseudonyms that protect the anonymity of respondents.

13. The size of land allocated to each family depends upon the crops for which there are different norms. These are 5 ha for wheat, 1.1 ha for rice and 1.7 ha for cotton. The labor power available to households is also taken into account.

14. There are currently 20 cotton brigades, 5 rice brigades, 2 wheat brigades, 2 sugar beet brigades, and 2 animal fodder brigades. The delivery contract for cotton the previous year, for instance, was 4,600 tons. This was divided among the 20 cotton brigades, which comprise 957 family leaseholders. The yields expected from each family leasehold, are set according to production norms for the different crops.

15. The administration of the *shirkat* continues to be relatively large and consists of salaried personnel who receive their wages from the proceeds of the *shirkat*. These are; the *shirkat* head, his deputy, bookkeepers, technical personnel (agronomists, machinists, machine repairers, water engineers) and brigade chiefs. The last echelon in the administrative structure to receive salaries are the brigade chiefs. It is difficult to reach an estimate of the level of over staffing in these salaried positions.

16. A number of governmental decrees introducing punitive measures (including surveillance by mounted militia) have been introduced since 1994 to prevent crop damage due to grazing. This appears to have had little effect since enterprise managers tend to turn a blind eye to this infraction.

17. Here the holders of chequebooks are the brigade chiefs who act as intermediaries between family leaseholders and the *shirkat* management. There is considerable confusion over the use of these chequebooks and a great deal of bitterness on the part of leaseholders who complain that the *shirkat* fails to provide them with timely inputs of fertilizer and technical support and yet holds them responsible for their yields.

18. This data was obtained from earlier fieldwork in 1997-98. See Kandiyoti (1999) "Rural domestic economy and female labor supply in Uzbekistan: Assessing the feasibility of gender-targeted micro-credit schemes", Final report, DFID, ESCOR Unit, Grant no. R6978.

19. These debts were owed to the providers of various inputs, such as MTPs (machine-tractor parks), the state petroleum company and agrochemical firms and amounted roughly to 50,000 sum per ha for each farmer with five years to repay the debt.

20. However some respondents reported shorter leases. If after two years the farms fail to keep to the terms of their contract, their leases may be revoked and the land reallocated, pointing to a probationary period in this instance.

The Rural Nonfarm Economy in Transition Countries: Findings from Armenia

Dirk J. Bezemer and Junior R. Davis

There has been an increasing recognition recently that the rural economy is not confined to the agricultural sector, but embraces all the people, economic activities, infrastructure and natural resources in rural areas (Barrett et al., 2001; World Bank, 2000; Reardon et al., 1999, Reindert, 1998). Since the 1970s, a large number of studies have investigated the role of nonagricultural economic activities in rural development. There is evidence that economic diversity in the countryside has the potential to foster local economic growth, and alleviate the rural-urban income gap and rural poverty.

These findings are relevant to the post-socialist transition countries, where typically a large part of the population lives in rural areas, and economic growth and the reduction of poverty are significant challenges. This is particularly true for those transition countries outside Central Europe. Analysis of the transition process in general and of transition in the agricultural sector has generated a large literature, but less has been specifically devoted to the wider rural non-farm economy.

However, studies in this field are now being undertaken, since it has been recognized that in the longer term the development of the rural economy is key to providing rural employment and income (Bleahu and Janowski, 2001; Breischopf and Schreider, 1999; Deichmann and Henderson (2000); Chaplin, 2000; Sarris et al., 1999). This chapter focuses on analyzing the development of the rural nonfarm economy (RNFE) in the context of a transitional economy, using detailed fieldwork carried out in Armenia.

A large proportion of the population of the Balkans and the CIS live in persistent poverty (the actual percentage depending on varying definitions of poverty). Using an expenditure measure, 10 percent of the population were persistently in extreme poverty in 1998, implying malnutrition. These poverty problems have started to be addressed (with varying degrees of success) in some economically advanced CEE countries such as the Czech and Slovak Republics, Poland, Hungary, and Slovenia, but hardly in the Balkans and CIS (Milanovic, 1998).

The RNFE has a role to play in poverty reduction during two stages of the transition process. In the first stage of impoverishment and economic decline, it acts as a "defensive" survival strategy for the rural poor. Most Balkan and CIS nations are still at this stage. For instance, limited off-farm earning opportunities are given as one of the main reasons for stagnant rural incomes in Georgia, together with the scarcity of rural credit, poor market access for domestic products, unequal access to inputs complementary to labor, and barriers to land consolidation. In countries such as Romania, where agriculture is acting as a buffer against unemployment and hidden unemployment is widespread and increasing (Davis and Pearce, 2000), development of the RNFE is vital. The Romanian government is aware that in order to improve the motivation of people to seek rural nonfarm employment, the quality of life in rural communities needs to be improved with better education and infrastructure (Turnock, 1998).

In the Central European countries, the second stage of economic growth and development has started. Many well-educated people are moving out of agriculture to seek higher incomes elsewhere. Rural areas are left with proportionally more elderly people. Gradually, a process of farm consolidation is getting underway. Large farms contract, and fragmented small farms are being amalgamated into larger, more viable units, with more mechanization. Both these developments are expected to result in the shedding of excess agricultural labor.

The promotion of rural nonfarm enterprises is seen as having the potential to absorb this excess farm labor, stimulate rural development and overcome rural poverty (Christensen and Lacroix, 1997). One could envisage jobs supporting this process–repairing machines, developing and maintaining rural roads and other infrastructure, local food processing (e.g., cheese-making, wine production and the like), and providing rural services (accounting, banking, distribution, teaching, etc.). Due to a lack of data it is difficult to measure the rate of growth of these activities (Davis and Pearce, 2000).

Remittances form part of rural income and are of importance in some of the transition economies, such as Albania (Ibid). By contrast, in a Ukrainian survey (Lerman and Csaki, 2000), remittances from abroad were found to be negligible. This was also observed in the chapter on Bulgaria by Kopeva et al. in this volume. Clearly, during the early post-socialist recession period, most nonfarm activities were low paid, labor intensive and/or basically survival strategies. This remains the case for many CIS and Balkan states.

The RNFE in Post-Socialist Countries

It is difficult to obtain evidence on income shares from nonfarm sources, firstly because nonfarm income is not recorded in the statistics of most countries in the region, and secondly due to the unwillingness of survey respondents to provide information on their incomes. However, there is growing evidence that rural households in the CEE may obtain 30 to 50 percent of their income from nonfarm sources (Davis and Gaburici, 1999; Greif, 1997). For example, in Poland, agriculture is the main source of income for only 29 percent of village households, whereas nonagricultural income is the main source for 30 percent of village households (Christensen and Lacroix, 1997). In Ukraine, 76 percent of the income of private farmers' families is from agriculture, while 16 percent is from off-farm sources and 8 percent from business (Lerman and Csaki, 2000). Thus it is likely that the nonfarm sector is generally more significant in the CEE than CIS, and also possible that income from the nonfarm sector is underestimated. Some observations may place these figures in perspective.

First, these percentages, though larger than many would expect, are in fact not high compared to the Western world. In the USA for instance, about 75 percent of farms are relatively small. In these businesses farming is a loss-making activity, and the main source of income is nonagricultural. For medium, large and very large farms, nonagricultural income is still close to 70 percent, 40 percent and 20 percent, respectively (Edelman, 1997). In the European Union, farmers derive typically only between one half and two-thirds from agricultural production.

Second, although there are reasons to expect the share of nonagricultural income to rise further, it is not a foregone conclusion that this convergence to Western figures signifies progress towards the Western economic model. The underlying forces differ dramatically. In Western countries the rise of the RNFE occurred during a period of increasing affluence and seems sustained currently by the declining importance of agriculture, in combination with the desire of rural (as well as originally urban) populations to live in the countryside. In transition countries the RNFE has grown during the post-socialist transformational recession and seems stimulated by a combination of the decline of agriculture and lower income levels.

Third, and related, although the RNFE may offer a wider range of livelihood options to the rural populations in transition countries, it does not thereby signify healthy economic development. Economic development has traditionally been associated with specialization of labor and increases in labor productivity. In the transition countries, especially in the Balkans and CIS, there has generally been a de-specialization of labor. The farming population is (or may be) diversifying from food production into nonfood production, which boosts the RNFE. At the same time, urban households diversify from nonfood production into food production (e.g. Bezemer, forthcoming, 2002; Caskie, 2000; Tho Seeth et al., 1998). These joint developments could also be interpreted as a general trend amongst the poorest transition countries, where the specialization of labor in the socialist system, under the pressure of increasing poverty, is being replaced by diversification as a subsistence (survival) strategy. This is primitivization (i.e. a decrease in value-added in the economy–see Hedlund and Sundstrom, 1996; Ellman, 2000), not development of the economic system. Although this interpretation is open to question, the opposite view, where the RNFE is seen as part of a resumption of growth after the transitional recession, is likewise questionable.

Fourth, even if the size or importance of the RNFE has increased recently, this does not imply that there is now more diverse economic activity in post-socialist rural areas than prior to the reforms. One social objective of socialism was to transcend differences between towns and the countryside. In this policy framework, industrial employment in rural areas was created, either by locating industrial concerns in rural areas (e.g. agro-industrial complexes in Bulgaria) or by encouraging agricultural cooperatives to diversify into nonagricultural activities (e.g. computer hardware manufacturing cooperative "firms" in the Czech Republic). The former strategy was most common in Central European and Balkan countries that were pre-industrial before the central planning era, e.g. Albania, Slovakia, Bulgaria, Romania, and most of the CIS. However, the development of nonagricultural businesses with agricultural cooperatives was also practiced there–around 88 percent of Slovak agricultural cooperatives were engaged in nonagricultural activities as compared to 78 percent in the Czech Republic, and 58 percent in Poland by the 1980s (Swain, 1999). Rural nonfarm employment existed during socialism on a larger scale than in Western Europe. Much of that activity was reduced or disappeared during the transformational recession. The RNFE now observed, may well comprise people, assets, and activities that were traditionally owned or managed by socialist farms and other rural firms. To the extent that this mechanism is at work, the emergence of the RNFE in post-socialist countries is in fact a re-emergence.

The RNFE in Armenia during Transition

Armenia is the smallest former Soviet Republic outside the Baltic States. It is a mountainous country located in the Trans-Caucasus, bordering Turkey, Georgia, Azerbaijan, and Iran. Its population is 3.7 million, with another five million Armenians living outside the state territory.

During the Soviet era, as in many socialist countries, Armenia was an industrialized country with a large rural population. In 1990, the year preceding Armenian independence and economic reforms, industry employed 20 percent of the labor force, contributed 33 percent to value-added, and 45 percent to gross output. Agriculture employed 13 percent of the labor force, contributed 17 percent to value-added, and 13 percent to gross output. About 20 percent of the population were rural residents.

Following independence, the reforms introduced in 1991-1992 comprised the privatization of many productive resources and organizations, a large degree of liberalization of trade and prices, and decentralization of economic decision-making. Importantly for the rural economy, Armenia was one of the few former Soviet Republics to privatize agriculture effectively and swiftly during 1991-1992: the overwhelming majority of agricultural land and output is now in small family or peasant farms (Lerman and Mirzakhanian, 2001).

The macroeconomic and structural reforms introduced in 1991-1992 led to a severe economic contraction, followed by a resumption of growth. In 1993, GDP had declined to 43 percent of its 1990 level, and subsequently climbed to 62 percent in 1998. In addition to the shock of system change, violence and natural disaster contributed to a sharp decrease in welfare. In 1990-1994, Armenia was involved in a territorial war, absorbed a large inflow of refugees, and experienced an earthquake affecting 40 percent of its territory and a third of its population. In 1997 a severe drought followed. Per capita levels of income sank during the initial economic decline from US $1,590 in 1990 to US $169 in 1994. Also the composition of income changed. In 1991, salaries comprised 55 percent of incomes. This decreased to 25 percent in 1994. Salaries were replaced by income sources such as humanitarian aid, remittances, and income in-kind. The quality of the average Armenian's diet deteriorated: food consumption declined from 2,181 K-calories in 1991 to 1,599 K-calories on average in 1994, and 97 percent of the population was in so-called 'absolute poverty' in 1994, with a daily per capita income of less than US $1. In 1999, the situation had slightly improved again, with the poor accounting for 55 percent of the population, the "very poor" for 28 percent, and the "extremely poor" for 10 percent. Poverty is concentrated in the cities and among landless rural residents. Since 1993, 500,000 Armenians have emigrated.

Contemporary data on the Armenian rural economy as a whole were, to the best of the authors' knowledge, not available at the time of writing. However, in 1998 a large survey of rural households was implemented, sponsored by the World Bank. The survey covered 75 villages and 7,000 people in 1,500 households, which is 0.5 percent of all Armenian farm households. The following information is based on these survey findings, summarized in Lerman and Mirzakhanian (2001).

The demographic profile of rural Armenia is 35 percent children and youths below 18 years of age, 50 percent of adults between 18 and 59 years of age, and 15 percent of people older than 60. Education levels, inherited from the Soviet system, are high, with 75 percent of men and 45 percent of women having secondary of higher education.

Agricultural underemployment is widespread, but this does not imply a vibrant nonfarm economy: 50 percent of adults do not work full-time on the farm, but only 20 percent have off-farm incomes, either as salaries or in self-employment. Nonfarm income accounts for 72 percent of cash income and half of total income. The main sources are salaries (40 percent) and pensions (23 percent). Remittances from abroad are also quite important (18 percent). Cash savings are held by only 10 percent of respondents, but never in a bank. Only a tenth of respondents saved money in the month prior to the survey.

Rural market development appears very limited, if information provided by farm families is taken as indicative. Land holdings are small, and trade in land is absent. Most (56 percent) farm output is consumed by the farm household, or bartered (5 percent). Produce that is traded (25 percent) is usually sold to individuals rather than to enterprises. Also inputs are almost always bought from private individuals. Food processing occurs on 60 percent of farms, rather than in separate, commercial enterprises. Credit from banks or credit associations is virtually unheard of, although two-thirds of respondents had outstanding, usually small, debts. The source of this borrowing is most often family and friends, who lend against zero or low interest rates and small, usually liquid collateral if at all.

About 45 percent of respondents report they have experienced a serious economic crisis that has endangered the well-being of their family. Rural poverty, even among food producing households, is apparent in the survey. Approximately 40 percent of respondents maintain that their family's diet is poor. Nearly two-thirds eat no meat at all, almost half have two meals a day, and 28 percent skipped meals weekly or daily during the four months preceding the survey. The pattern of these responses is replicated in reported incomes, with an average per capita income of US $1,200 for those reporting a good diet and US $600 for those reporting poor diet. In these data there is a sharp dichotomy between a small group of better-off respondents and the poorer majority; and the same is true for reported housing quality, especially in the former earthquake zone.

As a consequence, 65 percent of respondents complain that they have not enough money for food and basic necessities, and 25 percent have just enough. In comparison, over half considered themselves comfortably off in 1990 and another 30 percent think they had then enough money for food and basic necessities. A widespread coping strategy is mutual assistance. About a fifth of respondents had recently received and extended material or practical help to friends or family.

The Findings from the Field

In the remainder of this paper the findings from a survey conducted in June 2001 in Armenia will be presented, followed by some analyses and implications. The survey research was initiated by the National Resources Institute, and implemented in cooperation with a local survey team. The aim was to gain insight into the nature of the rural nonfarm economy in the country. The focus in this research is now nonfarm rural enterprises. For that purpose, 21 rural communities in three regions (known as *marzes* in Armenian) were non-randomly selected. These *marzes* were Ararat, Gegharkunik and Syunik. Since a prime motivation of the research is to study the potential of the RNFE to alleviate rural poverty through rural nonfarm employment, selection criteria included poverty levels and the level of development of the RNFE. In the three *marzes*, 45 entrepreneurs active in the RNFE were surveyed, 15 from each region[1]. It is hoped that the data will provide a basis for a larger survey of the RNFE in the near future.

We will now provide an overview of the characteristics of micro, small and medium-sized enterprises (SME) in the survey sample. The aim is to explore what the barriers and facilitating factors for SMEs in rural Armenia are, and how features of these enterprises and of the economic environment influence their capacity to contribute to rural employment and incomes.

Personal Data

The average entrepreneur in the sample is a middle-aged, local male of Armenian ethnic background with a high level of education. Over half (24) the respondents have completed higher education, and of the rest, most (19) have completed secondary education (mostly general, in 4 cases professional). The age of respondents was varied: 14 are in the 24-35 age group, 14 in the 36-45 group, 15 in the 46-55 group, and two are over 55 (65 and 77). They were most frequently (39 cases) male and Armenian (44 cases), and mostly have lived in the local area all their life (41 cases). Half (22) the entrepreneurs have dependent children. Most (35) describe their business location as "very" (23) or "moderately" (12) rural. Only one reports living in an urban area.

Unsurprisingly, by far the most important reason for having the business is to provide a main source of income (rank 8 of 10). Also important are the ability to do this work and live in a rural area, to develop a personal interest, and to create jobs (ranks 6, 5, and 5 respectively). The reported present aims of the entrepreneur do, on average, hardly differ from those reported as motivations for starting up the business. There are some motivations that are likely to be satisfied once a business is started, and will then become less important. This is true for the provision of additional income, developing a personal interest, providing employment to family members, and finding a more suitable business. In line with conventional notions of entrepreneurship, obtaining a main source of income remains of paramount importance. Preventing unemployment appears to have become more important, although the importance attached to this change is limited by the small change in score levels that underlies it.

The small average changes in scores and ranking reflect the fact that many respondents do not report changes at all. Studying the subset of respondents who did change their ranking of aims between starting the business and the moment of surveying shows that there are a few significant shifts (scores changing more than one point). The importance of providing an additional source of income rose most dramatically in this group, while that of providing a main source of income fell correspondingly. Providing employment to family members became less important, and being able to spend time in the preferred way became more important. The picture that emerges is that, after the start-up phase, a significant minority of entrepreneurs shift their business priorities away from income and economic security, and towards lifestyle preferences; although this does not affect the primacy of the business as a main income source, even within this group.

Enterprise Characteristics

The enterprises in the sample are specialized. Asked to rank 13 activities in order of importance, only a few respondents use rank 2, and ranks 3-13 are absent. They are all fully involved in nonagricultural activities, but for one respondent who spends a fifth of his time in agricultural production. Most frequently, main activities as reported by the respondents are trade (19 cases) and agricultural processing (10). When classified by product, over half (26) the respondents are linked to the agricultural sector, in almost all cases through food processing or trade in food products.

Most (34) enterprises were established in 1997-2000, and none before 1989. Most (42) were also started by a single person rather than taken over from a family member (1, in 1997) or bought (2, in 1997 and 1999). Most (39) business facilities are owned, the rest are leased. Only nine respondents reported on their firm's legal status, all of whom were classified as self-employed. Sales are most often to individual customers and households (39 cases) and to shops (17 cases). Sales to enterprises and the public sector are more rare (16 cases). The *share* of sales is also largest for those to individual customers and households (72 and 66 percent, respectively). Of the other options only sales to a wholesaler, reported by five respondents, are of similar importance (67 percent). Almost all (40) respondents report a large share (77 percent on average) of customers within a distance of 25 kilometers, and a fifth (9) report that half their sales go to customers more than 150 kilometers away. No export sales were reported.

Suppliers are also mostly located in the local area: 30 respondents report an average 86 percent of inputs suppliers located less than 25 kilometers way, while 21 report large input shares (about two thirds on average) coming from between 25 and 100 kilometers. Two respondents have their inputs supplied from abroad: one from the CIS, the other from EU and other countries (for 85 percent of total inputs).

Labor, Capital, and Finance

Most (28) businesses have other workers besides the entrepreneur. In only five cases this is the spouse, in 24 cases there are nonfamily members in full-time employment. In these 24 enterprises, there are most often (14 cases) up to three employees, with an average of six. Only two respondents are also shareholders in another business, two others have been business owners in the past, and two are employed by someone else.

Table 1. Expenditures and Income in 2000

| Expenditure category | Region averages (1,000 dram) | | | Whole sample (n=45) |
	Syunik (n=15)	Gegharkunik (n=15)	Ararat (n=15)	Mean (SD)
Salary expenditure	568	1,726	416	944 (3,108)
Total expenditure	3,832	3,993	2,450	3,392 (4,984)
Income	1,088	4,706	1,111	2,302 (5,054)
Charges	334	941	331	545 (1,376)
Taxes	2,498	1,111	290	1,299 (4,384)

Note: For the first three columns, one outlier value in Gegharkunik was removed, with expenditures and income around 100 million dram.

About half (21) the respondents report that their workload is roughly the same each week, and nearly a third (13) has seasonal variation. Just over half (24) the respondents work between 41 and 45 hours weekly in their enterprise, with the rest evenly distributed over longer and shorter work hours. About two thirds of the enterprises reported on their registered capital in 2000 and their turnover in 1999. These were 4.3 million dram (n = 29) and 3.7 million on average, but with a large spread (a standard deviation of 9.2 and 8.4 million dram respectively)[2]. Average salary expenditures, total expenditures, and income during the year

2000 were reported by most respondents. Variations across respondents and regions in these variables were large (table 1).

Respondents also reported on their purchases during the year 2000. The items they mentioned were categorized as food (including health) expenditures[3], energy expenditures (electricity, petrol, wood) nonfood purchases (stones, "photography materials"), and other expenditures (e.g. "goods"). Most frequently mentioned are food expenditures (63 times). Productive goods and energy were equally frequent (16 times), and other goods slightly less often (12 times). Expenditure levels follow a similar ranking.

Expenditure patterns varied widely between respondents, with standard deviations between three and seven times average values. Also regional variations were observable. Enterprises in Ararat appear more often engaged in food processing, and have larger input expenditure levels overall (table 2).

Sales reports over the year 2000 confirm that most enterprises are specialized: 36 of 43 respondents reported the sale of one product, four reported two products, and another four reported selling three or more products. Sales are categorized as food products (in all cases processed, e.g. bread, flour, cheese, sausages, and vodka), and nonfood products. Nonfood products include agricultural inputs such as seed and pesticides, industrial products such as bricks and petrol, and craft products such as carpets. Some products are obviously traded rather than produced, such as in the case of petrol, or of the one respondent who buys and sells "photography materials."

Table 2. Expenditure on Inputs in the Year 2000

Input categories	Region averages (1,000 dram)			Whole sample (n=45)
	Syunik (n=15)	Gegharkunik (n=15)	Ararat (n=15)	Mean (SD)
Food products	478	496	1,279	776 (1,396)
Energy	0	260	213	156 (551)
Non-food inputs	48	124	468	225 (638)
Other inputs	195	62	133	129 (434)

Note: Outlier values (expenditures over 10 million dram) were removed.

Over half (27) of the respondents sell food products, in three cases in combination with nonfood products, which are sold by 23 respondents. Food sales, if calculated on the basis of sales volume and unit prices, average 188 million dram, nonfood sales are 166 million dram on average per respondents, both with standard deviations of about four times the average. Fourteen respondents report that they consume some of the produce themselves, the shares varying between one and 50 percent, with an average of 11 percent.

If these sales findings were representative for the Armenian rural economy in general, two things seem most worth noting. The nonfarm rural economy is strongly agriculture-related, mainly through processing but also by providing inputs. The policy question is not what the trade-off between agricultural and nonagricultural employment and incomes is, but what the constraints and incentives for enterprises in the nonagricultural part of the agri-food sector are. Second, rural nonfarm enterprises vary greatly in size as measured in revenue levels. Policies designed to support them should be accordingly flexible. For instance, some of the smaller enterprises might benefit primarily from micro credit schemes, while the medium-sized enterprises may well benefit more effectively from institutional support that develops their marketing capacities, negotiation skills, and accounting practices. While this study suggests that it is unlikely that one hat fits all even in this small sample, the exact nature of such policy differentiation is a matter for further research.

Institutional Environment

For SMEs the distance to key institutions, suppliers, and customers may have a significant impact on a firm's development. Poor infrastructure and telecommunications can retard both SME and village level economic development opportunities. The great distances to key institutions and markets may be an obstacle to the development of competition and/or collaboration between rural enterprises. Therefore, we aimed to address this issue in our SME survey.

It appears that those institutions most frequently used (suppliers, bank, and post office) are in the local economy. Institutions supplying additional services are generally more remote. The considerable standard deviations imply large differences in these factors over respondents. It should be noted that, given the lack of data on transportation infrastructure and relative distance, it is hard to assess to what extent these findings indicate that the factor distance to institutions is a barrier for business operations. Business support, to the extent that it was sought, is mostly found in the private sector. Over the last few years, of the 45 respondents to this question, many had approached a consultant or accountant (reported in 20 cases), a bank manager (17), family and friends (15), trade and professional organizations (14), and contacts in industry (12). Among the public institutions, the local council (13) and *marz* council (12) are most often mentioned, other bodies much less frequently.

The type of assistance sought was most often (21 of 30 responses) financial. Only one respondent had access to the Internet. Given the plausibly considerable need for advice and information and, apparently, still limited role of the public sector in providing this, these figures may be interpreted to suggest that there is scope for expansion. The desirability and effect of this would depend on the extent to which rural entrepreneurs are presently excluded from such support because they cannot afford private sector assistance. This is something that the present data provide no information about.

The reported usefulness of different types of business support appeared much larger in two *marzes* (Gegharkunik and Syunik) than in the third (Ararat).[4] Background data on these regions could provide an interpretation to this finding, and a more detailed regional analysis of this topic, not pursued here, appears promising. First, considering the usefulness in the past, present, future, or in general taken together, support in the area of "new technology" is found to be most often mentioned overall. Least frequently mentioned are "employing staff," "management organization" and "computing." These are understandable findings in a sample from micro-businesses with low technological requirements and virtually no access to information technology. The other ten business support options are mentioned with very similar total frequencies.

The incidence of nonresponse in the second column suggests that respondents seem to have been less aware of past needs, than of present and, particularly, future requirements. With regard to the past, business strategies and staff training and development are, understandably for (then) starting businesses, ranked highest. The main present need is reportedly negotiating skills, while support in obtaining technology and developing new products and services are seen as the most important future requirements. In general, market research and support in financial topics is deemed most helpful. These findings appear to fit well in a sample of relatively young businesses just out of the starting phase, and could be used to guide the development of policies in support of the Armenian nonfarm rural economy.

Of the 45 entrepreneurs, 40 responded to a question about the importance of various local factors for their business. Most factors (which were ranked in descending importance, at a scale from 10 to 1) are much more often deemed of high than of medium importance. This is true for the top seven factors ('electricity costs' down to 'access to water'). Most factors are considered of medium importance, only one is deemed highly important, and no factor is considered of low importance on average (i.e. has a mean higher than 2.5). Many factors are considered about equally important (mean 1.7-1.9). The high importance of electricity costs suggests that many businesses are energy-intensive. This is probably not true for the 19 trade businesses in the sample, but would fit better with the 10 processing enterprises.

Legal safety in Armenia is assessed as low by most (28 of 42) respondents, and of medium quality by the rest. Almost all (43) respondents rank the importance of various local development factors. The two most general options elicited the most positive response on average, and were nearly equal in average score: nonagricultural development was most uniformly supported as most important, while agricultural development was more often assigned slightly less importance. The more abstract rural development goals (locally suitable projects; community effort; local autonomy) were seen as less important, the more concrete projects generally as more important (but for tourism). Development goals not directly related to the local community (reform progress and foreign cooperation) ranked, understandably, low.

Credit

Capital shortage reportedly inhibits business growth in 20 cases, of which 13 also plan to expand their business. For 12 respondents capital shortage is no constraint, of whom only five also plan to expand. Most of those who are capital-constrained feel this hinders an increase in turnover (14) and in acquiring fixed assets (12). One respondent would expand business staff if there were better access to capital. The most frequently mentioned reason for capital shortage is a lack of own capital or of collateral to attract it (17 cases) ("lack of funds," which appears to refer to the same, is also mentioned twice). Also attitudes to debt appear to be important: over half (11) of capital-constrained respondents report they "do not like borrowing." Five give as the constraining reasons that they are already in debt, thirteen mention high interest rates, three think the bank assessed the risk attached to their business as too high, and eight have problems obtaining a grant.

In sum, limitations in access to credit or other funds are quite general, and derive from a number of factors. On the demand side there is a limited debt-carrying capacity (in turn caused by lack of collateral and by debt-averse attitudes). On the supply side, possibly insufficient risk assessment skills in banks, and high interest rates appear to play a role. The findings suggest that relaxation of the capital constraint would probably result in output expansion, but not clearly in more rural employment.

Indeed, the only constraint on production reported is capital, not labor, land, buildings or other factors offered as answer options. Of those indicating a capital constraint, over two-thirds (33) specify that working capital is the bottleneck. The amount needed to solve the problem is reported at 11.2 million dram on average. The other respondents say capital for investment is needed (4.9 million dram on average).

Many respondents are also liquidity-constrained: most (34 of 45) respondents think profit is insufficient to cover costs for equipment replacement, premises refurbishment and such; another 10 feel they can cover those costs by profits, but with difficulty. Still, the majority (30) have not applied for a loan in the past five years. Those who did apply were evenly distributed over successful loan applications (7) and loan refusals (8). The average loan sum obtained was 7.5 million dram (with observations varying between 0.5 and 2.7 million dram), most often (in 5 cases) from a bank. Only three out of 45 respondents had applied for a grant in the last five years, and unsuccessfully so far: one was refused, two had not yet received a reply.

Only six of 45 respondents applied for a loan in the year 2000. Half of them did not receive credit; in two cases because of a lack of collateral, and once because nobody would guarantee the loan. The most frequent (26 of 39) reason for not applying for credit at all is that assessment criteria are deemed too severe. The severity of credit allocation criteria is most often (15) specified as overly high interest rates, and half as often (8) as lack of collateral. Six respondents indicated their income to be too low to meet repayment demands. The only other reason for not applying that is mentioned with some frequency (5) was good access to funds via friends and family. The rest of the answer options are never used more than twice in the sample.

Five respondents who did not obtain a loan from an institution, borrowed from friends or family in 2000. The amounts borrowed (in 1,000 dram) were 6,871, 100, 165, 500, and 130. The first two of these were obtained at zero interest rates; the last three at 5 percent. No bribes or gifts were given in exchange for obtaining the loan. A fifth (9) of the respondents had saved from their enterprise profits in 2000. The levels varied widely, both between respondents and over time. Only one of the respondents held these savings in a bank, at an annual interest rate of 26 percent.

Plans

Most respondents are optimistic but cautious with regard to the near future: 19 planned a slight business expansion over the next two years, 13 aimed at stability in that period. Of the other 13, 6 did not know about their plans. Over the longer term, respondents in large majority (39 of 44) aim at stability, while five plan slight expansion.

Nearly a third (13) of respondents think there is demand for increased production, but more respondents (19) deem demand to be a constraint on business expansion. The large number of respondents (13) who do not know the answer may signify considerable uncertainty about market conditions. Most (32) enterprises work below production capacity, and also a large minority (18) plan to expand the business. The numbers of respondents who are not planning to expand, or in doubt about this, are about similar (13 and 14). The main determinant of this attitude may be demand: most (11) of those who hesitate about expansion also report to be uncertain about market demand for increased production. Problems with finding space is an expansion constraint for nine respondents, most (6) of whom are actually planning to expand. In five of these nine cases, refused permission to expand is the reason of the constraint. In the other cases space on the business premises is too limited. None of the respondents report staffing problems as a constraint.

Analysis: Profit, Employment, and Income

In addition to this overview of the characteristics of rural enterprises and the experiences of rural entrepreneurs, it would be useful to explore the determinants of enterprise performance in the setting of the Armenian rural economy. The modest size of the data set obviously limits the scope for statistically valid inferences. Still, it is possible to go a bit beyond mere description and explore the links between performance, factor endowments, and economic environment. We will here investigate possible determinants of profit and employment. Profit is a traditional enterprise performance indicator, while the capacity of rural enterprises to generate employment is an important factor in the development of the rural economy and the income level of the rural population.

Table 3. Enterprise Characteristics in Survey by Region

	Syunik	SD	Gegharkunik	SD	Ararat	SD	Total sample	SD
Number of firms	15		15		15		45	
In retail	10		12		8		10	
Employment (full-time equivalents)	3.7	(2.9)	9.6	(13.1)	3.7	(3.3)	5.6	(8.3)
Salaries	416	(281)	3,277	(7,734)	568	(352)	1,577	(4,963)
Non-salary expenditures	2,034	(1,832)	6,784	(17,720)	4,336	(5,384)	4,392	(11,291)
Profit	43	(911)	1,007	(1,687)	513	(1,030)	522	(1,301)
Sapital stock	2,957	(2,137)	11,687	(26,570)	16,927	(43,359)	10,226	(28,417)

Note: The reported figures are averages and, in parentheses, standard deviations. Financial figures are in 1,000 Dram and reported on a monthly basis.

Profit

A prime enterprise performance measure is profit. What determines firm profit in our sample? A simple profit model based on a Cobb-Douglas production function is specified. Independent variables include EMPLOY (total employment)[5], EXPEND (reported expenditures other than salaries), and CAPITAL (the reported value of the capital stock), as independent variables. The dependent variable is PROFIT, the reported level of profit.[6] All variables relate to the year 2000. The exponential Cobb-Douglas profit function is transformed into a linear regression equation by taking logarithms of all variables. The model fit with a logged Cobb-Douglas specification is found to be much better than for a simple linear specification. The estimation results are presented in table 4.

In this specification, coefficient values can be interpreted as measures for return to factor inputs.[7] It is interesting to note that capital expenditures generate the highest return, followed by capital stock and labor. This conforms to the general notion that capital is more productive than labor.

Table 4. An Estimated Profit Function

Dependent variable ln (PROFIT)	Standarized coefficient values	t-values	Signifi-cance	Adjusted R^2
Independent variables (C = -3.401)[*]				0.81
Ln (EMPLOY)	0.298	3.201	0.003	
Ln (EXPEND)	0.424	4.037	0.000	
Ln (CAPITAL)	0.360	3.666	0.001	

[*]C is the constant.

It was also noted earlier that most respondents are capital but not labor constrained. By implication, this constraint significantly hinders the generation of profit increases, which would derive more from investment than from labor additions. However, the credit constraint is likely to constrain employment indirectly, since capital investments may be accompanied by an increase in the labor force. This will be explored below.

Is amount of input the only determinant of output? Many theories on firm production suggest the role of human capital, institutional and regional variables. On the basis of this production-model approach, a series of specifications introducing these factors were explored. However, none of these variables had coefficient estimates that had values comparable to the above; and none of the coefficient estimates was statistically significant ($p < 0.10$). It appears that the profit function of enterprises in the sample mainly contains the conventional factors of production (although this still leaves a fifth of profit variations unaccounted for). In exploring the impact of institutional and regional factors, one would therefore more usefully investigate their relation to the level and efficiency of factors of production, rather than their impact on profit levels directly. This is left for future work.

Employment

Employment is not traditionally seen as an enterprise performance indicator. However, in the context of enterprises as potential motors of rural development, the idea is relevant. Enterprises that are able to generate more employment are more useful in combating unemployment and generating rural incomes. Here we explore the determinants of employment in our sample. Table 5 presents four relevant variables that appeared to explain most of the variation in employment levels in an ordinary least squares (OLS) regression estimation. These are RETAIL (the share of enterprise output sold to households and individuals, rather than to enterprises), BANKLOAN (a binary variable indicting whether the enterprise has obtained a loan in the last 5 years), CAPITAL, and EXPEND.

Table 5. Factors Controlling Employment Level

Dependent variable: EMPLOY	Standardized coefficient values	t-values	Signifi-cance	Adjusted R^2
Independent variables (C = 4.314)[*]				0.86
RETAIL	-0.137	-2.192	0.036	
BANKLOAN	0.133	2.107	0.043	
EXPEND	-0.123	-4.104	0.000	
CAPITAL	2.092	6.992	0.000	

[*]C is the constant.

The largest estimated coefficient is associated with the amount of capital goods. Thus, it turns out that the constraint on finances to invest in capital may also be a major barrier to employment expansion, as was suggested above. It may be noted that this is in line with respondents' own replies, although in an indirect manner. Most of them reported that they would use extra funds for investment rather than employment. The estimation results suggest that via investment extra employment would be generated.

Respondents' access to credit over the last five years is also associated with higher employment, although less clearly than in the case of capital stock. This appears to lend some support to the prominence of credit allocation in thinking and research on rural development (see e.g. Heidhues et al., 1999 for an application to transition economies). It should however be noted that the causality here can also run the other way. Larger enterprises with more employment often have better access to credit for reasons of social capital and political economy.

Other, but clearly less important, determinants are negative. They include the level of expenditure on flexible inputs (which are apparently substitutes for labor), and the sector: retail enterprises employ fewer people than other enterprises. We have observed that most enterprises sell to individual customers. This is in line with the general prevalence of small retail and services businesses in the private sector in transition economies. Obviously this feature of the non-agricultural private economy in Armenia, and plausibly elsewhere, limits the scope for employment creation.

As to policy, this raises the eternal question of whether support programs should focus just on program objectives–e.g. employment creation–or on constraints imposed by the economic environment. We think that the design of employment creation programs would need to take existing entrepreneurial choices into account. Retail firms are apparently preferred by rural entrepreneurs themselves, and can therefore be assumed to be best suited to this particular economic environment. We argue that employment programs should 'follow the market' in this respect in order to create sustainable improvement. Even though non-retail firms were found to create more employment, they should not be promoted for this reason only. Enterprises must be able to survive also when program support is withdrawn, and the best indication in these data is that retail firms would be most viable.

Employment, Income, and Enterprise Size: A Regional Exploration

It is useful to note that some variables in the sample did not appear to influence employment levels, although they might be expected to. This includes the size of the enterprises in terms of revenues or profit level. This finding is in line with the large variation in capital intensity and associated labor intensity over firms in the sample. While the above results show the link between, particularly, capital investments and employment, earlier findings suggest there are large differences in the strength of this link over regions and sectors in the rural economy.

It was not possible to explore this using regression analysis because of the small size of the sample. As an alternative method of exploration, the average of the ratio of employment over capital stock, non-salary expenditures, revenue level, and profit was computed for each region. Apart from employment, the same was done with the variables "income" and "total salaries" in the nominator of the ratio. All in all, for each region twelve ratios were calculated, i.e. all combinations of employment, income, and salaries in the nominator and capital stock, non-salary expenditures, profit, and sales in the denominator.

The limited size of the sample did not allow significant differences between most ratios in comparisons between the regions. The only significant differences were in three ratios: of employment over revenues, of entrepreneurial income over capital stock, and of income over non-salary expenditures. Differences between these ratios in comparisons of the regions Gegharkunik and Ararat were not significant. In comparisons of the regions Syunik and Ararat, as well as Syunik and Gegharkunik, there were significant differences. These findings are presented in Table 6.

These findings must be seen as tentative given the nature of the data, and can be summarized as follows. First, enterprises in Syunik are less labor-intensive and generate less income per unit of capital goods than in the other two regions. Second, enterprises in Gegharnukik generate much more income relative to expenditures than enterprises in Syunik and Ararat (although this last observation is not supported in terms of statistical significance).

One implication appears to be that growth of the rural nonfarm economy in Gegharkunik in terms of revenue, capital stock, or in terms of capital expenditures, would result in a clearly larger increase in income and employment than is the case in Syunik (and probably also Ararat). Although the small sample size makes these sorts of inferences difficult, the results are indicative for the relevance of enterprise structures for the income and employment effects of rural economic development.

Table 6. Regional Differences in Employment and Income Relative to Capital and Revenue Level

	Regions			
	Syunik	Gegharkunik	Ararat	Whole sample
Employment divided by sales	0.39	0.90*	0.51*	0.61
Income divided by capital stock	0.61	1.76*	1.62	1.32
Income divided by Non-salary expenditures	2.81	9.14*	2.60*	4.90

*These values are significantly different relative to Syunik at 0.05 level; the differences between Gegharkunik and Ararat are not significant.

Conclusions

In this paper a general overview of issues and findings on the rural non-agricultural economy in the transition countries was combined with a study based on primary data from Armenia. Countries in the post-socialist transition have suffered from initial contraction and subsequently from often insufficient growth. In addition, inequality in incomes and other welfare components has generally increased substantially. A general result, particularly in the Balkan and FSU states, is a significant increase in poverty. In rural areas, these trends were in many instances (though not always and everywhere) exacerbated by the rural-urban income gap and by the collapse of socialist-era rural industries. The agricultural sector, most often the largest in the rural economy, is not likely to become a motor of rural economic growth in view of longer-term trends in developing and developed countries, and also because of its continuing post-socialist restructuring challenge. These observations suggest that the role of non-agricultural rural economy in rural development, and more specifically poverty alleviation and regionally balanced economic development, is a useful research topic.

The substantial literature on rural nonfarm development lends some support to this expectation, although findings are clearly country and situation-specific. A finding that can be generalized appears to be that public investment (in education, in the quality of infrastructure, and in market structures) is an important determinant of the capacity for rural growth, and of its effect on income inequality.

Two stages in rural economic growth are discerned. In one, rural non-agricultural incomes are a refuge from poverty, and rural diversification a defensive strategy that implies a shift to low-return activities in order to preserve household income, generally without achieving local economic growth. This description applies generally to the CIS and Balkan countries. The other, and subsequent, stage has been entered by most Central European countries. Here rural manufacturing, trade, and services are a response to new market opportunities, bring higher returns than agricultural production, and signify genuine rural economic growth.

Although the rural nonagricultural sector in transition countries has been found to be substantial, the above observations indicate that the significance, in economic terms, of the sector is not unambiguous. These ambiguities, combined with the plausibly large size and potential of the rural nonagricultural sector, warrants more research into this issue.

This is taken up in the second part of the paper, where survey data on non-farm enterprises in rural Armenia are studied. A sample of 45 businesses in three regions was surveyed in the summer of 2001. The findings can be summarized as follows:

- Nearly all enterprises are specialized, profit-oriented businesses providing a full income to the entrepreneur and employees.
- The capacity for salaried employment is limited per enterprise to a few employees; but in many cases entrepreneurial income sustains people in and beyond the entrepreneur's household through unpaid labor.
- There are very large variations in the financial features of enterprises, including cost, revenue, and profit levels.
- There are strong links with the agricultural sector through food processing or trade in food products.
- Marketing channels are generally in the local economy and small-scale, with most firms in retail.
- Liquidity and capital constraints are general, and the most important constraint to expansion, or indeed operation, is access to credit.
- The role of public institutions in business support appears very limited, although there is much to be improved in factors that are usually in the domain of public action, such as legal safety and infrastructure quality.

The data are also used to undertake some basic explorations of the determinants of profit, employment, and incomes generated in the enterprises. Profit levels are satisfactorily explained by conventional inputs: labor, fixed capital, and inputs. Of these, employment is of special interest from a rural development point of view. It appears that the size of the labor force, though modest in all cases, is linked to the level of fixed capital, and to access to credit. It is also negatively associated with the share of retail sales, and with capital input expenditures.

There appear to be important regional differences in the relation between employment and income on the one hand, and businesses' capital stock and levels of revenues and expenditure on the other. This confirms the idea that expansion of the rural nonfarm sector is likely to have very different implications for rural employment and rural incomes in different regions. The findings show both how this type of research can be relevant for directing policy on rural development, and the limitations imposed by a relatively small sample.

Notes

The study was prepared as part of the Natural Resources Institute project entitled "Characterization and Analysis of the Nonfarm Rural Sector in Transition Economies" undertaken for the World Bank and Department for International Development (DFID).

1.   The communities surveyed were, in Marz Ararat: Hovtashen, Kaghtsrashen, Ajgepar, Mkhchyan, Dzorak, Dashtavan, Ararat. In Marz Siunik: Tolors, Uts, Akhlatyan,

Shake, Ishkhanasar, Akner, Verishen. In Marz Gegharkunik: Ljashen, Tsovazard, Gandzak, Karmir Gyugh, Noraduz, Chkalovka, Sarukhan.

2.   The Armenian currency, the Dram, which was introduced in 1993. After initial hyperinflation, the Dram value had been quite stable since 1995. Its value is about 500 dram to the US dollar (in 1998).

3.   Food items mentioned include agricultural products, bakery products, medicines, black oil, fish, bread, flour, cigarettes, food products, fat, meat, milk, syrup, bread, salt, wheat, vodka, cigarettes, spices, water, salt, yeast, sugar, garlic, and vegetables.

4.   The 30 respondents from Gegharkunik and Syunik all provide an answer to each of the 14 sub questions. The 15 respondents from Ararat have many missing values.

5.   The entrepreneur's labor input in hours per week was divided by 50 in order to get full-time units. Spouse, family and non-family were recorded as one full-time unit (full-time employee and active partner), 0.5 (part-time or frequently helping out) or 0.25 (occasionally helping out) per person. Then all was added to get total labour input in full-time equivalents. Because many enterprises have less than one full-time equivalent of labour (resulting in negative log-values), EMPLOY was measures in tenths of full-time labour equivalents. Replacing employment by salaries as independent variable increasing the adjusted R^2 to 0.78, and gives a large (0.403) and very significant (0.001) coefficient estimate for ln (SALARIES). However, since SALARIES does not account for non-paid labour, EMPLOY is a better measure for labour input.

6.   The validity of this variable was checked by calculating gross margins on the basis of reported sales and revenues. Reported profit was always smaller than gross margins, and in the same order of magnitude. This supported the validity of reported profit. The distribution of ln (PROFIT) is skewed. Therefore 0.2 is raised to the power of ln (PROFIT). The resulting variable is approximately normally distributed and used in the linear regression estimation. This implies that the values of coefficients need to be transformed in order to show their impact on profit. Since we are only interested in the values of coefficients relative to each other, these results are not discussed.

7.   Because the coefficients are standardized and differences in value between them are significant, their values can be meaningfully compared.

Rural Credit Institutions in Kyrgyzstan: The Practice of Transition Aid

Mathijs Pelkmans

During the first half of the 1990s Kyrgyzstan was repeatedly praised for its speed in reforming its political and economic structures. The Western press and especially representatives of multilateral organizations portrayed the country as the "Switzerland of Central Asia," "an example for most countries in the world,"[1] and as the 'wonder-child in the CIS.'[2] Now, ten years after independence, little resembles these fairy-tale like images. Kyrgyzstan received more transition aid per capita than any other Central Asian state, but it is unclear what the influence of this aid has been. The supposed transition to democracy and capitalism seems to have been only partially successful, especially considering the reports of nepotism and widespread corruption, and indications that recovery of the sharply reduced economy remains shaky and uncertain.[3]

The capitalist experiment in Kyrgyzstan illustrates many of the problems connected with the implementation of a Western development model in societies with barely any experience with a market economy. As such, Kyrgyzstan is an interesting case to illuminate the collision of Western development efforts and post-socialist reality.[4] The aim of this paper is to reflect on both the limits and possibilities of transition aid, using the *Participatory Poverty Alleviation Project* (PPAP) started by UNDP in 1998, as an example. The main goal of this project was to initiate a structure that would enable credit disbursement to broad layers of the population, in order to stimulate small-scale economic initiatives. The project's trajectory will be analyzed to show some of the complexities inherent in initiating economic change, and to provide insight into the role of and interaction between the state, financial institutions and the local population.

Reforming the Kyrgyz Economy

Like all republics in the FSU, Kyrgyzstan faced severe economic problems in the early 1990s. Kyrgyzstan was constrained by its lack of raw materials and unfortunate geographical location. These constraints–coupled with the economic crises of 1991 and 1992, which led to a sharp reduction in production in industry and agriculture–convinced the government that economic development could only be achieved with foreign aid and investment. It was assumed that rapid adoption of market reforms and the creation of a law-governed democracy would give Kyrgyzstan a head start in a region otherwise rather wary of market reform.

Kyrgyzstan opted for a shock therapy-type of transition strategy and closely cooperated with the IMF and the World Bank. The principles of structural adjustment were laid down in successive agreements, bearing a strong focus on reducing inflation and budget deficits, regulation of the foreign debt, and large-scale privatization of the still sizable state sector (UNDP, 1997: 4-5). These reforms were deemed highly successful and as early as 1994 a representative of the IMF noted that everything was in place at the macroeconomic level–the introduction of the new currency had been successful, inflation had been tamed and trade had been fully liberated.[5]

However, in the middle of the 1990s some observers remarked that the macroeconomic reforms were merely a facade for chaos at the micro level. Spoor (1995) concluded that instead of using the terms "shock therapy" or "fast reformer," it would be more applicable to speak of "hasty" or "unprepared reforms." These hasty reforms often had disastrous consequences for the economy. The dismantling of the socialist economy had in fact only been partially accompanied by factual restructuring of the economy. In the course of a few years the entire infrastructure deteriorated, energy distribution became problematic and new laws were not only poorly designed, but also often unknown to those who had to implement them.

Economic recovery was very slow and, except for the numerous small-traders, levels of economic initiative were disappointing. Moreover, macroeconomic stabilization did not prevent the further decline of living standards. The percentage of the population living below the poverty line increased from 45 percent in 1993 to 60 percent in 1996 and recent information suggests that the trend is continuing.[6]

Problems in the Rural Sector: Lack of Financial Sources

The privatization of the rural sector is a typical example of the haphazard way the economy was transformed. New privatization laws were adopted quickly–in line with the demands of multilateral organizations–but without having secured consensus within the government. Moreover, the government neglected to provide the population with sufficient information on the reforms. Lack of transparency within the privatization process resulted in great irregularities, which generally meant that the local elite with access to information and with connections in the administration was able to get hold of most assets.[7] As a result of the general confusion and as a response to the uncertainty concerning the status of property, many former *kolkhozniki* decided simply to slaughter their own cattle. The half-hearted reforms resulted in dramatic decreases in agricultural production.[8] A quick recovery of the rural sector did not take place and the rural population returned to subsistence agriculture rather than to produce for the market (Anderson, 1999; Spoor, 1995).

One of the largest problems for renewed rural development was the lack of adequate financial structures that would enable investment in small agricultural farms. Although in the 1990s a multitude of commercial banks were established, their services were mostly restricted to the capital Bishkek and fell short of covering actual demand in the rest of the country. Thus, in 1998, it was estimated that 70 percent of the population did not have access to financial institutions (Wadhwa, 1998: 8).[9]

Moreover, as a result of continuing inflation and high default rates, interest rates remained endemically high. Private lenders asked interest rates of 20 to 30 percent per month, while commercial banks applied rates of 50 to 100 percent per year. Such percentages greatly exceeded the relatively small profit margin of agricultural activities, especially because investments in animal husbandry or crop cultivation only generate profits after a year or longer.

Without a radical change in the financial structure it was improbable that credit services would become accessible to the majority of small farmers. In fact, poor small farmers were simply not interesting clients for commercial banks. Both technical and psychological factors were responsible for this situation. In order to guarantee repayment, banks generally demanded a large number of official documents from their clients, which made the costs of receiving small loans disproportionally high.[10] Small farmers could simply not afford to apply for such credits.

Moreover, under conventional credit practices administrative costs were too high to make disbursement of small credits (of a few hundred dollars) profitable for banks. Another reason that explains the bank's reluctance to grant loans to farmers was a general distrust of poor villagers. They reasoned that since rich clients had so many problems repaying loans, poor villagers would probably not repay at all and enforcing repayment would be either too costly or impossible.

The Participatory Poverty Alleviation Project: Structure, Characteristics, and Goals

In 1998 UNDP and the Kyrgyz Agricultural Finance Cooperation (KAFC) signed a cooperation treaty to jointly provide micro-credit to groups of poor farmers. The KAFC was responsible for the actual disbursement of loans and had received a long-term interest-free credit from IFAD of 1.5 million dollars for this purpose.[11] For its part, UNDP was responsible for the social aspects of the project. In other words, it prepared groups for credit eligibility and monitored the credit process. In order to guarantee the sustainability of the micro-credit approach, the project had to address two major issues. First, it was necessary to design new micro-credit mechanisms that could replace the conventional crediting policies used by the KAFC. Second, in the villages where the project would be introduced, there was a need to create social structures that would facilitate the preparation of credit groups and that would deal with problems of repayment level.

The KAFC was the successor to the Soviet *Agroprombank*, which had collapsed in the beginning of the 1990s. Although the KAFC was an independently operating financial institution, it was closely linked to the Kyrgyz government, which had established the KAFC to address the lack of financing in the rural sector. Given this background, it is not surprising that, until 1998, the KAFC had disbursed credit solely to large agro-business and cooperatives. Nevertheless the bank was selected as a partner in the project for several reasons. It had a relatively young management with a positive attitude towards alternative credit management. In fact, the KAFC had already received technical aid for this purpose from TACIS. Moreover, the bank possessed a large number of branches throughout the country, which was a necessary precondition for micro-credit operations.[12] To allow for the disbursement of credits of 5,000 som per person (approximately US $150) it was necessary to introduce new credit mechanisms that would minimize both transaction costs and repayment risks. The applied principle was based on social collateral.

To circumvent the need for physical collateral, loans were disbursed to groups of five to twelve people who were responsible for repayment as a group. Moreover, future credit disbursement within a given village was made dependent on the timely and complete repayment of already financed credit groups.[13] Another measure taken to reduce administrative costs was assessment and approval of the applications by local village associations.

The structure outlined above enabled the KAFC to apply relatively low interest rates. The rates of 28 percent and 32 percent per year covered inflation and the administrative costs of the financial institution but did not include a profit margin. The KAFC expected that if clients were successful, they would take out larger follow-up loans and that these loans would generate profit.

The implementation of such a financial structure strongly depended on a social network that could guarantee the coordination and functioning of the implicated activities. The task of the UNDP staff was to establish such structures in designated pilot villages and small towns. Their work started at grassroots level by initiating or strengthening informal groups made up of former colleagues, neighbors, or, for example, ex-classmates. Participants received short courses in bookkeeping, and marketing and financial mechanisms. Potential credit groups were also required to attend workshops and informal meetings to develop their group structure and to write a business plan.

This preparation phase lasted six months on average. The goal of the preparations was not simply to teach practical skills–some of them were quite redundant–but rather to enhance and test group cohesion. During this period special attention was given to the obligatory informal savings funds that were set up within the groups. The savings funds were meant to create an internal emergency fund and more importantly, the way a group managed these funds served as a reliable indicator of their relative cohesion.[14]

A crucial and tricky element in the project design was to organize village associations in order to regulate coordination between the various groups. These associations consisted of representatives of each group and several respected community-members, usually elderly men (*aksakals*). In due course the village associations were expected to take over the coordination of credit disbursement in their villages by forming a link between the affiliated farmers and the financial institutions. Credit services would be sustainable after a period of four years–the life span of the UNDP project–only if these structures operated well.

The model outlined above was not an externally prescribed blueprint, but instead evolved from discussions between the various groups involved and was repeatedly adjusted during the first year of the project. However, this does not mean that it was successful in all cases. Problems frequently arose during application. These problems can best be illustrated by reference to specific cases, showing progress and setbacks in a small industrial town and in a more or less typical rural setting. The town of Kok-Jangak and the village of Bai-Munduz are both located in Jalal-Abad province in Southern Kyrgyzstan, where the project was initiated in fourteen villages and small towns.

Surviving in Kok-Jangak

The economic decline that followed the disintegration of the Soviet Union turned Kok-Jangak into a ghost town. By 1998 approximately 3,000 miners had already lost their jobs in the destitute coal mine, while the textile and radio factories had long closed their gates. Of the 25,000 people that had inhabited Kok-Jangak at the end of the 1980s, approximately 16,000 had left the town for good. Because of the deplorable living conditions Kok-Jangak quickly attracted the attention of aid agencies. They tried to alleviate the problems with grant and emergency aid, but they had very little lasting effect. In fact, the combination of severe economic decline and an overwhelming amount of uncoordinated and ill-prepared aid projects turned out to be a dangerous mix. Within a few years a wide variety of local NGOs had been set up in Kok-Jangak. They were hardly known by the majority of the population, but they received one grant after the other from international donors.[15] The leaders of these newly established NGOs often saw foreign aid agencies as a lucrative source of income that—with some ingenuity—could easily be tapped.[16]

Given these circumstances, it is hardly surprising that the implementation of the *Poverty Alleviation Project* was problematic in Kok-Jangak.[17] Various NGOs and influential people tried to advance their own interests. In fact, at one point the police commander visited the regional UNDP office, and demanded that a special credit group be set up for *his* men.[18] Eventually the project started to work with eight groups. Six were formed after several informal visits to two neighborhoods, during which the mechanisms of the project were explained and discussed. The other two groups, in contrast, were nominated by local NGOs. These two groups were initially accepted because they genuinely consisted of poor inhabitants and seemed to meet the criteria of the project—but also because the UNDP fieldworkers did not want to strain relations with local NGOs.

One of the poorest credit groups in Kok-Jangak had adopted the name *Yntymak* ("friendship"). The group consisted of eight female neighbors who had already developed close contacts of mutual aid. As single or divorced mothers they barely survived the economic changes. They relied on irregular and insufficient state allowances and poorly paid administrative jobs for their income. In terms of the project *Yntymak* formed the ideal group. The group cohesion was strong, the members were highly motivated and they freely expressed their ideas during noisy group discussions. As was pointed out before, the project demanded that the groups established their own internal savings fund. Although in principle, they were free to define the terms of such a fund, like most groups, *Yntymak* set up a rotating savings fund. The women borrowed the accumulated sum in turn, but only after having written down how the money would be used. Every two weeks the women discussed the results and the amount—with 5 percent interest added—was allocated to the next member in line. During one of these discussions a woman said that she had used the money to make pastries and sold these on the market, but that she had hardly made any profit. The other women were ready with advice and discussed innovative ways of producing cheaper pastries without incurring complaints from customers.

Nevertheless, application for credit turned out to be problematic. In their business plans, the majority wished to use the credit for the purchase of cows. The reason for their choice was understandable. Having young children at home, fresh milk was a desirable addition to the sober diet. However, simple profit analysis showed that keeping a cow would not be profitable in their case. The application that the KAFC eventually accepted was a compromise. The women collectively bought one cow, but used the bulk of the loan for the purchase of poultry. The remaining 25 percent of the loan was set aside to enlarge their internal rotating fund for individual trading activities. Repayment of the credit did not raise any real problems and at the end of the year the group had a net profit of one cow and 120 chickens.

Not all credit groups were equally successful. Nurlan Kabaev was the leader of a group of former miners and in all modesty he had given the group his own first name. The group enrolled in the project on the recommendation of a local NGO, of which Nurlan's wife was an active member. Whereas most groups had difficulties in formulating their future economic activities, the *Nurlan* group already possessed a solid business plan, which contained detailed calculations and timetables on the management of a beef and poultry farm, and the organization of corn and potato cultivation. Stables for the animals had already been arranged, consisting of an abandoned apartment complex that the local authorities had allocated "free of cost" to Nurlan.

On paper everything looked fine, but in practice problems quickly rose. After the group had met a few times, it turned out to be virtually impossible for Nurlan to get all his members together. Likewise, the set up of an informal savings fund turned out to be problematic for the group. Although amounts were meticulously written down in a log, in reality no money was saved. Eventually the credit application was turned down by the KAFC. The main problem was that the majority of the members showed little interest or initiative. The group was constructed on the principle of patronage that resembled the Soviet way of doing things. One person takes the initiative, gathers a number of people and of course also receives the bulk of the profit. Because the KAFC granted the loans on the basis of social collateral, this hierarchical structure involved a high risk as it prohibited strong internal group cohesion.

Joint Effort in Bai-Munduz

Bai-Munduz is a small rural community with approximately 200 houses, located along the edge of the Ferghana Valley. Most of the local people used to be employed in the local collective farm (*kolkhoz*), whose administrative buildings were located in the neighboring village. The dismantling of collective agriculture had harsh consequences for the village. Because most farmers had no financial reserves, dependency on costly agreements with brokers greatly increased. Generally, these agreements meant that the broker financed fertilizer, pesticides and transport on condition that the farmer would sell the harvest at a greatly reduced price. Even those villagers who had no need to enter in such unequal relations, still had great difficulty in improving their economic position. The limited diversification of Kyrgyz agriculture, the lack of storage facilities and the fragmented character of markets, resulted in extreme fluctuations in the prices of the most important crops. Villagers without sufficient financial resources were forced to sell their produce at the moment that prices were lowest, while agricultural inputs like fertilizer, seeds, pesticides and petrol were bought when prices were highest.

In spite of these problems the prospects of the inhabitants of Bai-Munduz seemed promising. The village was located along the main transit road, not far from one of the bigger regional markets. The fields were fertile, allowing the cultivation of cotton and tobacco, both relatively profitable crops. In several respects Bai-Munduz was the opposite of Kok-Jangak. The former *kolkhozniki* had been left alone since the *kolkhoz* was disbanded, which meant that daily life was less interwoven with bureaucratic structures. Although there were several "rich" villagers, the difference in living standards was much less pronounced than in Kok-Jangak. Moreover, the villagers had no experience with aid organizations, which paradoxically eased the implementation of the project.

One of the groups in Bai-Munduz had adopted the name *Maksat* ("hope"). The members were of the same age group and had known each other since childhood. They had already applied for credit through the KAFC once before, but this attempt had failed because of their inability to provide sufficient collateral. The men stressed that the main reason for the refusal to grant them credit was that corrupt bank employees would only provide a loan in exchange for the payment of an additional 10 percent on top of the regular interest rate.

Maksat's business plan was very simple. They intended to rent four hectares of land to cultivate cotton. During the assessment of their plan a KAFC credit specialist asked them whether they understood that they had to pay interest on the credit. After all, they would receive money in January, but the bulk of expenditures would be made in April or May. This meant that during the first three months—according to their business plan—interest would accumulate on unused credit. This question started a heated discussion, which showed that the group had planned in detail how to invest the money. From January to April they would raise young bulls and sell these again around the time that agricultural inputs for the cultivation of cotton had to be purchased. The group knew exactly how to proceed, but it had been too difficult for them to translate this formally into writing. The KAFC decided nevertheless to grant them the credit on the basis of their simple business plan. After four months of buying and selling cattle, the group had already made enough money to repay the bank, but preferred to stick to the repayment schedule in order to be able to further expand their economic activities.

In Bai-Munduz, as in every village where the project was operating, a village association was created, consisting of representatives of the credit groups and respected elderly men. The effectiveness of this specific village association became clear when a conflict arose in one of the groups. This group had already received credit, but decided at the last minute not to trust one of its members. This member made his dissatisfaction clear to one of the representatives of village association, who in turn demanded a special meeting. The association decided that the group did not have to give the money to the distrusted member, but instead had to return the money to the KAFC within a week in order to prevent problems of future financing in the village.

The creation of village associations filled a social vacuum that was created after the collapse of the FSU. In several villages, including Bai-Munduz, these new village associations became active in addressing village problems. Access to credit was only one of the issues that could be handled collectively. In the course of the project several village associations started to coordinate other economic issues and activities. The association in one village bought an oil-press for the production of sunflower oil; elsewhere a plan was developed for the renovation of the village waterworks. In Bai-Munduz the association focused on marketing services and aimed to solve some problems with regard to the purchase and sale of agricultural assets. By organizing these transactions collectively they were able to reach more profitable markets (in Uzbekistan as well as Northern Kyrgyzstan), which reduced their dependency on disadvantageous agreements with rich middlemen.

Analysis of Problems and Successes

The mining town of Kok-Jangak and the rural community of Bai-Munduz differed in many respects and the problems of implementing micro-credit services varied accordingly. The former miners and civil servants in Kok-Jangak obviously had more difficulty in setting up viable businesses than the farmers in Bai-Munduz, not only because of their professional background, but also because of the differential access to markets, the fertility of the soil and the availability of land. Moreover, the pervasiveness of bureaucratic and hierarchical structures in Kok-Jangak made the implementation of a project based on horizontal grassroot initiatives more problematic than in Bai-Munduz. However, these are differences more of scale than of nature, and therefore make a comparison possible. By pointing at both similarities and differences in the implementation of the project, it will be possible to acquire further insights into the wider process of economic reform and the collision of international agencies and local circumstances.

A first obstacle in the implementation of the PPAP, for both the financial institution and the recipients, was unfamiliarity with the credit mechanisms. The initial designs of projects were regularly not economically viable. Members of potential credit groups were often motivated by the daily needs of their families, such as milk, or by concerns originating from social status, for example to own cattle, rather than profit margins. This problem was particularly urgent in small industrial towns, where until recently inhabitants had the security of monthly wages and for whom private economic activities had mainly meant additional income and less dependency on inadequate distribution systems. More often though, the difficulties of business planning were related to the problem of translating complex thoughts into flat black and white paper. As such it reflected the difficulty of *planning* activities in an environment of uncertain and changing economic opportunities and bureaucratic restrictions, rather than a lack of knowledge among the villagers.

A more urgent problem was the inclination towards hierarchical group formation, with persons with a higher social and economic status being chosen as chairmen, as was the case in the *Nurlan* group. This tendency is understandable, as such leaders have better access to local authorities and can therefore ease operations in the economic and political arena. However, these vertical group structures increased the possibility of power abuse and unequal profit sharing, and proved disastrous in a credit scheme based on social collateral because they undermined the principle of shared responsibility. Moreover, they did not correspond to the ideal of poverty alleviation of the aid organization.

As the *Maksat* group made clear, not all groups trusted the KAFC–or any official financial institution for that matter–and accusations of corruption were frequently expressed. Although such allegations have to be understood in the context of a widespread tendency to attribute all kinds of problems to "the Mafia" or to corruption in official institutions, the charges were certainly well-founded in a number of cases. The problem of corruption is of course not new in this part of the world, but one has to be careful in seeing it automatically as a legacy of the Soviet past. On the contrary, the involvement of donor organizations and the implementation of aid projects have to be considered. The dilemma was very visible in the implementation of the PPAP. On the one hand the project aimed to "empower" local communities, so that their dependency on authorities and other influential people would be lessened. On the other hand, the interference in the financial flows meant an increased risk of corruption. Because the credits had been partially subsidized, the KAFC could apply lower interest rates than commercial banks. This difference in interest rates put local bank employees in a tempting situation, because they were able to capitalize on the difference. The KAFC attempted to restrict corruption among its staff by adopting a rule that employees were not allowed to work in the same district for longer than two or three years. This would prevent their personal networks from becoming too large. UNDP adopted a similar policy and sent its Kyrgyz employees to regions where they had no relatives. In addition, the modest size of the loans and the involvement of several organizations in realizing the projects provided a certain guarantee that bribing and corruption remained on a fairly low level.

Despite the problems outlined above–or perhaps because they were not ignored–the PPAP has a fairly good reputation within the 'aid world.'[19] The latest reports indicate that the project is successful in its own terms. Contrary to expectations and fears, repayment did not pose serious problems at the end of the first credit cycle. At the end of 2000, the repayment rates were still very high (99.92 percent), and micro-credit had become one of the KAFC's major activities. Meanwhile, over a thousand credit groups totaling 6,500 members were receiving credit. At least as important is that in a number of pilot villages the village associations have taken over UNDP's role and mediate directly with the KAFC to streamline credit services in their villages. This provides reasonable hope that the established financial structure will also prove sustainable after UNDP's planned retreat in December 2002 (UNDP, 2000: 50).

The unexpected but nevertheless understandable conclusion that can be drawn from this project is that farmers' unfamiliarity with economic principles forms a relatively small obstacle. They only had difficulties in places where people lacked experience with market forces, such as in Kok-Jangak, whereas in Bai-Munduz it was mainly an issue of teaching farmers to speak the "right" language. Indeed, most farmers quickly picked up the principles of micro-credit and applied inventive strategies to deal with the new economic realities. However, long-term success is certainly not guaranteed. One of the main issues to be confronted in the future is how to elude established power structures and to prevent local authorities and elite groups from interfering with financial institutions and aid projects. Authorities in the post-socialist era are accustomed to having influence on economic initiatives, and since the political chaos that arose after 1991, both the possibilities and the wish to do so (lack of resources) have grown. No development project can harbor the illusion of fully circumventing these problems, and dangers of nepotism and corruption form a continuing threat.

Another consideration is how this bottom-up approach relates to the general development of the rural economy in Kyrgyzstan. One reason for the success of the PPAP was its limited scale. Because of the general deficit of financial resources among small farmers, providing loans to a limited number of people automatically gives them an advantage over others. This advantage disappears when a larger percentage of the population gains access to credit facilities. Although even in this scenario the establishment may still have the effect of reducing independence on local elite groups and brokers, sustained development can only be achieved if the rural market overcomes its present isolated and local character.

Aid Organizations, the Rural Sector, and the Transition

Considering the number of projects that fail or turn out to be counterproductive, one may well question the value of development aid in general. This issue is not only relevant in the West, where time and again voices are raised advocating the complete withdrawal of Western assistance, but also in Kyrgyzstan itself. Ten years of rhetoric and unfulfilled promises have resulted in a lack of trust in both the country's government and in the intentions of foreign aid organizations. In the Jalal-Abad province–which borders on the more authoritarian but perceived as more thriving Uzbekistan–calls for a strong but just government are particularly loud.

One can justifiably question the wisdom of the shock therapy approach, which paid insufficient attention to the path-dependency of development. Introducing free-market principles without paying attention to societal forces resulted in the dismantling of the Soviet economy but certainly not in the development of an economy in which all groups have equal chances. In the case of Kyrgyzstan the rhetoric of "democracy" and the "free market" served as a veil for existing power structures, without providing any alleviation for the majority of the population.[20] Critiques of neo-liberal approaches to development are especially strong in anthropology, where scholars have become disillusioned with "development" in general. Though the criticisms of the neo-liberal approach in the 1990s provide accurate analyses of the drawbacks of imposing change, this should not lead to a distancing from the problems. The changes that were introduced in Kyrgyzstan have simply made "development" a reality for its inhabitants. The adoption of structural reform policies engendered many undesirable effects. It remains important then to find ways to counter or alleviate these negative effects.

This brings us back to the approach followed by UNDP. The PPAP and similar projects are in fact belated attempts to compensate for the excesses that resulted from ill-considered and one-sided reforms. An important reason for the moderate success of this case is that outsiders did not impose the project's form as a blueprint. For development projects to succeed it is very important to achieve an understanding of local power structures and to use this knowledge to enable a more equal development of the economy. In this respect the presence of aid organizations can have a positive influence, on condition that they have enough knowledge of societal structures and are able to monitor the aid for considerable periods of time. Because outsiders are not already entwined in established social structures, they can be instrumental–especially in a period of rapid change, such as during "transition"–to make sure that the changes are not monopolized by small elite-groups.[21]

However, this approach can only be successful if simultaneous steps are taken on a higher level. Markets do not simply emerge, but depend on the infrastructure provided by the state. How effective the government will be in curbing corruption, in controlling inflation and in establishing circumstances that enable local and regional trade remains a significant question, not least because of the regional tensions that have become more problematic over the last couple of months. Until then however, it remains important to try and assist local people by giving them weapons to deal with the highly insecure and problematic new realities.

Notes

An earlier and shorter version of this paper was published in Dutch as "Kleinschalige kredietverlening in Kirgizie: Een casestudie naar de praktijk van transitiehulp." *Oost Europa Verkenningen*, no. 163 (March 2000): 73-87.

1. From an interview with the former president of the World Bank, in: *NRC Handelsblad*, 17 December 1994.
2. Spokesman of the IMF, cited in: *Internationale Samenwerking*, no. 12 (1994).
3. See for example: Eschment (2000).
4. The strong symbolism of the West's involvement has been amply described by Wedel (2001: 16). The symbolic meaning was not only phrased in catchy terms such as democracy, freedom, markets and civil society, but that the "transition" itself was perceived as a "return to Europe" and as "lost child returning home."
5. *Internationale Samenwerking*, no.12 (1994).
6. See Anderson (1999: 81). UNDP even classified 84 percent of the population in 1999 as poor, compared to 12 percent in the late 1980s (Freedom House 2001: 376).
7. There are no analyses available of the extent of these misappropriations. However, every Kyrgyz can give ample anecdotal examples. The term *privatizatsia* was in common speech often referred to as *prikhvatizatsia*, which combines the words for privatization and grabbing.
8. Production decreases particularly affected animal husbandry. In the period 1990 to 1997 the number of sheep and goats decreased by 65 percent, the number of cattle by 30 percent, birds by 86 percent and pigs by 80 percent (Mudahar 1998: 31).
9. Although there are approximately 20 functioning banking institutions in Kyrgyzstan, only the SSC (State Accounting and Savings Company) and the KAFC have offices outside the largest towns.
10. In addition to some eight to ten legalized documents, commercial banks demanded a collateral of 120-200 percent of the size of the credit (UNDP, 1999:3).
11. In 2000 IFAD provided an extra 3 million US $ to the KAFC for its micro-credit activities.
12. It must be said that there were not many alternatives either. The only other potential candidate was the SSC but its employees were only trained in conventional bookkeeping. Another possibility would have been to set up a separate credit institution. Besides financial and legal constraints this ran against the ideology of UNDP, since the Programme aimed to provide only temporary technical assistance and refrained from being directly involved in commercial activities.
13. The credit period did not exceed 16 months for a first loan and the repayment schedule was adjusted to the profit expectations.
14. In the beginning most groups used these savings to finance individual activities on a rotating basis. In the future these savings should serve as collateral, which would mean that the level of credit is dependent on the amount saved.
15. The remarks of the director of a youth NGO in Jalal-Abad were a typical example. She confessed to me that the computer she had "won," was part of the equipment actually meant for a youth project she had initiated. According to her this

did not make the slightest difference, because everyone would have forgotten about the existence of the project within a year or so.

16. Development agencies usually have only limited possibilities–and little direct interest–to control the spending of delivered aid over extensive periods of time. Aid-workers are often only temporarily employed and are pressed to show quantifiable results. A former UNDP project in Kok-Jangak illustrates this dilemma. In 1996 UNDP allocated the management of revolving funds to a local NGO, which in its turn obliged itself to disburse this fund to the poorest layers of the population as micro-credit. A monitoring visit in 1998 showed that the entire operation had been a fiasco. The NGO no longer existed and the money had disappeared or was disbursed to family members of the organization's management.

17. See also Pelkmans (1999: 127-30).

18. This was certainly not the only case. Likewise, the wife of the mayor strongly urged the UNDP staff to arrange credit for her friends, and the director of the technical school insisted that a group of teachers–which he had personally prepared for credit–should be accepted by the project.

19. See also a recent article in the *New York Times*, in which the successes of the PPAP are praised.

20. The anthropologist Boehm (1999: 39-48) argued in this respect that the notion of "democracy" had become the equivalent of "financial aid." The adoption of democratic rhetoric should therefore not be seen as democratization in the Western sense of the word, but instead often leads in practice to the strengthening of existing power structures.

21. The term outsiders should not be mistaken for foreigner or westerner. First, foreign outsiders were usually of African or Asian decent. Second, outsider also refers here to the policy of KAFC and UNDP to send employees to regions where they lacked kinship networks, thus avoiding that they be entangled in corrupt networks.

Bibliography

AFE-USAID (1999), Farm Profitability, Sustainability and Restructuring in Russia. Moscow: Institute of Economies in Transition, Analytical Center of Agri-Food Economics and US Agency for International Development.

Akerlof, G. A. "The Market for "Lemons": Quality Uncertainty and the Market Mechanism." *Quarterly Journal of Economics* LXXXIV, no. 3 (August 1970): 488-500.

Anderson, J. *Kyrgyzstan: Central Asia's Island of Democracy?* Amsterdam: Harwood Academic Publishers, 1999.

Barrett, C., T. Reardon and P. Webb. "Non-farm Income Diversification and Household Livelihood Strategies in Rural Africa: Concepts, Issues, and Policy Implications." *Food Policy* 26, no. 4 (2001): 315-31.

Benjamin, C. "The Growing Importance of Diversification Activities for French Farm Households." *Journal of Rural Studies* 10, no. 4 (1994): 331-42.

Bezemer, D. "Russian Reforms: The Return of the Peasant?" in *Progress in Economic Research*, edited by F. Columbus. New York: NovaScience Publishers, Forthcoming, 2002.

Bezemer, D. *Structural Change in the Post-socialist Transformation of Central European Agriculture: Studies from the Czech and Slovak republics.* Unpublished Ph.D.-thesis. Amsterdam: Tinbergen Institute, 2001.

Blanchard, O. and M. Kremer. "Disorganization." *Quarterly Journal of Economics* 112, no. 4 (1997): 1091-1126.

Bleahu, A. and M. Janowski. "Factors Affecting Household-level Involvement in Rural Non-Farm Economic Activities in two Communities in Dolj and Brasov Judete." Unpublished mimeo. Bucharest, Romania, 2001.

Bloch, P. C. and K. Rasmussen. "Land Reform in Kyrgyzstan." Pp. 111-35 in *Land Reform in the Former Soviet Union Eastern Europe*, edited by S.K. Wegren. London and New York: Routledge, 1998.

Boehm, C. "Democracy as a Project: Perceptions of Democracy within the World of Projects in Former Soviet Kyrgyzstan." *Anthropology of East Europe Review* 17, no. 1 (1999): 39-48.

Breitschopf, B. and G. Schreider. "Rural Development in Transition Economies–The Cases of Two Counties in Romania." Paper presented at the 48th International Atlantic Economic Conference, Montreal, 7-10 October 1999.

Brooks, K. and Z. Lerman. "Land Reform and Farm Restructuring in Russia." *World Bank Discussion Paper*, no. 233, Washington: The World Bank, 1994.

Brooks, K., E. Krylatykh, Z. Lerman, A. Petrikov and V. Uzun. "Agricultural Reform in Russia. A View from the Farm Level." *World Bank Discussion Paper*, no. 327, Washington: The World Bank, 1996.

Bruszt, L. "Constituting Markets: The Case of Russia and the Czech Republic." Pp. 197-219 in *Democratic and Capitalist Transitions in Eastern Europe*, edited by M. Dobry. Dordrecht: Kluwer Academic Publishers, 2000.

Brydon, J. and R. Bollman. "Rural Employment in Industrialized Countries." *Agricultural Economics*, 22 (2000): 185-97.

Canco, G., B. Musabelliu, M. Meci, E. Skreli, E. Petrela, and D. Baku. "Land Fragmentation in Albania." Unpublished mimeo, Tirana, 2000.

Carley, P. M. "The Price of the Plan: Perceptions of Cotton and Health in Uzbekistan and Turkmenistan." *Central Asian Survey* 8, no. 4 (1989): 1-38.

Caskie, P. "Back to Basics: Household Food Production in Russia." *Journal of Agricultural Economics*, 51 (2000): 196-209.

Chaplin, H. "Agricultural Diversification: A Review of Methodological Approaches and Empirical Evidence." Imperial College at Wye, University of London: IDARA *Working Paper Series* 2/2, 2000.

Chaplin, H., S. Davidova and M. Gorton. "Non-Agricultural Diversification of Farm Households and Corporate Farms: Lessons from Central Europe." Paper presented at the NRI Workshop on Rural Non-Farm Employment and Rural Development in the CEECs and CIS, 6-7 March 2002.

Chirca, C. and E. Tesliuc, eds. *From Rural Poverty to Rural Development*. Bucharest: World Bank and National Commission for Statistics, 1999.

Christensen, G. and R. Lacroix. "Competitiveness and Employment: A Framework for Rural Development in Poland." *World Bank Discussion Paper*, no. 383, Washington: The World Bank, 1997.

Craumer, P. "Agricultural Change, Labor Supply and Rural Out-Migration in Soviet Central Asia." Pp. 132-80 in *Geographic Perspectives on Soviet Central Asia*, edited by R. A. Lewis. New York: Routledge, 1992.

Craumer, P. *Rural and Agricultural Development in Uzbekistan*, London: The Royal Institute of International Affairs, 1995.

Csaki, C. "Agricultural Reform in Central and Eastern Europe and the Former Soviet Union: Status and Perspectives." in *Agricultural Economics* 22, no. 1 (2000): 37-54.

Csaki, C. and J. Nash. "The Agrarian Economies of Central and Eastern Europe and the Commonwealth of Independent States: Situation and Perspectives, 1997." *World Bank Discussion Paper*, no. 387. Washington: The World Bank, 1998.

Csaki, C. and Z. Lerman. "Agricultural Transition Revisited. Issues of Land Reforms and Farm Restructuring in East Central Europe and the Former USSR." Pp. 61-96 in *Redefining the Roles for European Agriculture*, Plenary Papers VIIIth EAAE Conference, Edinburgh, 1996.

Csaki, C. and Z. Lerman, "Land Reform and Farm Restructuring in the Former Socialist Countries in Europe," *European Review of Agricultural Economics* 21, no. 3-4 (1994): 553-76.

Cungu, A. and J. Swinnen. "Albania's Radical Agrarian Reform." *Economic Development and Cultural Change* 47, no. 3 (April 1999): 605-19.

Davidova, S. and A. Buckwell. "Political Design of Land Reform in Central and Eastern Europe: Was it Backward Looking?" Paper presented to the Agricultural Economics Society Annual Conference, University of Edinburgh, 21-24 March 1997.

Davis, J. R., D. Pearce, and M. Janowski. *Characterization and Analysis of the Non-Farm Rural Sector in Transition Economies*. Chatham: Natural Resources Institute, 2000.

Davis, J. R. and A. Gaburici. "The Economic Activity of Private Farms in Romania during Transition." *Europe-Asia Studies* 51, no. 5 (1999): 843-69.

Davis, J. R. and D. Pearce. "The Rural Non-farm Economy in Central and Eastern Europe." *Discussion Paper*, no. 4, Chatham, U.K.: Natural Resources Institute, 2000.

De Melo, M. and A. Gelb. "A Comparative Analysis of Twenty-Eight Transition Economies in Europe and Asia." *Post-Soviet Geography and Economics*, 37, no. 5 (1996): 265-85.

De Melo, M., Denizer, C., and Gelb, A. "From Plan to Market: Patterns of Transition." *Policy Research Working Paper*, no. 1564, Washington: The World Bank, 1996.

Deaton, A. *The Analysis of Household Surveys*. Washington: The World Bank, 1997.

Deichmann, U. and V. Henderson. "Urban and Regional Dynamics in Poland." *Policy Research Working Paper*, no. 2457, Washington: The World Bank, 2000.

Deiniger, K. and P. Olinte. "Rural Non-farm Employment and Income Diversification in Colombia." *World Development* 29, no. 3 (2001): 455-65

Delehanty, J. and K. Rasmussen. "Land Reform and Farm Restructuring in the Kyrgyz Republic." *Post-Soviet Geography* 36, no. 9 (1995): 565-86.

EBRD. *Ten Years of Transition, Transition Report 1999*. London: European Bank for Reconstruction and Development, 1999.

EBRD. *Transition Report 2000*, London: European Bank for Reconstruction and Development, 2001.

EBRD. *Transition Report Update 2001*, London: European Bank for Reconstruction and Development, 2001.

EC. "Agricultural Situation and Prospects in the Central and Eastern European Countries. Bulgaria, Agriculture and Rural Development." Brussels: DG Agriculture, 1998.

Edelman, M. "The Adequacy of Rural Capital Markets: Public Purpose and Policy Options." Written Testimony, U.S. Senate Committee on Agriculture, Nutrition and Fishery. Ames: Iowa State University, 1997.

Efimova, A. "Rastet rol' krestyanskikh podvorii." (Increasing Importance of Peasant Enterprises). *Ekonomika s/kh Rossii*, no. 2 (1997): 5.

EIU. *Country Reports, July, September, October: Kazakhstan, Kyrgyz Republic, Uzbekistan*, London: Economist Intelligence Unit, 2001.

Ellman, M, E. Gaidar and G. Kolodko. *Economic transition in Eastern Europe*. Oxford: Blackwell, 1993.

Eschment, B. "Democratie onder Vuur: Autoritaire regimes in Centraal-Azië." *Oost Europa Verkenningen*, no. 161 (September 2000): 70-81.

Fadeeva, O. "Sel'skie rynki truda i semeinye strategii." (Agricultural Labour Markets and Household Strategies). Paper presented at the International Conference of Economic Sociology, Moscow, 2000.

Fierman, W. "Political Development in Uzbekistan: Democratization?" Pp. 360-408 in *Conflict, Cleavage and Change in Central Asia and the Caucasus*, edited by K. Dawisha and B. Parrott. Cambridge: Cambridge University Press, 1997.

Fischer, S., R. Sahay, and C. Vegh. "Stabilization and Growth in Transition Economies: The Early Experience." *Journal of Economic Perspectives* 10, no. 2 (1996): 45-66.

Foster, C. "The Impact of FDI in the Upstream and Downstream Sector on Investment in Agriculture in the NIS." Pp. 198-211 in *Agricultural Finance and Credit Infrastructure in Transition Economies*. Paris: OECD, 1999.

Frantz, D. "A Chicken in Every Kyrgyz Pot." *New York Times*, 2 December 2000.

Freedom House. *Nations in Transit 1999-2000: Civil Society, Democracy & Markets in East Central Europe and the Newly Independent States*, edited by A. Karatnycky, A. Motyl and A. Piano. New Brunswick and London: Transaction Publishers, 2001.

Gleason, G. "The Political Economy of Dependency under Socialism: The Asian Republics in the USSR." *Studies in Comparative Communism* 24, no. 4 (1991): 335-53.

Gleason, G. *The Central Asian States: Discovering Independence*. Boulder, Colorado: Westview Press, 1997.

Goskomstat Pskov. *Sel'skoe khozyaistvo Pskovskoi Oblasti*. (The agriculture of Pskov Region). Pskov: Goskomstat, 2000.

Goskomstat Russia. *Sel'skokhozyaistvennaya deyatel'nost' khozyaistv nacelenaya v Rossii*. (The agricultural state of household enterprises in Russia). Moscow: Goskomstat, 1999.

Goskomstat Russia. *Sel'skokhozyaistvennaya deyatel'nost' krestyanskikh (fermerskikh) khozyaistv v Rossii*. (The agricultural state of peasant farms in Russia). Moscow: Goskomstat, 2000.

Gow, H. and J. Swinnen. "Agribusiness Restructuring, Foreign Direct Investment, and Hold-Up Problems in Agricultural Transition." *European Review of Agricultural Economics* 25, no. 4 (1998): 331-50.

Gow, H., D. Streeter, and J. Swinnen. "How Private Contract Enforcement Mechanisms can Succeed where Public Institutions Fail: the Case of Juhocukor a.s." *Agricultural Economics* 23, no. 3 (2000): 253-65.

Greif, F. "Off-farm Income Sources and Uses in Transition Economies." Unpublished mimeo. Vienna: Federal Institute of Agricultural Economics and Rome: FAO/REU, 1997.

Griffin, K, ed. *Poverty Alleviation in Mongolia*. Report for UNDP, Ulaan Baatar, 2001.

Grossman, G. "Informal Personal Incomes and Outlays in the Soviet Urban Population." Pp. 150-70 in *The Informal Economy*, edited by A. Portes and M. Castells. Baltimore: The Johns Hopkins University Press, 1989.

Hann, C.M., ed. *Property relations: Reviewing the anthropological tradition*. Cambridge: Cambridge University Press, 1998.

Heidhues, F., J. R. Davis and G. Schrieder. "Agricultural Transformation and Implications for Designing Rural Financial Policies in Romania." *European Review of Agricultural Economics* 25, no. 3 (1998): 351-72.

Herman, M. "Sustainable Agricultural Reform–the Case of Uzbekistan." Pp. 84-95 in *Central Asia 2010: Prospects for Human Development*. New York: UNDP, 1999.

Huffman, W. "Farm and off-farm work decisions: the role of human capital." *The Review of Economics and Statistics* 62, no. 1 (1980): 14-23.

Humphrey, C. *Marx Left, but Karl Stayed Behind. A Revised Edition of Karl Marx Collective. An Ethnography of a Soviet Collective Farm*. Cambridge: University Press, 1996 and Ann Arbor: The University of Michigan Press, 1998.

Ickes, B., R. Ryterman. "From Enterprise to Firm: Notes for the Theory of Enterprise in Transition." Pp. 83-104 in *The Postcommunist Economic Transformation: Essays in Honor of Gregory Grossman*, edited by R. Campbell. Boulder: Westview Press, 1994.

Ilkhamov, A. "Divided Economy: Kolkhoz System vs. Peasant Subsistence Economy in Uzbekistan." *Central Asia Monitor*, no. 4 (2000): 5-14.

Ilkhamov, A. "*Shirkats, Dekhqon* farmers and others: farm restructuring in Uzbekistan." *Central Asian Survey*, 17, no. 4 (1998): 539-60.

IMF. *Republic of Uzbekistan: Recent Economic Developments*. IMF Staff Country report No. 98/116. Washington: International Monetary Fund, 1998.

INSTAT. *Results of Household Living Condition Survey*. Tirana: INSTAT (*Republica e Shqiperise Instituti Statistikes*), 2001.

Johnson, S. "Institutional versus Policy Reform in Transition Countries." Pp. 17-28 in *The Importance of Institutions for the Transition in Central and Eastern Europe*, edited by Frohberg, K. and W. R. Poganietz. Halle/Saale: IAMO,1998.

Kandiyoti, D. "Poverty in Transition: An Ethnographic Critique of Household Surveys in Post-Soviet Central Asia." *Development and Change* 30, no. 3 (1999): 499-524.

Kandiyoti, D. "Rural Domestic Economy and Female Labour Supply in Uzbekistan: Assessing the Feasibility of Gender-targeted Micro-credit Schemes." Final report, DFID, ESCOR Unit, Grant no. R6978, 1999.

Kandiyoti, D. "Rural livelihoods and Social Networks in Uzbekistan: Perspectives from Andijan." *Central Asian Survey*, 17, no. 4 (1998): 561-78.

Karatnycky, A., Motyl, A., and B. Shor, eds. *Nations in Transit 1997: Civil Society and Markets in East Central Europe and the Newly Independent States*. New Brunswick and London: Transaction Publishers, 1997.

Khan, A. R. and Ghai, D. *Collective Agriculture and Rural Development in Soviet Central Asia*, London: Macmillan, 1979.

Khan, Azizur R. "The Transition to a Market Economy in Agriculture." Pp. 62-92 in *Social Policy and Economic Transformation in Uzbekistan*, Geneva: ILO, 1996.

Kodderitzsch, S. "Reforms in Albanian Agriculture." *World Bank Technical Paper*, no. 431. Washington: The World Bank, 1999.

Kopeva, D. "Farm restructuring in Bulgaria." *Working Paper* ACE Phare Project P-96-6090-R. Sofia: University for the World Economy, 1999.

Kopeva, D. and N. Noev. "Subsistence Farming in Bulgaria: between Tradition and Market Requirements." Paper presented at the 76th EAAE Seminar *Subsistence Agriculture in Central and Eastern Europe: How to Break the Vicious Circle?*, IAMO, Halle/Saale, May 6-8, 2001.

Kornai, J. "The Road to a Free Economy–Ten Years After." *Transition* 11, no. 2 (2000): 3-5.

Kostov, P. and Lingard, J. "Subsistence Farming in Transitional Economies: Lessons from Bulgaria." *Journal of Rural Studies* 18, no.1 (2002): 83-94

Leibenstein, H. Allocative Efficiency vs. "X-Efficiency." *American Economic Review* 61 (June 1966): 392-415.

Leonard, C. "Rational Resistance to Land Privatization". *Post-Soviet Geography and Economics* 41, no. 8 (December 2000): 605-20.

Lerman Z. "Land Reform and Farm Restructuring: What has been accomplished to date?" *American Economic Review* 89, no. 2 (1999): 271-75.

Lerman, Z. "Does Land Reform Matter." *European Review of Agricultural Economics* 25 (1998): 307-30.

Lerman, Z. "Land Reform in Uzbekistan." Pp. 136-61 in *Land Reform in the Former Soviet Union and Eastern Europe*, edited by S. K. Wegren. London and New York: Routledge, 1998.

Lerman, Z. "Experience with Land Reform and Farm Restructuring in the Former Soviet Union." Pp. 311-32 in *Agricultural Privatization, Land Reform and Farm Restructuring in Central and Eastern Europe*, edited by J. Swinnen, A. Buckwell and E. Mathijs. Ashgate: Aldershot, 1997.

Lerman, Z. and C. Csaki. "Ukraine: Review of Farm Restructuring Experiences." *World Bank Technical Paper*, no. 459, Washington: The World Bank, 1997.

Lerman, Z. and A. Mirzakhanian. *Private Agriculture in Armenia*. Lanham, Maryland and Oxford, UK: Lexington Publishers, 2001.

Lerman, Z., C. Csaki and G. Feder. "Land Policy and Changing Farm Structures in Central Eastern Europe and the Former Soviet Union." *Policy Research Paper* 2794, Washington: The World Bank, 2002.

Lerman, Z. and C. Csaki. "Land Reform in Ukraine: The First Five Years." *World Bank Discussion Paper* 371, Washington: The World Bank, 1997.

Lerman, Z., J. Garcia-Garcia and D. Wichelns. "Land and Water Policies in Uzbekistan." *Post-Soviet Geography and Economics* 37, no. 3 (1996): 145-74.

Lerman, Z., Y. Tankhilevich, K. Mozhin and N. Sapova. "Self-Sustainability of Subsidiary Household Plots: Lessons for Privatization of Agriculture in Former Socialist Countries." *Post-Soviet Geography* 35, no. 9 (1994): 526-42.

Lin, J. Y. "Rural Reforms and Agricultural Growth in China." *American Economic Review* 82, no. 1 (1992): 34-51.

Lubin, N. *Labour and Nationality in Soviet Central Asia*. London: Macmillan, 1998.

Lusho, S. and D. Papa. "Land Fragmentation and Consolidation in Albania." Madison: Land Tenure Center, University of Wisconsin, *Working Paper* no. 25, 1998. <http://www.wisc.edu/ltc>

Macours, K. and J. Swinnen. "Causes of Output Decline in Economic Transition: The Case of Central and Eastern European Agriculture." *Journal of Comparative Economics* 28, no. 1 (2000a): 172-206.

Macours, K. and J. Swinnen. "Impact of Reforms and Initial Conditions on Agricultural Output and Productivity Changes in Central and Eastern Europe, the Former Soviet Union, and East Asia." *American Journal of Agricultural Economics* 82, no. 5 (2000b): 1149-55.

Macours, K. and J. Swinnen. "Patterns of Agrarian Transition." *Economic Development and Cultural Change* (forthcoming, 2002).

Mathijs, E. and I. Beka. "Micro-economic Analysis of Farm Restructuring in Central and Eastern Europe: Albania." EU Phare ACE Programme. Unpublished mimeo, 2001. <http://www.agr.kuleuven.ac.be/aee/clo/ace97.htm>

Mathijs, E. and J. Swinnen. "Production Organization and Efficiency during Transition: An Empirical Analysis of East German Agriculture." *The Review of Economics and Statistics* 83, no. 1 (February 2001): 100-107.

Mathijs, E. and J. Swinnen. "The Economics of Agricultural De-collectiviztion in East-Central Europe and the Former Soviet Union." *Economic Development and Cultural Change* 47, no. 1 (1998): 1-26.

Mathijs, E. and J. Swinnen. "Agricultural Privatization and De-collectivization in Central and Eastern Europe." *Transition* (26 July 1996): 13-16.

McMillan, J. "Markets in Transition." Pp. 210-39 in *Advances in Economics and Econometrics: Theory and Applications,* edited by D. Kreps and K.F. Wallis, vol. 2. Cambridge: Cambridge University Press, 1997.

Milanovic, B. "Income, Inequality, and Poverty during the Transition from Planned to Market Economy." *World Bank Regional and Sectoral Studies*, Washington: The World Bank, 1998.

MOAF. *The Green Strategy*. Tirana: Ministry of Agriculture and Food, Agrofood Information Center, 1998.

Mudahar, M. "Kyrgyz Republic: Strategy for Rural Growth and Poverty Alleviation." *World Bank Discussion Paper*, no. 394, Washington: The World Bank, 1998.

Nerlove, M., K. L. Bachman. "The Analysis of Changes in Agricultural Supply: Problems and Approaches." *Journal of Farm Economics* 42: 531-54

Network. "Social Security Systems and Demographic Developments in Agriculture in CEE Candidate Countries." IAMO, *Assessment Report* no. 7, Network of Independent Agricultural Experts on the CEE Candidate Countries. Unpublished mimeo, 2002.

NSI. *Statistical Reference Book 1997*. Sofia: National Statistical Institute, 1997.

NSI. *Statistical Yearbook*. Sofia: National Statistical Institute, 2000.

NSO. *Mongolian Statistical Yearbook 1998*. Ulaanbaatar: National Statistical Office, 1999.

NSO. *Mongolian Statistical Yearbook 2000*. Ulaanbaatar: National Statistical Office, 2001.

O'Brien, D. J., V. V. Patsiorkovski and L. D. Dershem. *Household Capital and the Agrarian Problem in Russia*. Burlington, Singapore and Sydney: Ashgate, 2000.

OECD. *Agricultural Policies in Transition Economies: Monitoring and Evaluation 1997*, Paris: Centre for Cooperation with the Economies in Transition. 1997.

OECD. *Review of Agricultural Policies: Bulgaria*. Paris: Organization for Economic Cooperation and Development, 2000.

Osborne, S. and M. Trueblood. "An Examination of Economic Efficiency of Russian Crop Output in the Reform Period." Unpublished mimeo, 2001.

Pelkmans, M. "Dwingende Gastvrijheid." Pp. 127-30 in *Etnografiche Miniature*, edited by H. Driessen and H. de Jonge. Nijmegen: Sun, 1999.

Phillipson, J., M. Gorton, P. Lowe, A. Moxey, M. Raley and H. Talbot. "Farms as Firms in the new Rural Economy: an Analysis of Rural Microbusinesses in the North East of England." Paper presented at the 73rd EAAE Seminar on Policy Experiences with Rural Development in a Diversified Europe, 28-30 June 2001.

Pingali, P.L. and V.T. Xuan. "Vietnam: Decollectivization and Rice Productivity Growth." *Economic Development and Cultural Change* 40, no. 4 (1992): 697-718.

Pomfret, R. "Agrarian Reform in Uzbekistan: Why Has the Chinese Model Failed to Deliver?" *Economic development and Cultural Change* 48, no. 2 (2000): 269-84.

Pomfret, R. *The Economies of Central Asia*, New Jersey: Princeton University Press, 1995.

Poppe, K. "A note on the Need for Micro-economic Household Data in Agriculture for International Policy Analysis." Presentation to the Workshop on Farm Household-Firm Unit: its Importance in Agriculture and Implications for Statistics, Imperial College at Wye, 12-13 April, 2002.

Praust, R. Y. *Razvitiya razlichnykh form khozyaistvovaniya v agrarnom sektore pskovskikh* (The development of different forms of enterprises in the agrarian sector). Moscow: Russian Academy of Sciences, 1998.

Reardon, T., K. Stamoulis, M. E. Cruz, A. Balisacan, J. Berdegue and B. Banks. "Rural Non-Farm Income in Developing Countries." in *The state of food and agriculture*

1998: Part III. Rome: Food and Agricultural Organization of the United Nations, 1998. <http://www.fao.org/docrep/w9500e/9500e02.htm>.

Reinert, K. "Rural Non-Farm Development: A Trade-Theoretic View." *Journal of International Trade and Economic Development* 7, no. 4 (1998): 425-37.

Rizov, M., D. Gavrilescu, H. Gow, E. Mathijs and J. F. M. Swinnen. "Transition and Enterprise Restructuring: The Development of Individual Farming in Romania." *World Development* 29, no. 7 (2001), 1257-74.

Roland, G. and T. Verdier. "Transition and the Output Fall." *Economics of Transition* 7, no. 1 (1999): 1-28.

Roy, O. "Kolkhoz and Civil Society in the Independent States of Central Asia." Pp. 109-21 in *Civil Society in Central Asia*, edited by M. Holt Ruffin and Daniel C. Waugh. Washington: Centre for Civil Society International and University of Washington Press, 1999.

Roy, O. *The New Central Asia: The Creation of Nations*. London: I.B. Tauris, 2000.

Rozelle, S. "Gradual Reform and Institutional Development: The Keys to Success of China's Agricultural Reforms." Pp. 197-220 in *Reforming Asian Socialism. The Growth of Market Institutions*, edited by J. McMillan and B. Naughton. Michigan: The University of Michigan Press, 1996.

Rumer, B. Z. *Soviet Central Asia: A Tragic Experiment*. Boston: Unwin Hyman, 1989.

Sachs, J. Poland's jump to the market economy. Cambridge MA: MIT), 1993.

Sachs, J. and W.T. Woo. "Structural Factors in the Economic Reforms of China, Eastern Europe and the Former Soviet Union." *Economic Policy* 18 (1994): 101-45.

Sarris, A. H. "Agriculture and Integration: Trade Liberalization versus Migration." Pp. 171-86 in *Agriculture and East-West European Integration*, edited by J. G. Hartell and J. F. M. Swinnen. Aldershot: Ashgate, 2000.

Sarris, A., T. Doucha, and E. Mathijs. "Agricultural Restructuring in Central and Eastern Europe: Implications for Restructuring and Rural Development." *European Review of Agricultural Economics* 26, no. 3 (1999): 305-30.

Sarris, A. H., T. Doucha and E. Mathijs. "Agricultural Restructuring in Central and Eastern Europe: Implications for Competitiveness and Rural Development." *European Review of Agricultural Economics* 26 (1999): 305-29.

Schleifer, A. "Government in Transition." *European Economic Review* 41, no. 3-5 (1997): 385-410.

Sedik, D. J., M. A. Trueblood and C. Arnade. "Corporate Farm Performance in Russia, 1991-1995: An efficiency analysis." *Journal of Comparative Economics* 27, no 3 (1999): 514-33.

Serova, E., N. Karlova, V. Petrichenko. "Russia: the Market of Purchased Inputs for Agriculture. In: Framework for Investigating Issues in Factor Markets and Economic Organization of Russian Agriculture." Conference Proceedings. Golitzino-II, July 2000. Moscow: Centre AFE, 2002.

Serova, E. and N. Karlova. "Liberalization and Decentralization in a Transition Economy: Regional Disintegration of the Russian Agro-Food Sector (the Case of Russia's Eastern Regions)." *Discussion paper* no.15. Series Russian Agri-Food Sector in Transition, Bonn, July 2000.

Serova, E. and I. Khramova. "Emerging Supply Chain Management in Russia's Agri-Food Sector." *Discussion paper* no. 14, Series Russian Agri-Food Sector in Transition, Bonn, July 2000.

Smith, A. *The wealth of nations*. Book 1. London: Dent, 1910 [1776].

Spoor, M. "'White Gold' versus 'Food Self-Sufficiency'? Agrarian Transition in FSU Central Asia." Pp. 57-74 in *Markets beyond Liberalization*, edited by A. Kuyvenhoven, H. Moll and A. van Tilburg. New York/London: Kluwer International.

Spoor, M. "Agrarian Transition in Former Soviet Central Asia: a Comparative Study of Kazakhstan, Kyrgyzstan and Uzbekistan." *ISS Working Paper*, no. 298. The Hague: Institute of Social Studies, 1999.

Spoor, M. "The Aral Sea Basin Crisis: Transition and Environment in Former Soviet Central Asia." *Development and Change* 29, no. 3 (1998): 409-35.

Spoor, M. *The 'Market Panacea': Agrarian transformation in developing countries and former socialist economies*. London: Intermediate Technology Publications, 1997.

Spoor, M. "Agrarian Transition in Former Soviet Central Asia: A Comparative Study of Uzbekistan and Kyrgyzstan." *The Journal of Peasant Studies* 23, no. 1 (1995): 46-63.

Spoor, M. "Transition to Market Economies in Former Soviet Central Asia: Dependency, Cotton and Water." *The European Journal of Development Research* 5, no. 2 (1993): 142-58.

Spoor, M. and O. Visser. "The State of Agrarian Reform in the Former Soviet Union." *Europe-Asia Studies* 53, no. 6 (September 2001): 885-901.

SSO. *Mongolian Economy and Society in 1994, Statistical Yearbook*. Ulaanbaatar: State Statistical Office, 1995.

Standing, G. *Russian Unemployment and Enterprise Restructuring: Reviving dead souls*. London: Macmillan, 1996.

Stark, D. "Path Dependence and Privatization Strategies in East Central Europe." *East European Politics and Societies* 6, no. 1 (1992): 17-54.

StatKom SNG. *Sodruzhestvo Nezavisimikh Gasudarstv v 2000 Godu* (Commonwealth of Independent States in 2000), Moscow: Statistical Committee of the CIS, 2001.

Stiglitz, J. E. "Whither Reform? Ten Years of Transition." Paper presented at the annual World Bank conference on development economics. Washington: The World Bank, April 1999.

Swain, N. "Post-Socialist Rural Economy and Society in the CEECs: the Socio-Economic Contest for SAPARD and EU Enlargement." Paper presented to European Rural Policy at the Crossroads Conference, The Arkleton Centre for Rural Development Research, University of Aberdeen, 29 June-1 July, 2000.

Swain, N. "Rural Development and Social Change in the Post-socialist Central European Countryside." *Zemedelska Ekonomika* 45, no. 2 (1999): 79-84.

Swinnen, J. F. M., H. Gow and I. Maviglia. "Modest Changes in the West, Radical Reforms in the East, and Government Intervention Everywhere: European Sugar Markets at the Outset of the 21st Century." *Sweetener Markets in the 21st Century*, edited by A. Schmitz, T. Spreen and W. Messina. Dordrecht: Kluwer Academic Publishers, forthcoming 2002.

Swinnen, J. F. M., L. Dries and E. Mathijs. "Constraints on Employment Growth and Development in Rural Areas in Transition Countries: Analysis and Policy Implications." Paper presented to the 73rd EAAE Seminar on Policy Experiences with Rural Development in a Diversified Europe, 28-30 June 2001.

TACIS/Government of Uzbekistan. "Pilot Integrated Development Programme, Bulungur District, Samarkand, Uzbekistan." Final Report BS6-Land Tenure, Tashkent, 1996.

Tarasov A. et al. *Lichnoye podsobnoye khoziaystvo naselenia* (Households' agricultural production). Rostov, 1998.

Tho Seeth, H., S. Chachnov and A. Surinov "Russian Poverty: Muddling Through the Transition with Garden Plots." *World Development* 26 (1998): 1611-23

Thurman, J. M. "The 'Command-Administrative' System in Cotton Farming in Uzbekistan 1920s to Present." *Indiana University Papers on Inner Asia*, no. 32. Bloomington, Indiana, 1999.

Trushin, E. "Uzbekistan: Problems of Development and Reform in the Agrarian Sector." Pp. 259-91 in *Central Asia: The Challenges of Independence*, edited by B. Rumer and S. Zhukov. New York: M. E. Sharpe, 1998.

Turnock, D. "Introduction." in *Privatization in Rural Eastern Europe*, edited by D. Turnock. Cheltenham, UK: Edward Elgar, 1998.

UNDP. "Empowering Communities for Alleviating Poverty in Kyrgyzstan. Annual Report." Gender in Development Bureau. Bishkek: UNDP Kyrgyzstan, 2000.

UNDP. "Project Document: KYR/99/007." Bishkek: UNDP, 1999.

UNDP. *Human Development Report Bulgaria 1999-2001*, Sofia: UNDP, 2001.

UNDP. *National Human Development Report of the Kyrgyz Republic, 1997.* Bishkek: UNDP, 1997.

Uvarovsky, V. and Voigt, P. "Russia's Agriculture: Eight Years in Transition–Convergence or Divergence of Regional Efficiency." *Discussion Paper* no. 31. Halle/Saale: IAMO.

Verdery, K. "The Obligations of Ownership: Restoring Rights to Land in Postsocialist Eastern Europe." in *Property in Question*, edited by C. Humphrey and K. Verdery. New York: Berghan Press, forthcoming 2003.

Wadhwa, S. "Micro Credit Development in Kyrgyzstan: Current trends, challenges and future opportunities." Paper presented at the Micro Credit Summit for Kyrgyzstan, Bishkek, 1998.

Wedel, J. *Collision and Collusion: The strange case of Western aid to Eastern Europe.* New York: Palgrave, 2001.

Wegren, S. K., ed. *Land Reform in the Former Soviet Union and Eastern Europe.* London and New York: Routledge, 1998.

Wheeler, R. and Lushaj, S. "Albania Land Consolidation Report." Report prepared for the World Bank, 1999.

Woldehanna, T., A. Lansink and J. Peerlings. "Off-farm work decisions on Dutch cash crop farms and the 1992 and Agenda 2000 CAP Reforms." *Agricultural Economics* 22, no. 2 (2000): 163-71.

World Bank. "Albania Agricultural Services Project Preparation Mission: Draft Aide Memoire." Unpublished mimeo. Tirana, The World Bank, 1999.

World Bank. "Albania Agricultural Services Project: Social Assessment." Unpublished mimeo. Tirana: The World Bank, 2000.

World Bank. "Food and Agricultural Policy Reforms in the Former USSR. An Agenda for Transition." *Studies in Economies in Transformation*, no. 1, Washington: The World Bank, 1992.

World Bank. "The Rural Non-Farm Economy: Report on Presentations and Discussions at the World Bank." Washington: World Bank, 2000. Internet Address: <http://www.worldbank.org/research/rural/workshop/May2000/RNFEmay.pdf>

World Bank. "Uzbekistan: Social and Structural Policy Review." *Technical Report* no. 19626, 1999.

World Bank. *World Development Report: From Plan to Market.* Washington: Oxford University Press, published for the World Bank, 1996.

Wyplosz, C. "Ten Years of Transformation: Macroeconomic Lessons." *CEPR Discussion Paper* No. 2254. London: Center for Economic Policy Research, 2000.

Zeddies, J. "Organization of Russia's Large Scale Farms." Pp. 471-93 in *Russia's Agrofood Sector: Towards Truly Functioning Markets*, edited by P. Wehrheim, E. V. Serova, K. Frohberg and J. von Braun. Dordrecht: Kluwer Academic Publishers, 2000.

Index

A

agricultural
  cooperatives, 56, 166
  development, 127, 175
  diversification, 103
  economy, 53, 141, 180, 182
  education, 111
  employment, 21, 105, 114, 173
  growth, 13, 37
  income, 109, 182
  individualization of, 12–15
  input, 2, 50, 172, 192
  labor, 21, 27, 29, 152, 164
  machinery, 68, 73, 137
  market, 37, 142
  output, 12, 13, 19, 21, 27, 28, 32,
    33, 57, 104, 108
  performance, 20–22, 56–58
  product, 12, 50, 53, 57, 59, 77,
    96, 149
  reform, 6, 21
  services, 123, 124, 127, 131, 133,
    141
  strategy, 125
  trade, 133
  transformation, 1
  transition, 16, 27, 34, 39
  workers, 10, 149
agriculture
  commercial, 1
  individualization of, 12, 13, 15,
    17, 20
  small-scale, 104
agri-food chain, 39, 61, 62, 66, 71,
  78, 80
agro-industrial complex, 166
Albania, 6, 10, 11, 23, 27, 34, 37,
  123–42, 164, 166
Armenia, 7, 11, 16, 23, 47, 163–83
Azerbaijan, 7, 12, 23, 166

B

banking system, 66, 73, 81
Belarus, 7, 8, 10, 23, 27, 28, 29, 31,
  32, 47
Bulgaria, 16, 22, 34, 103–22, 164,
  166

C

capital market, 81
CEE, 5–25, 27–45, 48, 103, 105,
  110, 116, 121, 164, 165
Central Asia, 5, 7, 8, 22, 23, 47–60,
  143, 158, 185
China, 27, 28, 29, 30, 31, 32, 33, 34,
  35, 36, 37, 42, 43, 44, 150
CIS, 2, 5–25, 52, 57, 164, 165, 166,
  171, 182
cotton, 50, 52, 56, 57, 59, 143–60,
  192
credit,
  access to, 179, 185–98
  agricultural, 72, 187
  commodity, 70, 71, 77
  constraint, 178
  institutions, 141, 176, 185
  market, 34, 52, 66, 132
  micro, 173, 187
Czech Republic, 16, 22, 27, 28, 29,
  31, 34, 39, 40, 41, 110, 114, 166

D

dekhan, 148, 149, 151
discriminant function, 117, 119

E

East/West divide, 7
enterprise
  collective, 15, 87, 144, 145, 147–
    59

About the Contributors

Max Spoor is Associate Professor of Transition Economics and Coordinator of the Centre for the Study of Transition and Development (CESTRAD), at the Institute of Social Studies (ISS) in The Hague. He has published widely on agricultural policies, environment and rural economies of developing and transition countries, with articles in international journals such as *World Development*, the *Journal of Agrarian Change*, the *Journal of International Development*, the *Journal of Development Studies*, *Food Policy* and *Europe-Asia Studies* (formerly *Soviet Studies*). In the past decade his research has focused in particular on the transformation of the rural economy and environmental problems in the Post-Soviet Central Asian states. His most recent books are: *The 'Market Panacea': Agrarian Transformation in Developing Countries and Former Socialist Economies*, London: Intermediate Technology Publications, 1997; and *Beyond Transition: Ten Years after the Fall of the Berlin Wall*, New York: UNDP/Regional Bureau for Europe and the CIS, 2000. He has worked as a development consultant and economist for many international agencies.

List of Authors

Bezemer, Dirk. Marie Curie Research Fellow, Imperial College at Wye, University of London, United Kingdom.

Chaplin, Hannah. Doctoral Researcher, Agricultural Economics and Business Management research section, Department of Life Sciences, Imperial College at Wye, University of London, UK.

Childress Malcolm. Associate Scientist, Land Tenure Center, University of Wisconsin, Madison, United States of America.

Davidova, Sophia. Senior Lecturer, Agricultural Economics and Business Management research section, Department of Life Sciences, Imperial College at Wye, University of London, UK.

Davis, Junior. Senior Lecturer, Natural Resources Institute, University of Greenwich, United Kingdom.

Doichinova, Julia. Professor, Department of Agribusiness, University of National and World Economy (UNWE), Sofia, Bulgaria.

Ellman, Michael. Professor, Faculty of Economics and Econometrics, University of Amsterdam, The Netherlands.

Gorton, Matthew. Lecturer, Agricultural Economics and Food Marketing Department and Assistant Director, Centre for the Rural Economy, University of Newcastle upon Tyne, UK.

Kandiyoti, Deniz. Reader, Deptartment of Development Studies, School of Oriental and African Studies (SOAS), University of London, United Kingdom.

Khramova, Irina. Senior Research Fellow of the Analytical Centre of Agri-Food Economics, Institute for Economies in Transition (IET), Moscow, Russia.

Kopeva, Diana. Professor, Department of Agribusiness, University of National and World Economy (UNWE), Sofia, Bulgaria.

Lerman, Zvi. Professor, Department of Agricultural Economics and Management, The Hebrew University, Rehovot, Israel.